IMAGES
of America

NEW GLOUCESTER

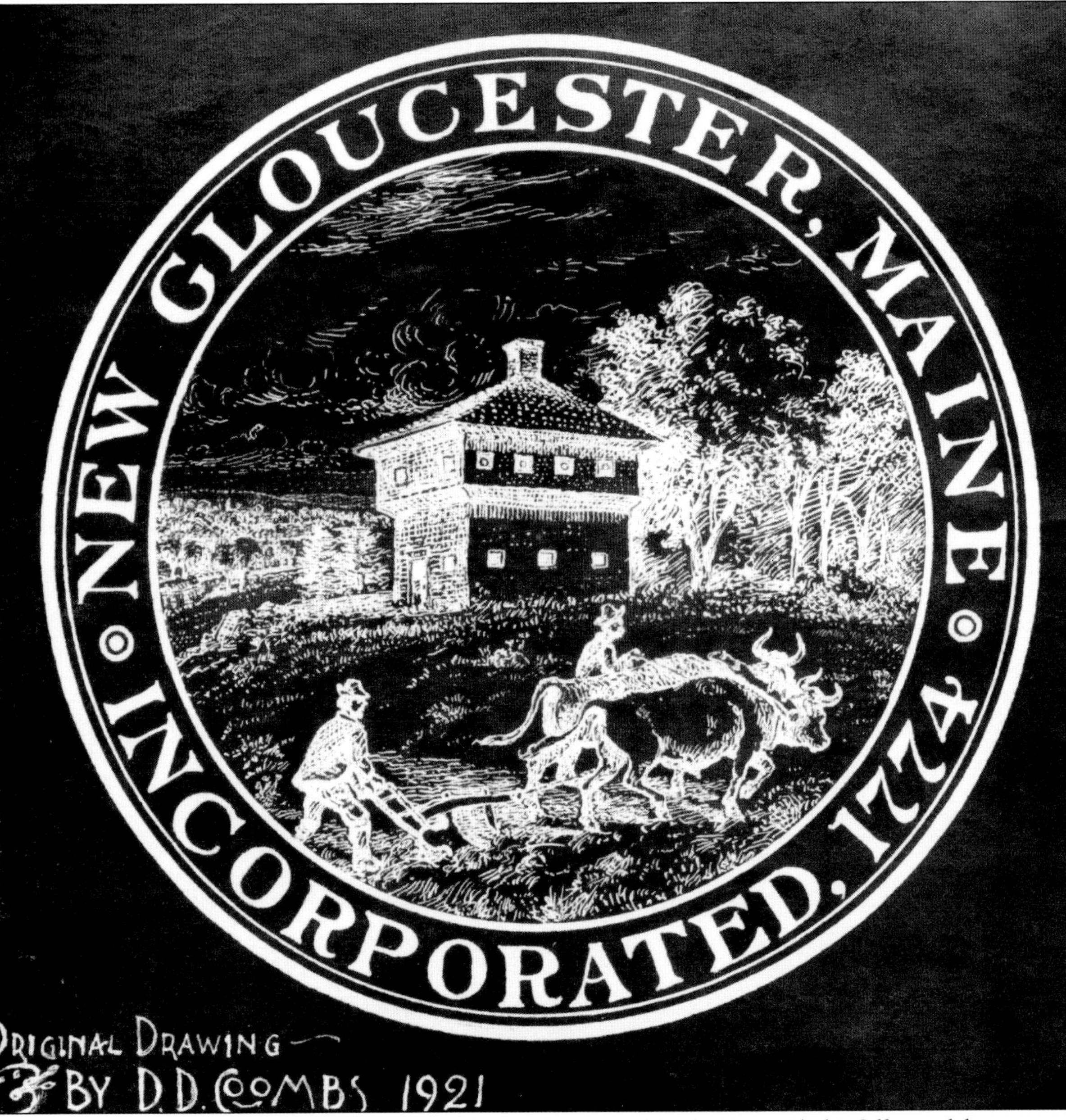

At the 1921 town meeting, it was voted "to purchase a Seal for the Town Clerk's Office and design for stationary." The town clerk at the time, John Woodman Rideout, had been considering a corporation seal for years. Local artist D. D. Coombs was paid $10 for his artistic rendering of Rideout's idea, and the seal made its debut on the cover of the 1922 annual report. (Courtesy of the New Gloucester Historical Society.)

On the cover: Oscar C. Stinchfield (above the horses on the left with the white collar) stands with his traveling sawmill, crew, and teams in 1910 at North Whitefield. A Penney Road resident, Stinchfield traveled throughout Maine and New Hampshire and set up his mill for weeks at a time. New Gloucester has a long history of sawmills and gristmills. (Courtesy of the Blake family.)

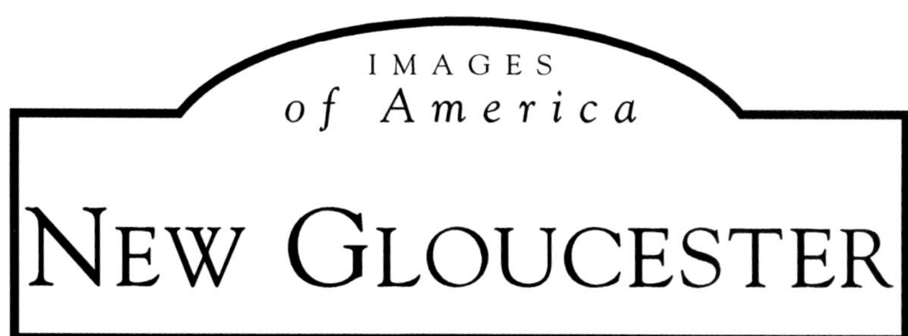

Thomas P. Blake
and the New Gloucester Historical Society

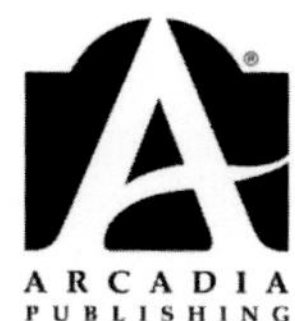

ISBN 978-0-7385-6583-5

Published by Arcadia Publishing
Charleston, South Carolina

Printed in the United States of America

Library of Congress Control Number: 2009921281

For all general information contact Arcadia Publishing at:
Telephone 843-853-2070
Fax 843-853-0044
E-mail sales@arcadiapublishing.com
For customer service and orders:
Toll-Free 1-888-313-2665

Visit us on the Internet at www.arcadiapublishing.com

This book is dedicated to my grandfather Everett Stinchfield Blake for countless stories of days gone by and for never throwing anything away.

Contents

Acknowledgments

Many thanks to the Town of New Gloucester for sharing its images and stories to make this history more complete. Thank you to Jean Libby for pushing the idea of making this book. Much gratitude to Ed and Betty True for sharing their volumes of collected photographs and information, and thank you to Earle Shettleworth of the Maine Historic Preservation Commission, Brother Arnold Hadd and Leonard Brooks at the United Society of Shakers, Stephen Chandler, Beverly Cadigan, Patti Mikkelson, Rick Andrews, Beverly Leighton, Margaret Parks, Mike Thompson, Debbie Emery, Colleen Anderson, and Everett Blake for the use of their photographs and the New Gloucester Public Library for loaning its collection.

The images in this book are from the archives of the New Gloucester Historical Society unless otherwise noted. There are many people who worked very hard through the 75 years of its existence to make the collection what it is today. Some of the notable names are John Woodman Rideout, the society's first president; Elizabeth Sedgley, the society's first honorary life member; Mortimer Blair; Alma Berry; Bill and Mal Greeley; Margaret True Racette; Ed and Betty True; Leonard Brooks; and current president Nancy Wilcox.

Thanks most of all to my family for their help and patience throughout this process, to my father, Phil Blake, for his assistance, and to my wife, Shelley, and son Isaac for still remembering what I look like. And special thanks to my editor, Hilary Zusman, for all her kind guidance along the way.

INTRODUCTION

In 1736, 60 men in Gloucester, Massachusetts, petitioned to the general court "for a grant of land, a township six miles square, exclusive of water, in the eastern part of the Province of Maine where it could be spared." The petition was granted on July 5, 1737, with the provision that, within five years, each of the 60 lots be settled on with a house and six acres cleared and have a minister and meetinghouse for worship. The proprietors met on February 17, 1738, to draw lots and chose the name of New Gloucester. John Millet swamped a road from North Yarmouth in 1739, allowing a few of the proprietors to settle. With the start of the French and Indian War, a blockhouse was erected in 1753 and 1754, which provided a home, fort, and church for 12 families for six years. The Town of New Gloucester was incorporated in 1774 and immediately formed a militia to prepare for the war with England.

New Gloucester has a rich religious history, starting with worship in the blockhouse. The first marriage solemnized in town was on December 27, 1759, between John Stinchfield Jr. and Mehitable Winship. In 1765, Rev. Samuel Foxcroft was ordained as the town minister and built his house, which still stands today. The town ended worshipping in the blockhouse and built a church/meetinghouse in 1772. The Baptist Society of New Gloucester was incorporated in 1803 and met for several years in the home of Rev. Ephraim Stinchfield, which still stands today on Penney Road. He was the town's first native-born clergyman and grandson of one of the builders of the blockhouse. The Baptists eventually formed two groups—the Freewill Baptists built a church at White's Corner in 1848, while the Calvinists built a church in Lower Village that now serves as a barn on Intervale Road.

The first schoolhouse was built in the center of town in 1764. After incorporation in 1774, the town was divided into four districts and into eight districts by 1803. The districts were abolished in 1877 to allow 11 schoolhouses to be managed by a committee. This system continued until the construction of Memorial School in 1950. The high school was built in 1903 and was used until 1962 when the town consolidated with Gray to form School Administrative District (SAD) 15 and built Gray-New Gloucester High School in Gray. The old high school now serves as the town's public library. The Opportunity Farm, a school for homeless boys, was incorporated on June 14, 1912, and became Opportunity Farm for Boys and Girls in 2001.

Lower Village (also called Lower Corner or Lower Gloucester) was built around the blockhouse and first burial grounds. The present town hall was built in 1886, while the old library (now the meetinghouse) was built beside it in 1896.

Upper Village (also called Upper Corner or Upper Gloucester) is home to the town's one traffic light and has several businesses. The current Masonic hall was built in 1903, replacing the original hall built in 1853. A racetrack was built in 1890 near the Royal River and became home to the New Gloucester and Danville Agricultural Association's annual fair.

The Intervale served as the farming and shipping center of the town, even having its own post office until the 1950s. The Royal River still meanders through the meadows on its way to Yarmouth. The Grand Trunk Railway (formerly the Atlantic and St. Lawrence Railroad) was placed through town in 1848, while the Maine Central Railroad was placed in 1870. These both had stations in town where the farmers shipped their crops to the cities. From 1914 to 1933, the Portland-Lewiston Interurban ran through town, providing luxurious passenger service. Now the Maine Turnpike goes through town, featuring one of the highway's three toll barriers.

The Shakers settled near Sabbathday Lake in 1782 in what was then called Thompson Pond Plantation. Shaker societies were set up in nine states, but the local one is now the only active Shaker community remaining. The dwelling house was constructed in 1794 and is one of 18 buildings on the community's 1,800 acres of land.

The Maine School for the Feeble-Minded was established in 1907, with the state purchasing 1,200 acres in New Gloucester, Gray, Pownal, and North Yarmouth. Most of the land and buildings are in New Gloucester. It later became Pineland Hospital and Training Center and closed in 1996. Pineland had over 40 buildings and 1,500 residents at its peak. It was purchased by the Libra Foundation and has been restored as a 19-building campus and 5,000-acre working farm.

Several interesting and notable people have called New Gloucester their home. Joseph E. Foxcroft, son of the town's first minister, Rev. Samuel Foxcroft, was original proprietor of the town of Foxcroft. New Gloucester served as a half-shire town with Portland from 1792 until 1805, with court being held in the old schoolhouse and jurors boarding at the Bell Tavern. Several lawyers lived and practiced here. U.S. representative Ezekiel Whitman practiced law in both Portland and New Gloucester. Pres. Abraham Lincoln's secretary of treasury William Pitt Fessenden and his father, abolitionist Samuel Fessenden (who studied law with Daniel Webster), were from New Gloucester. Maine's premier early mapmaker and author Moses Greenleaf grew up here on Peacock Hill and studied law here with Ezekiel Whitman.

One

The Blockhouse

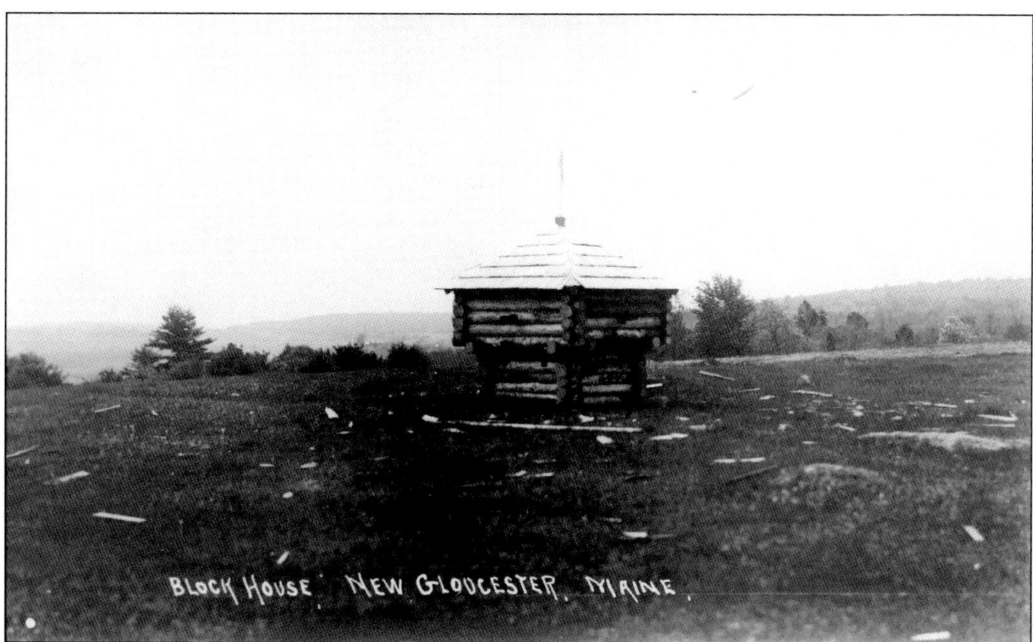

This postcard depicts the model of the blockhouse that still stands at the site of the original structure. The first settlers arrived here in 1739, but the settlement was abandoned during the Native American attacks of King George's War. The settlers returned in 1753 and began constructing the two-story fort that also served as a home and church to 12 families for six years.

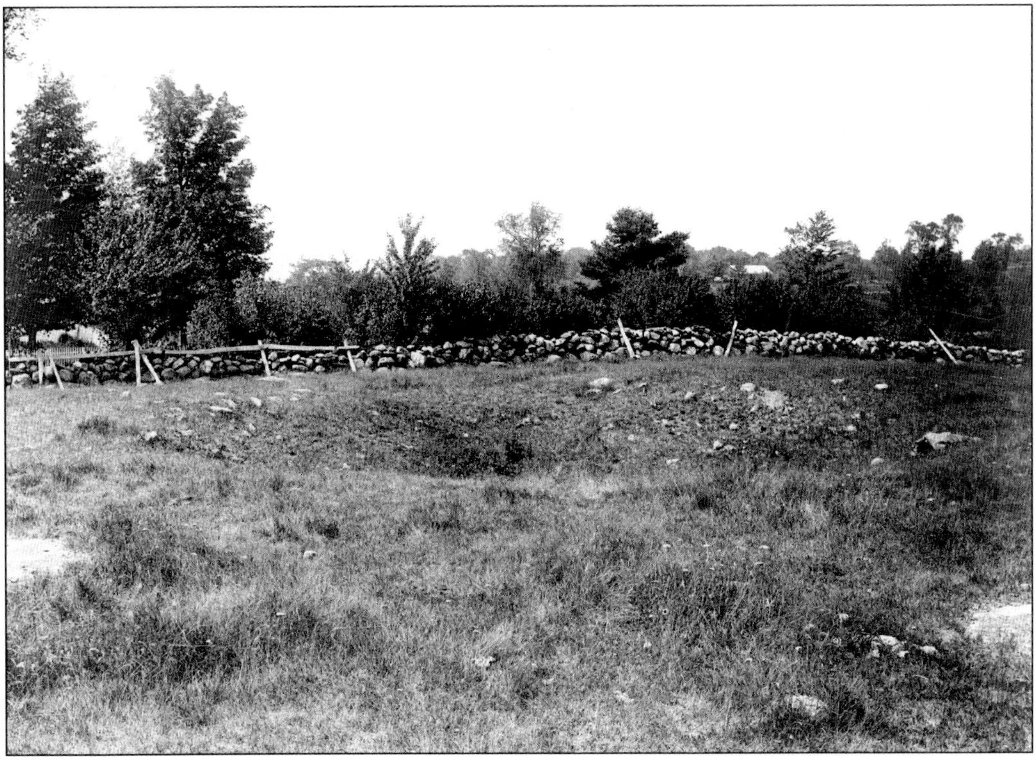

The cellar hole of the blockhouse built in 1753 and 1754 still remains. The men worked at clearing the surrounding 60 acres of common land under the protection of two swivel guns manned by a garrison of six soldiers. One attack was made upon the fort, resulting in one scalping and two men captured.

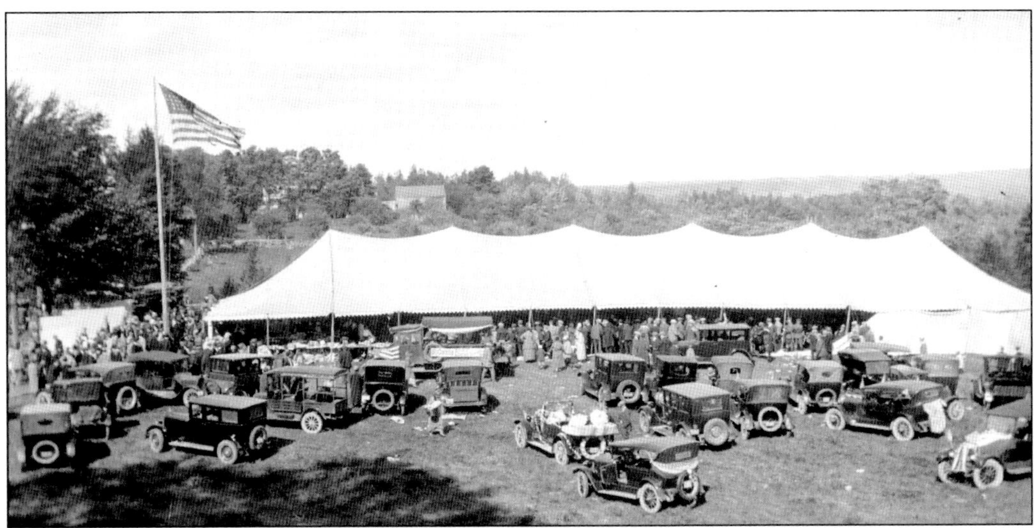

In 1924, New Gloucester celebrated 150 years of incorporation with one of the largest gatherings the town has ever seen. This view of the main tent (40 feet by 140 feet) on the blockhouse site was taken from the roof of William P. True's house at 80 Gloucester Hill Road. It was estimated that 1,500 people were in attendance.

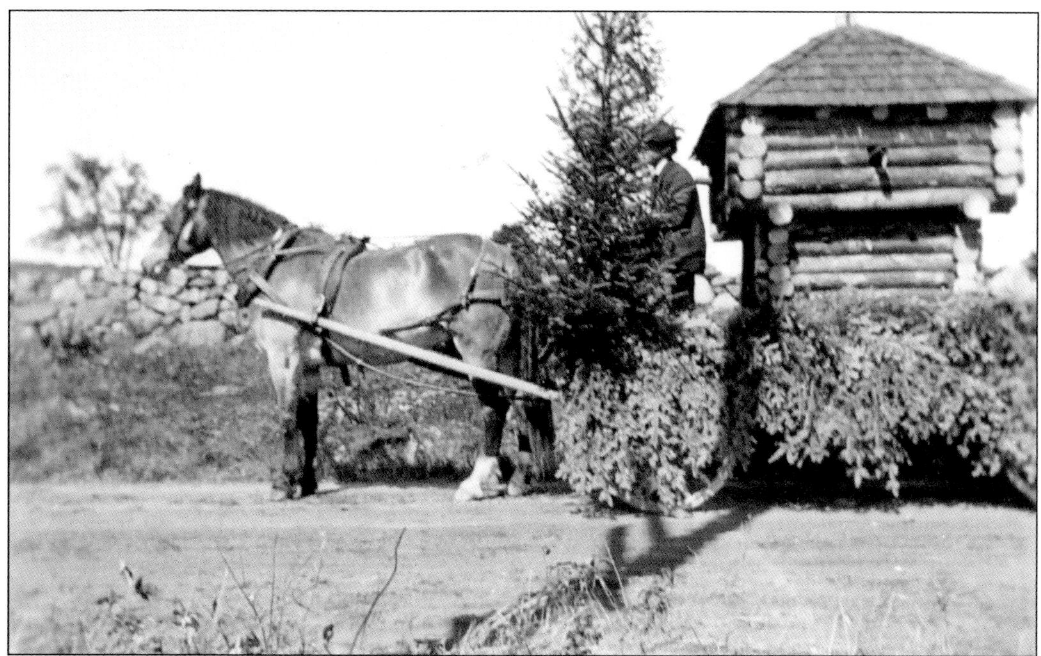

A parade consisting of 26 floats was held on Saturday, September 6, 1924, and began in front of the blockhouse site and proceeded through Lower Corner, up Intervale Road to Upper Corner, looped through Upper Village, and then went back to the starting point. The second float held the newly constructed miniature blockhouse, complete with two small guns, and was driven by Albert D. True.

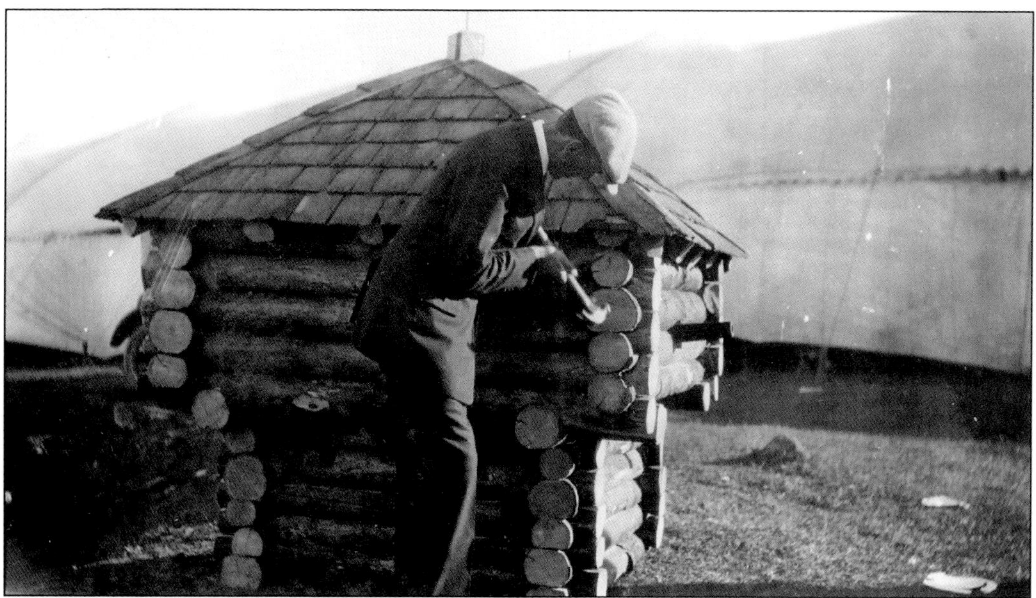

This is Harvey B. Hadley ensuring his display is complete alongside the main tent. Hadley constructed the blockhouse replica with Edgar K. Eveleth for the 1924 celebration. The original building was 50 feet on each side within a stockade that was 110 feet on a side. The palisades, 10 to 12 feet tall, were sharpened at the top.

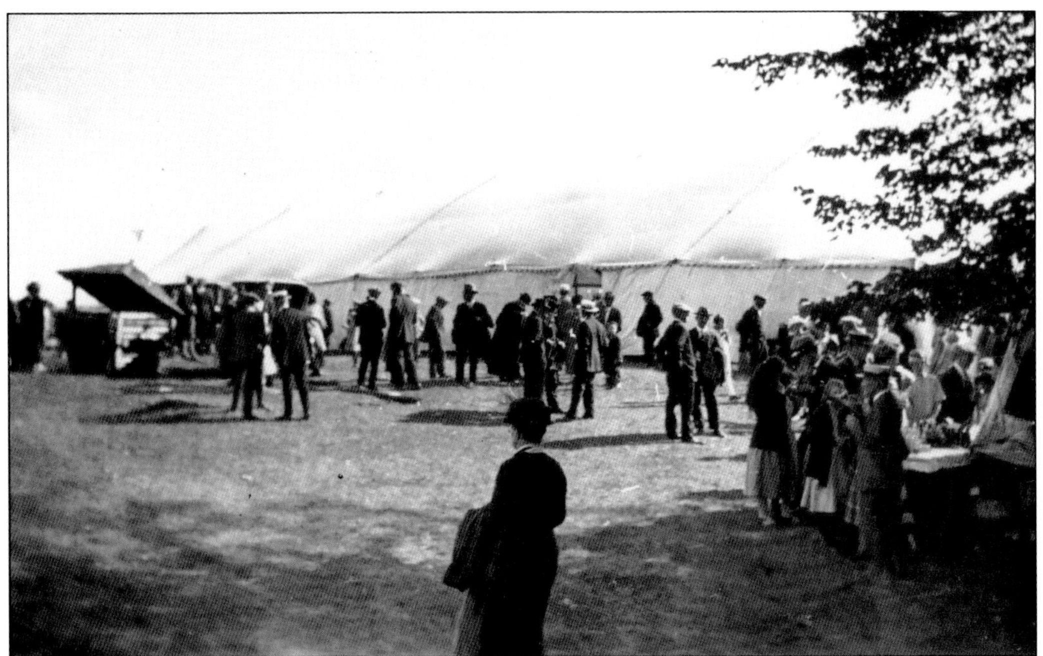

Here is a view of outside the main tent, with the refreshment tent on the right. Note the flip-top blockhouse on the left revealing the guns. Among the first guests to arrive were Mayor and Mrs. William J. MacInnis of Gloucester, Massachusetts. Maine Supreme Court justice Guy H. Sturgis, a New Gloucester native, was the key speaker.

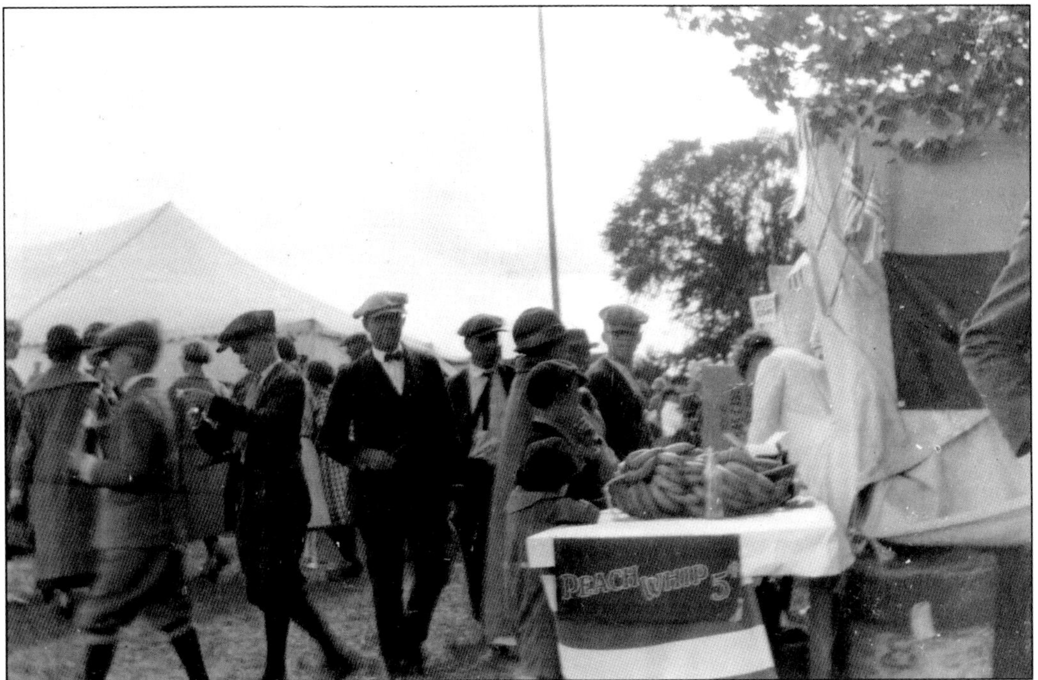

Ice cream, fruit, and drinks were served during the weekend-long celebration. This tent was run by Alice G. Nevins, assisted by Hattie E. Litchfield. The three other smaller tents were used for reception, registration, and the always-important restrooms.

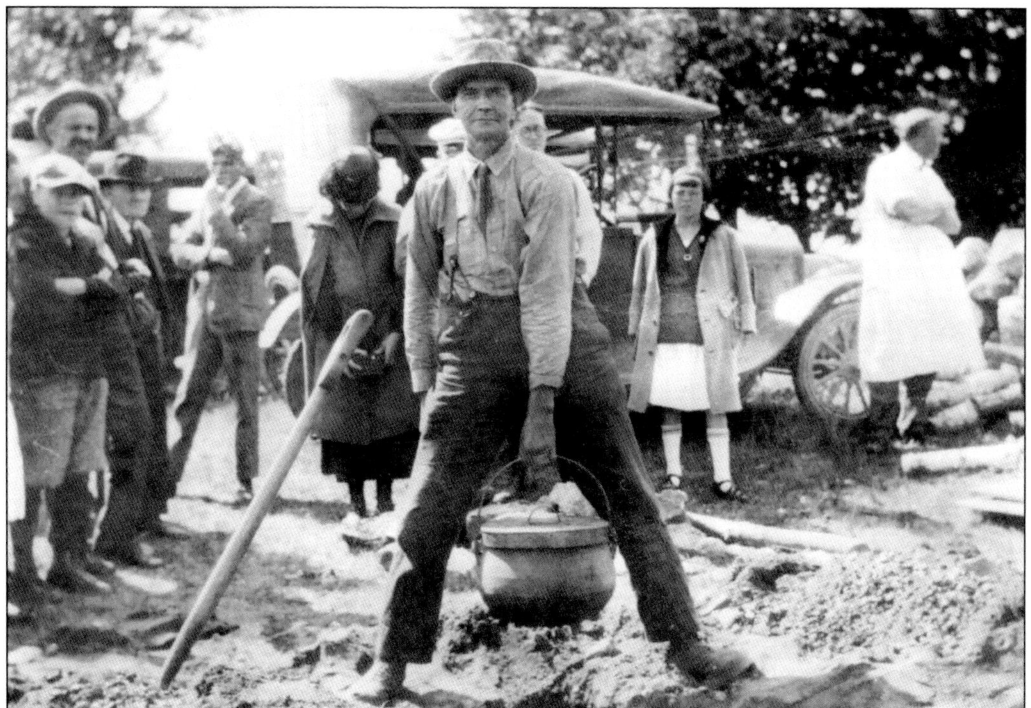

A big bean hole was made in which 12 pots of beans, containing two bushels of dry beans, were baked with 60 pounds of pork by expert bean baker Fred S. Packard of North Auburn.

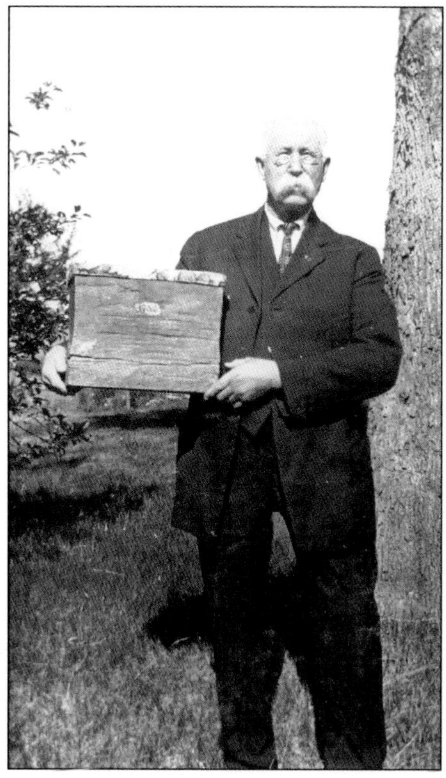

John Woodman Rideout was there displaying his box made from wood that came from the old blockhouse. He served as town clerk for 20 years, was postmaster of the Intervale Post Office, and was the first president of the New Gloucester Historical Society. By 1788, the blockhouse was no longer being used. It was sold to the highest bidder, John Woodman (Rideout's great-grandfather), for seven bushels of corn. It was taken down in sections to his farm on the Intervale, where he built a hog house.

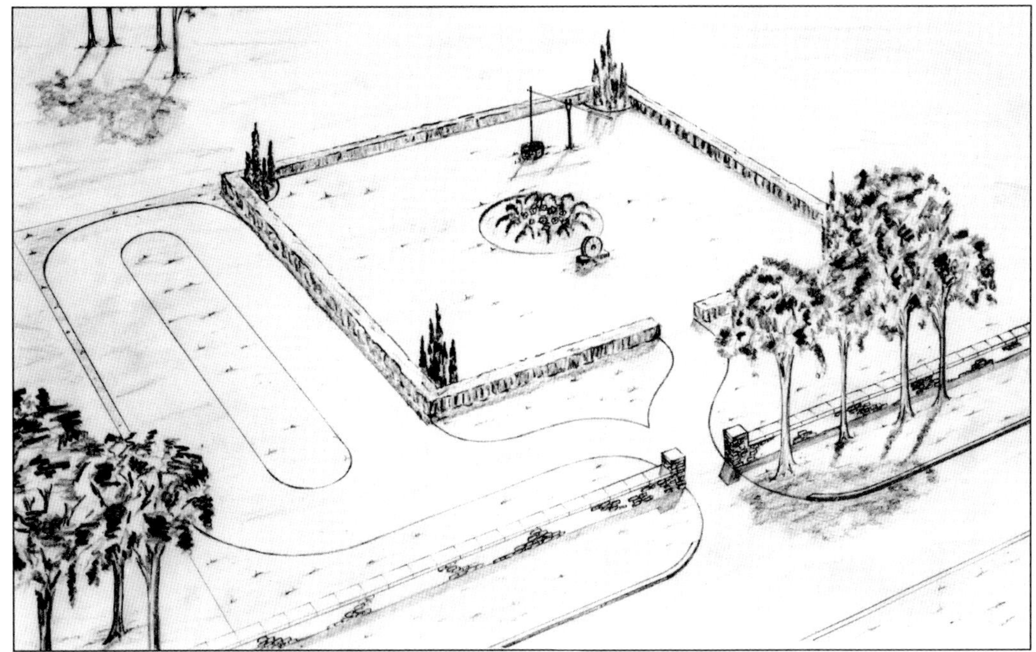

In 1952, plans were made to construct a commemorative blockhouse park. The New Gloucester Historical Society had recently purchased the 152-by-164-foot site from Donald C. Chandler. A hedge was to outline the old stockade, enclosing the replica and a new monument, while the well was to be restored.

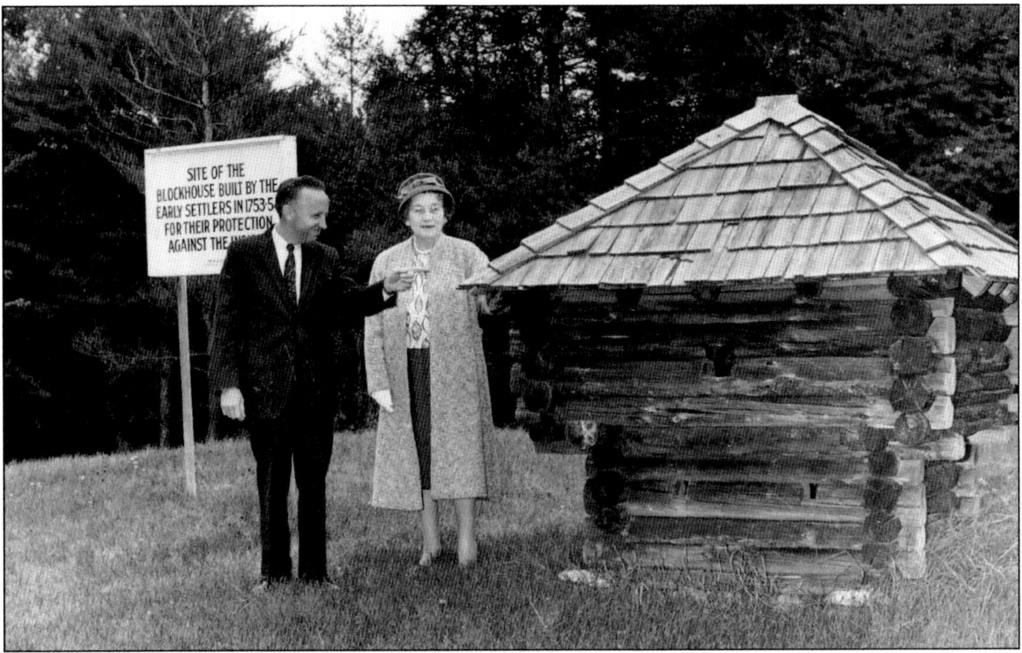

Rev. David Day and local historian Elizabeth Sedgley examine the replica during the 1965 celebration of 200 years of Christian congregations in New Gloucester. Day issued a book that year, titled *Born in a Block House, the Religious Heritage of New Gloucester*, with research by Sedgley.

Two

The Churches

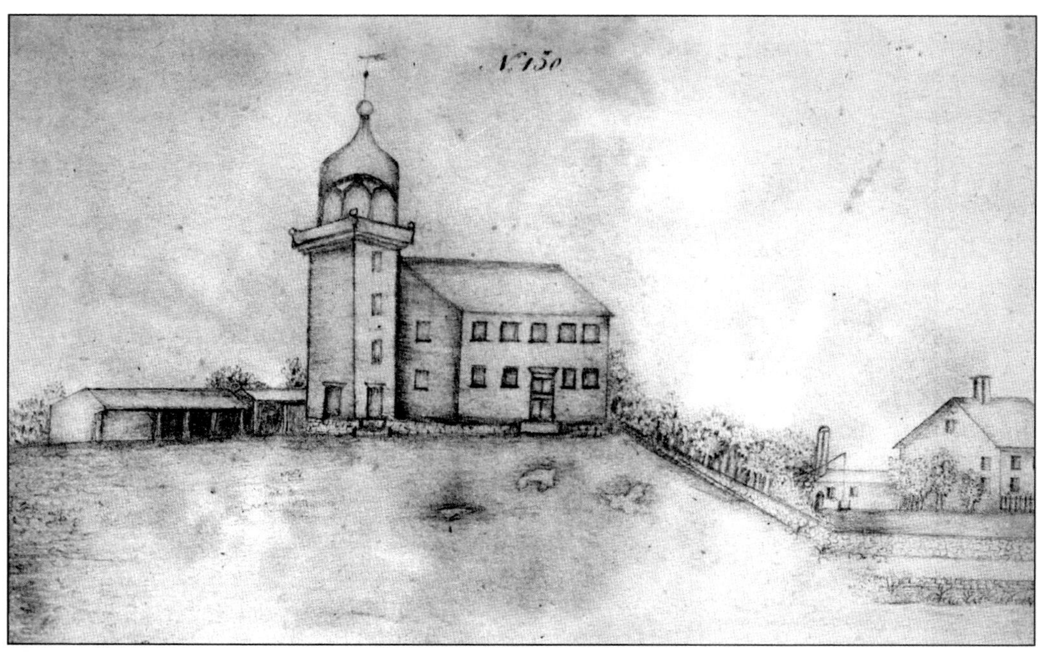

This 1838 hand sketch depicts the original church at the site of the current Congregational church. The church served as the town house, as all elections were held here. There were 26 small glass windows in two rows that let in little light. Many holes were drilled in the floor that served as ventilation but were also utilized by tobacco users for spittle. A stock of gunpowder was stored in a closet beneath the pulpit and was served out at the close of Sunday meetings. Building commenced in 1772 and was finally completed in 1798, and then the structure was razed in 1838. The blockhouse was used as the house of worship prior to this.

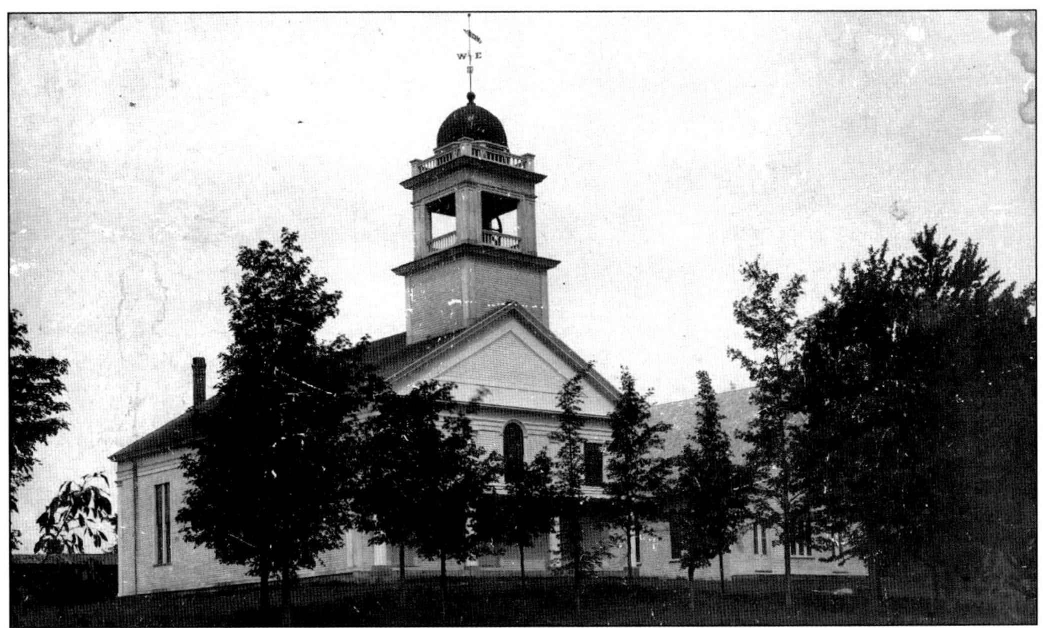

The 1839 Congregational church and 1871 vestry are seen with stables in the rear at 19 Gloucester Hill Road. This picture was taken after the 15 memorial stained-glass windows were installed in 1893 but before the town clock was installed in 1895. The clock was a gift to the town from Dea. Nelson Valentine. The maples are now much larger.

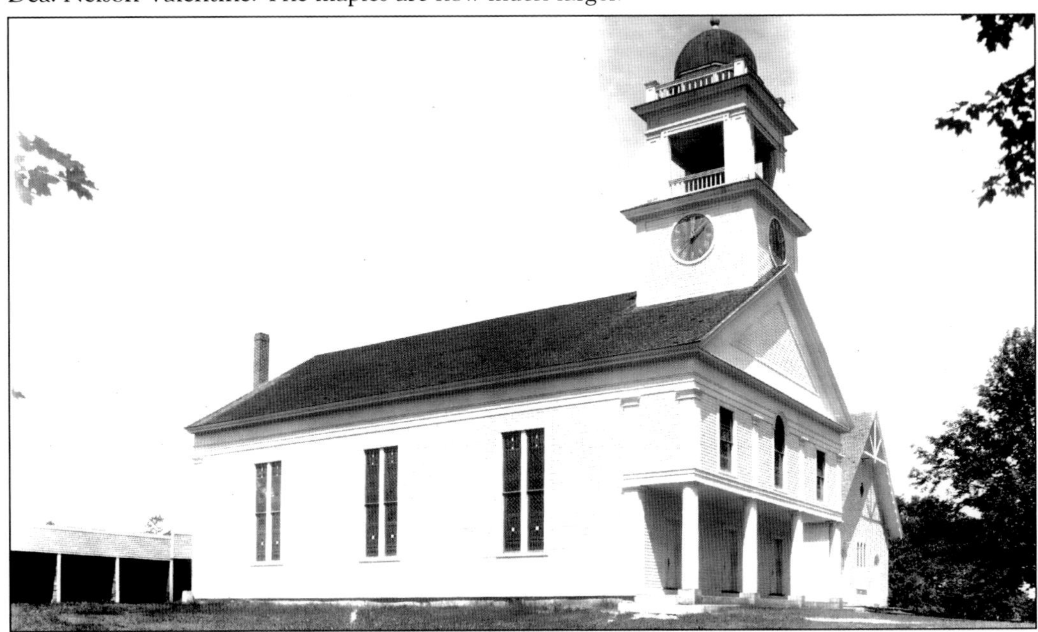

The bell was installed in 1840, weighing about 1,800 pounds and engraved, "I to the Church the living call, And to the grave summon all." After many years, a crack appeared, so townspeople contributed silver dollars to be melted and recast into the bell, resulting in a tone that is "clear and silvery." A choir was formally organized in 1856. At a parish meeting on May 27, 1853, it was voted "that no person be permitted to speak more than twice or over 5 minutes on any subject." (Courtesy of the True family.)

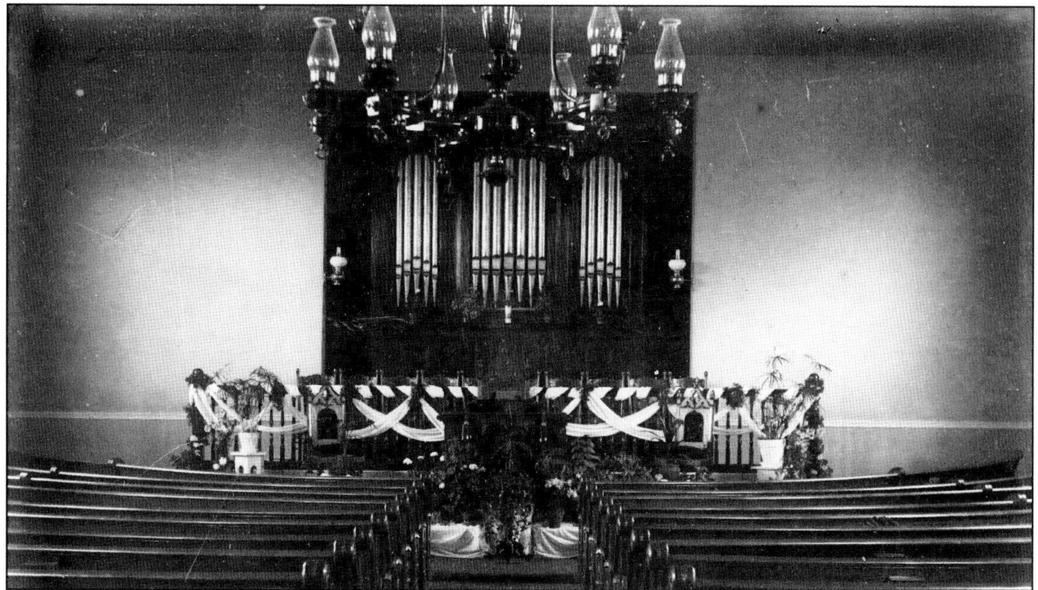

The interior of the church is shown with Palm Sunday/Easter decorations and potted plants. This was taken after October 1893 when the George Stevens pipe organ (installed in September 1857) was moved from the balcony to its current location in the alcove constructed by Benjamin Rideout. It was purchased through "the zeal and charity of a N. G. resident and Church member, Mr. S. H. Hurlbut, inspired by a healthy rivalry with the Baptist Church which also had a cabinet organ and he was resolved to outdo." In November 1964, an electric blower was installed to eliminate the need for a pumper boy.

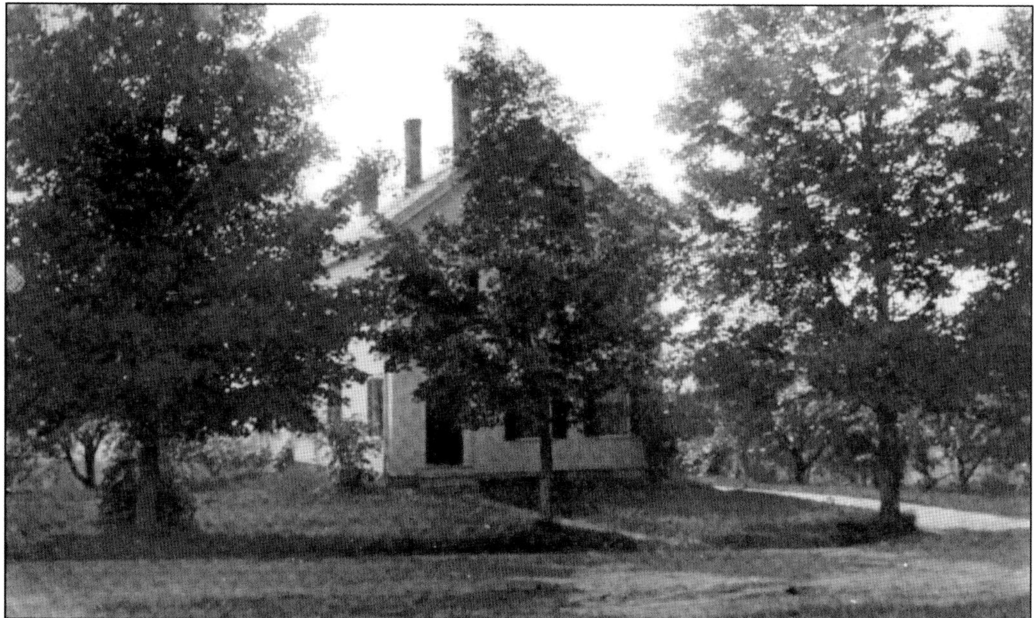

The present Congregational parsonage was built in 1866 for Rev. Wellington Cross. The church voted to install a Pine Tree Telephone and Telegraph Company telephone in April 1911. The members voted in March 1921 to have electric lighting installed in the parsonage and the vestry. It still serves as the parsonage at 30 Gloucester Hill Road.

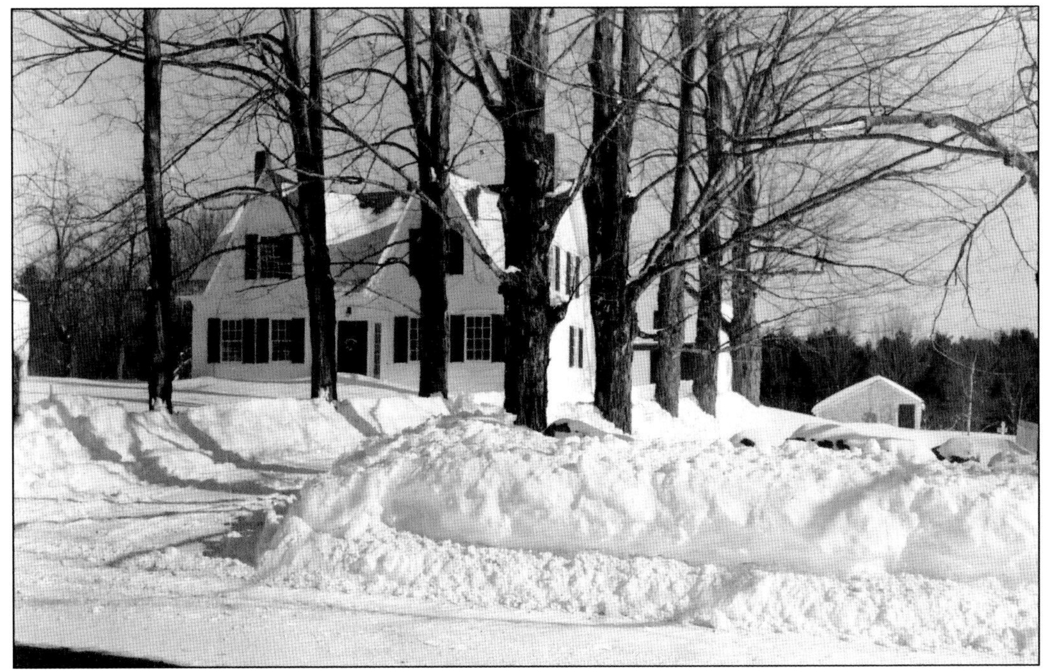

The first Congregational parsonage was the Caleb S. Haskell place and was purchased in 1855 from Seth L. Haskell and sold to Hannah Hancock in 1862 for $1,200. It serves as a residence at 34 Gloucester Hill Road beside the current parsonage.

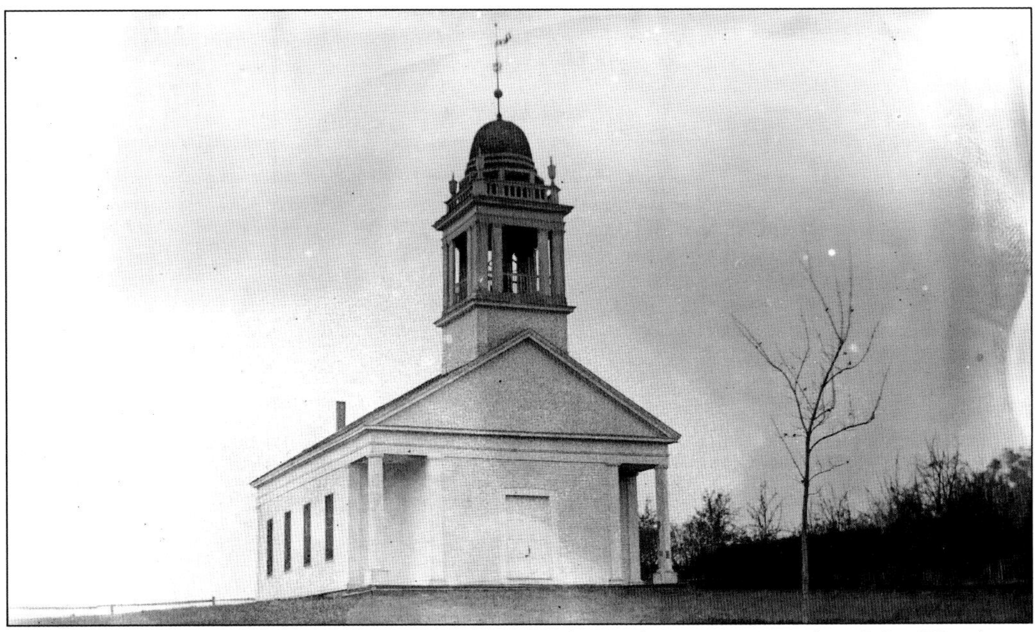

The Baptist Religious Society of New Gloucester and Gray began in 1790 when John Woodman and 72 others decided to part with the town church. This church was built in 1838. The original Baptist church was built in 1811 just below the Foxcroft house and purchased for a town house when the previous one was razed in 1838. It was then taken down in 1886 when the new town hall was constructed.

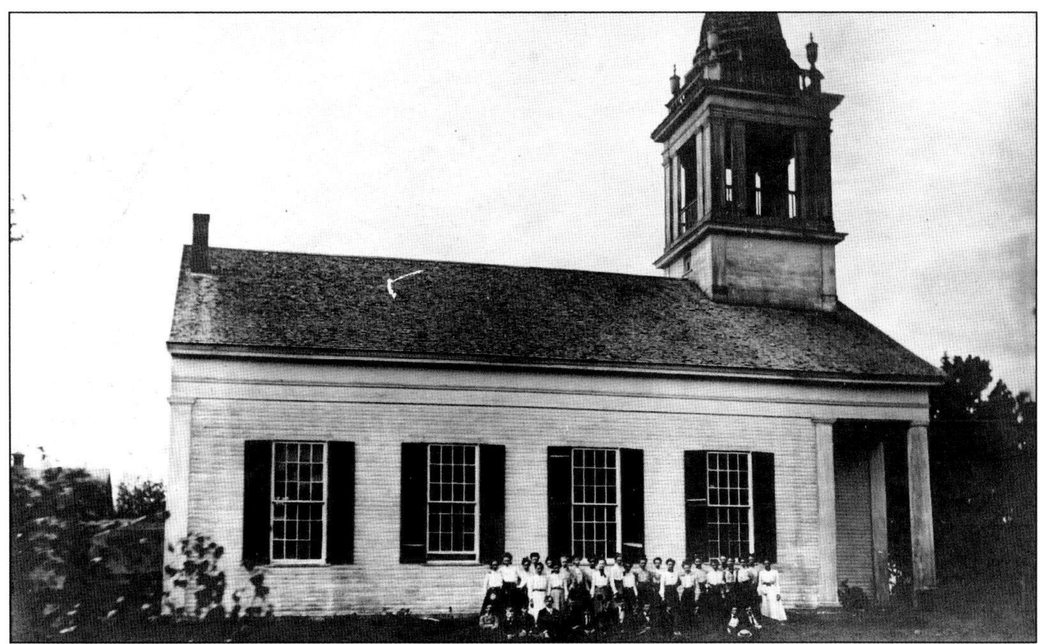

The 1838 Calvinist Baptist church is shown here when it was used as the high school between 1900 and 1902, at which time the new high school was erected. It was later turned back from the road and is now a barn at 337 Intervale Road. This church also had a parsonage across the road.

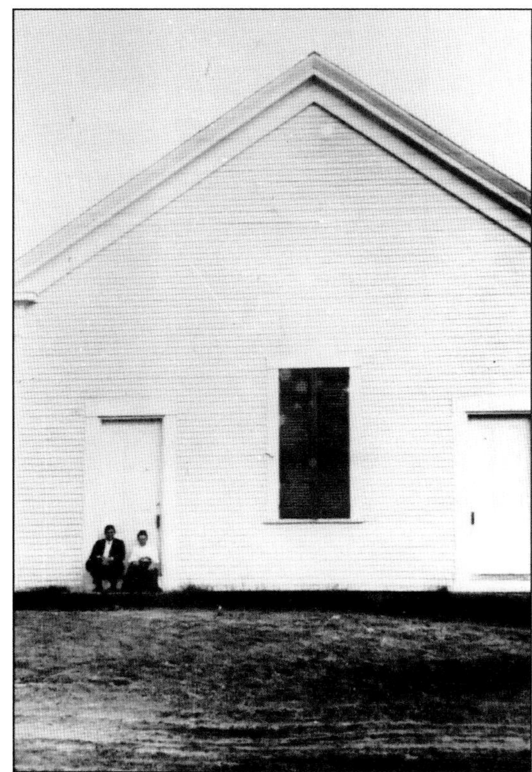

The Free Will Baptist Society was organized in April 1848, and this church was built in 1849 at White's Corner but destroyed by fire on February 8, 1929. It was rebuilt in 1930 on the same site and still sits at 211 Lewiston Road beside the Gloucester Hill Cemetery across from the current New Gloucester Bible Church.

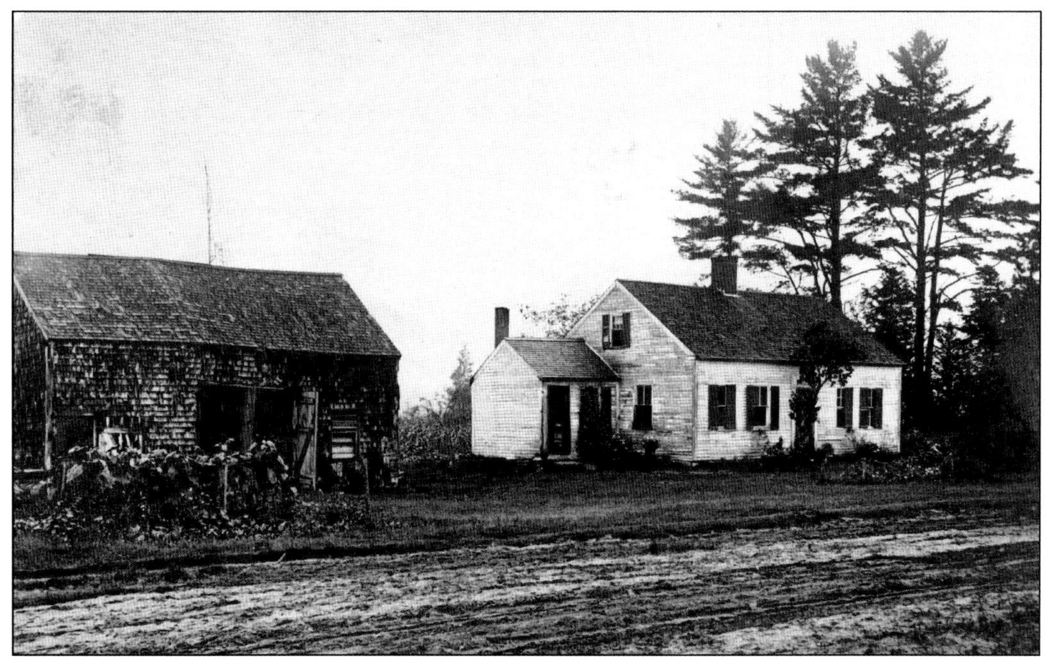

The first parsonage of the church at White's Corner was built in 1869 by Job White. The barn and shed are gone, but it is still located opposite Morse Road where it now serves as a dwelling at 72 Lewiston Road. A severe rainstorm in 1869 caused the road to suddenly cave in and create the deep gullies nearby.

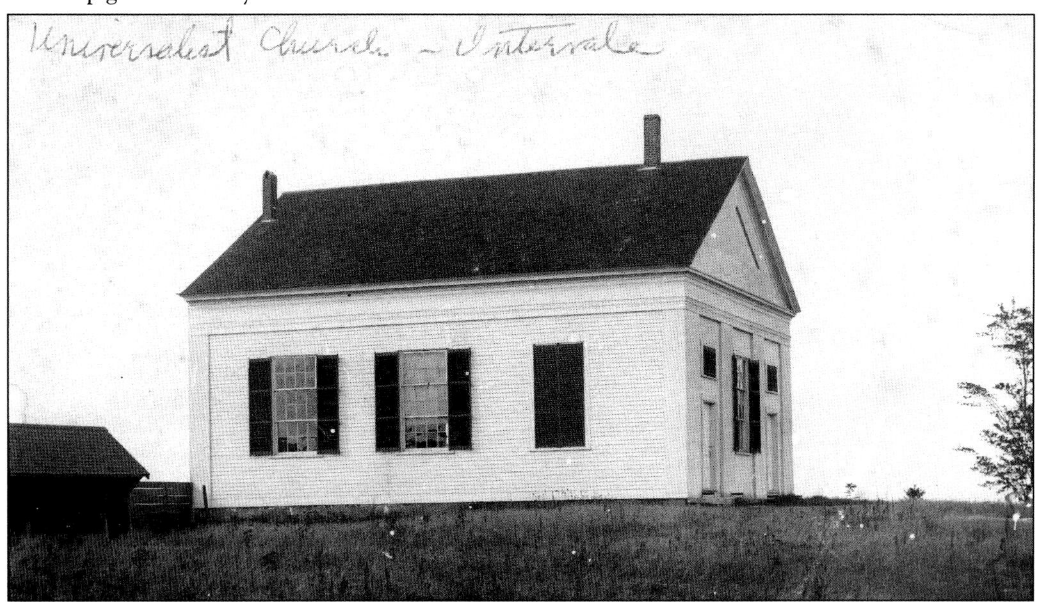

Built in 1839 by Jeremiah Cotton of nearby Pownal, the Universalist church still sits on its original site at 1131 Intervale Road. Pew No. 2, located in the first row directly in front of the pulpit, was deeded to Cotton. In 1969, the building was conveyed to the New Gloucester Historical Society, which still occasionally opens it for special functions. On June 23, 1988, the Universalist Meeting House of New Gloucester was entered on the National Register of Historic Places.

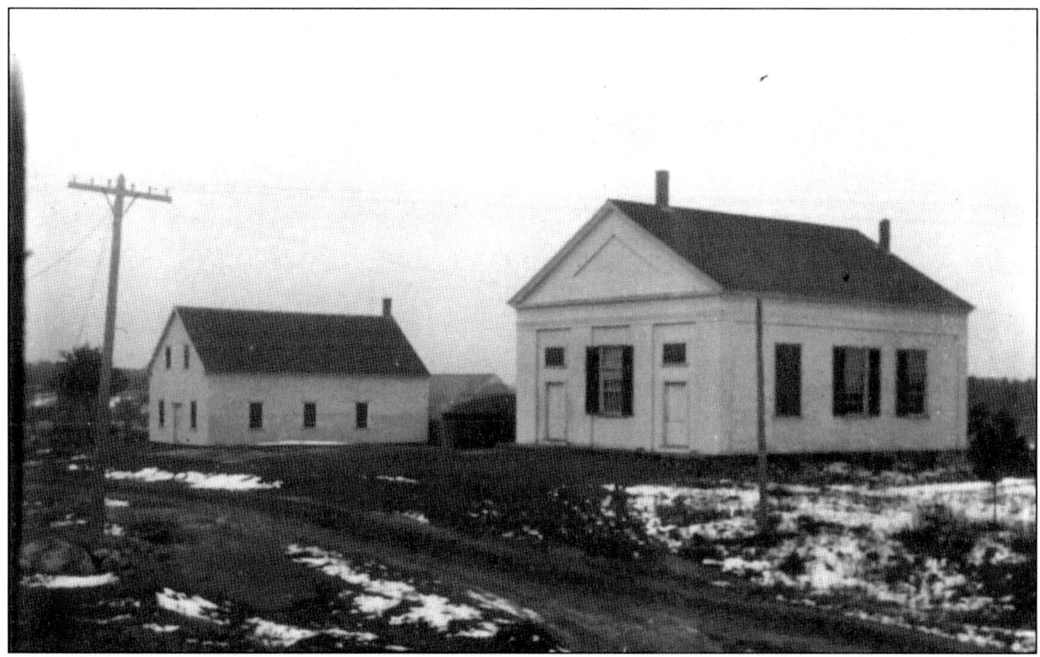

The 1904 vestry (left) consisted of a first floor, a stage, and an upstairs dining room. The church and vestry were erected upon a ledge, so they had no basements. The vestry was eventually wired for electricity, but the church never became that modern. The vestry was disassembled and moved to Grange Hall Road in 1973, where the lower floor was used by Thomas Moser for a furniture display room. A stable was also constructed in 1905 to accommodate 16 horses. (Courtesy of the Maine Historic Preservation Commission.)

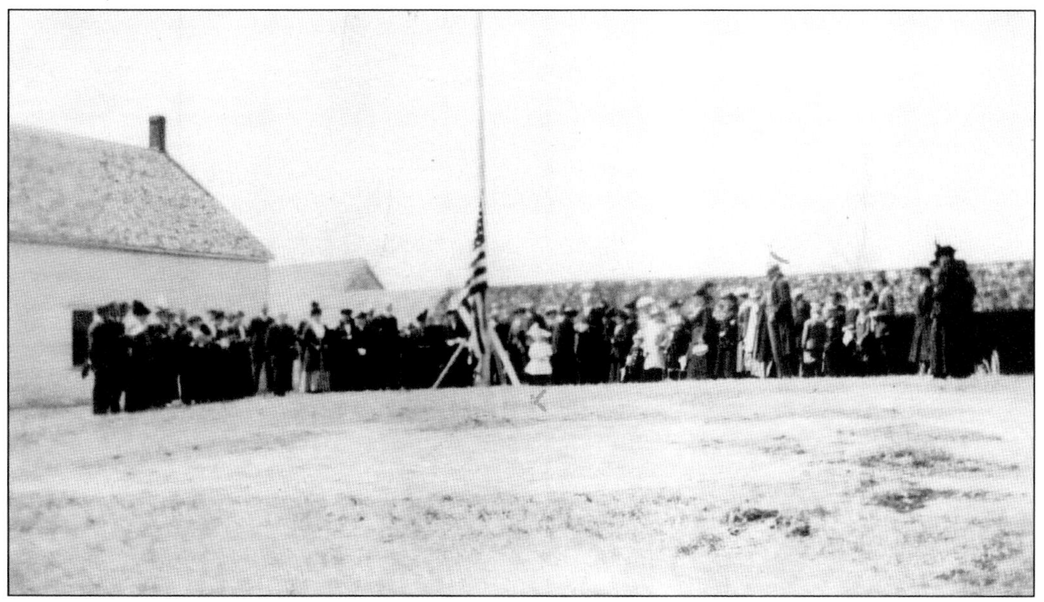

A flagpole, donated by S. Clifton Clark, was placed between the Universalist church and vestry for this ceremony held on April 22, 1917. Little Irma Jones (Cox), age four, was in charge of hoisting the flag. After repeatedly saying, "I can do it, I know I can do it!" she raised the flag without hesitation and was cheered as it rose.

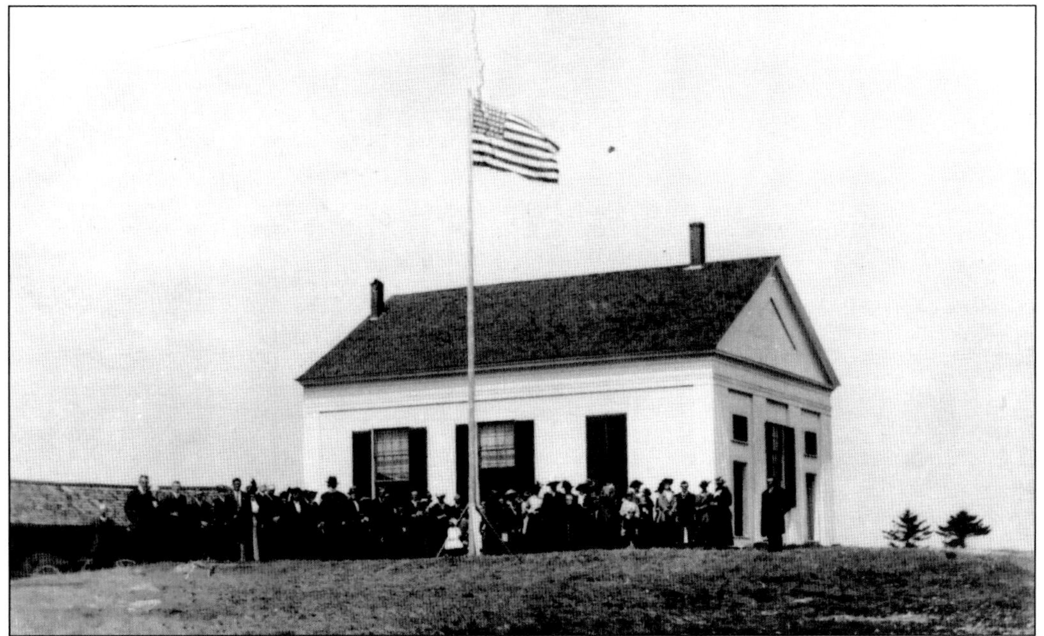

The formation of the First Universalist Society of Christians in New Gloucester in 1805 was one of the earliest formal associations of Universalists. Members from Gray, Poland, and Pejepscot were also included in 1830, when the society reorganized to become the First Universalist Society of New Gloucester and Pownal. Services were held regularly until the 1930s and sporadically until 1957. It is reportedly the oldest church of the denomination in the state.

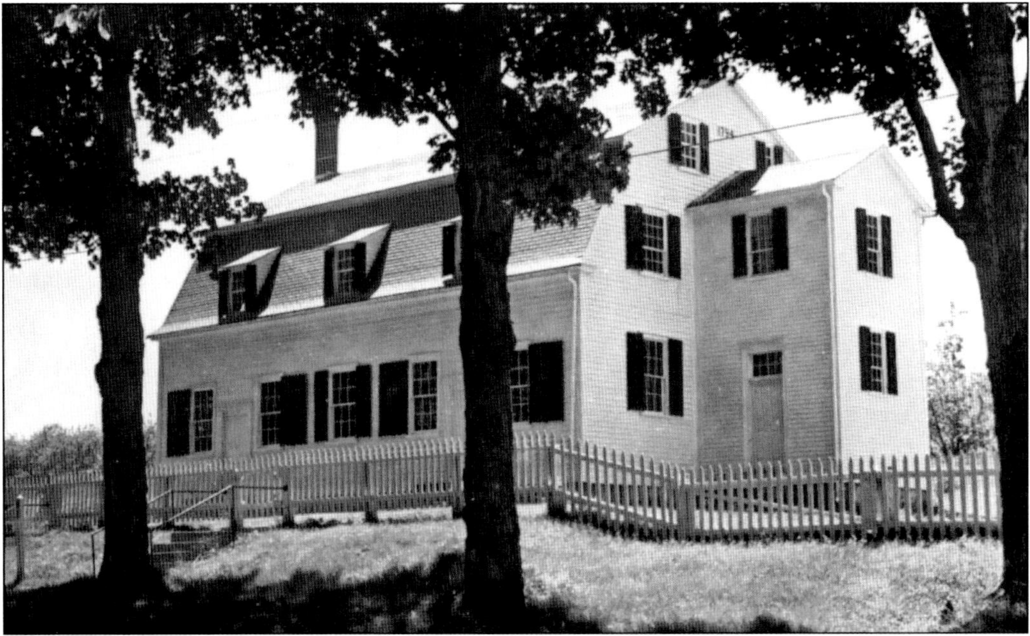

The first Shaker meeting ever held in New Gloucester was in a house owned by Gowen Wilson in 1782. The meetinghouse was built in 1794 by Moses Johnson and was one of several that he built at Shaker villages throughout New England. This building is still used today at the only active community remaining in the country.

Three

The Schools

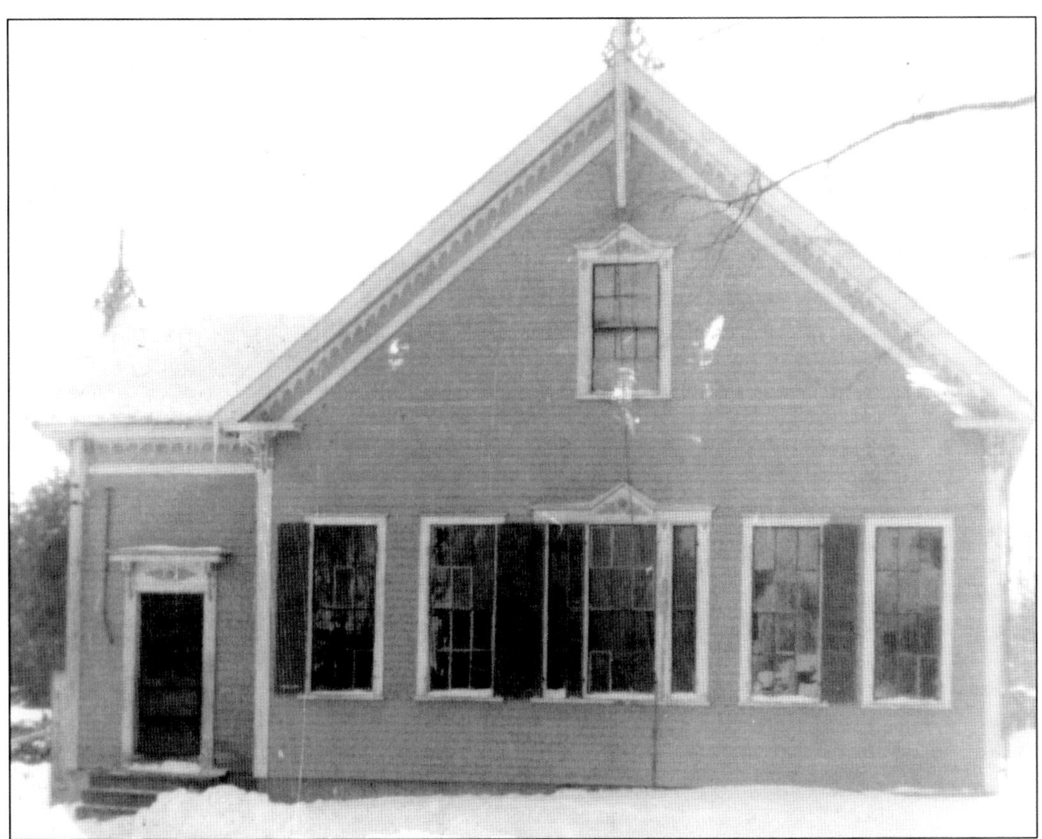

The Lower Corner Schoolhouse was built in 1883 in school district No. 1 on the site of the old town pound. It served as a school until consolidation and the opening of Memorial School in 1950. The town deeded the lot to New Gloucester Grange No. 28 in 1957, and it was released back to the town in 1978. The building was demolished in 1980, and the lot now sits vacant just below the Village Store. (Courtesy of the True family.)

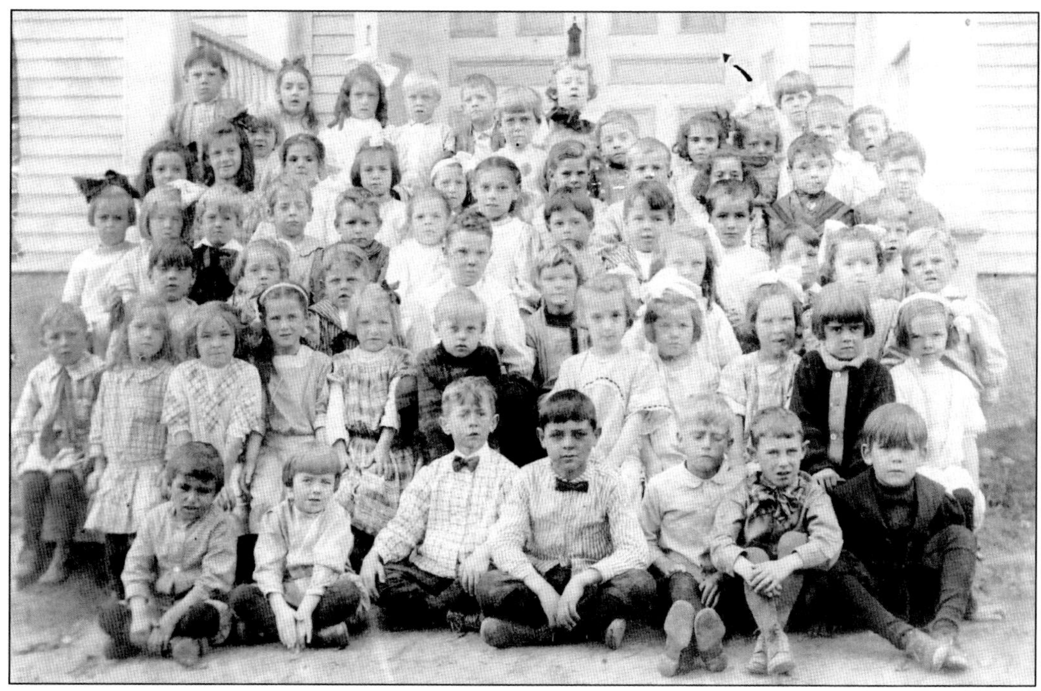

The boys used the front entrance and coatroom, and the girls used the rear. A woodstove sat at the front of the room, and boys and girls each had "two-holers" out back. This group of Lower Corner students taught by Minerva Quint is pictured on the front steps of town hall.

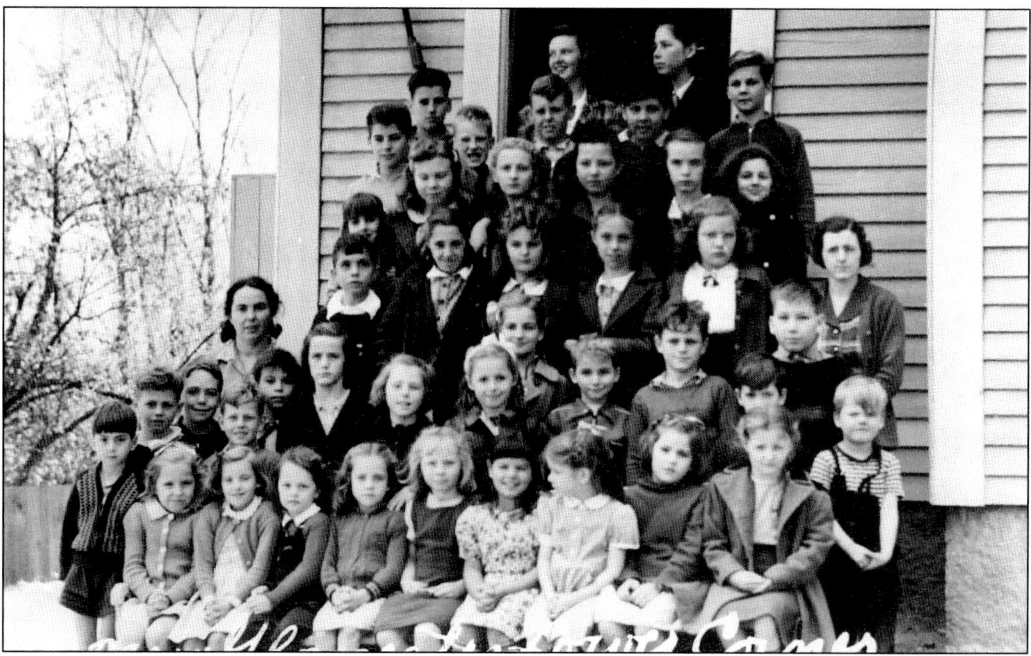

The front left steps of Lower Corner Schoolhouse are covered with students led by Ellen McCann and Ruth Burton Ayer in October 1941. A stone marks the corner of the school lot and was inscribed "1883" by Jabez and Elbridge True, builders of the schoolhouse. The previous schoolhouse sat across the road from this one.

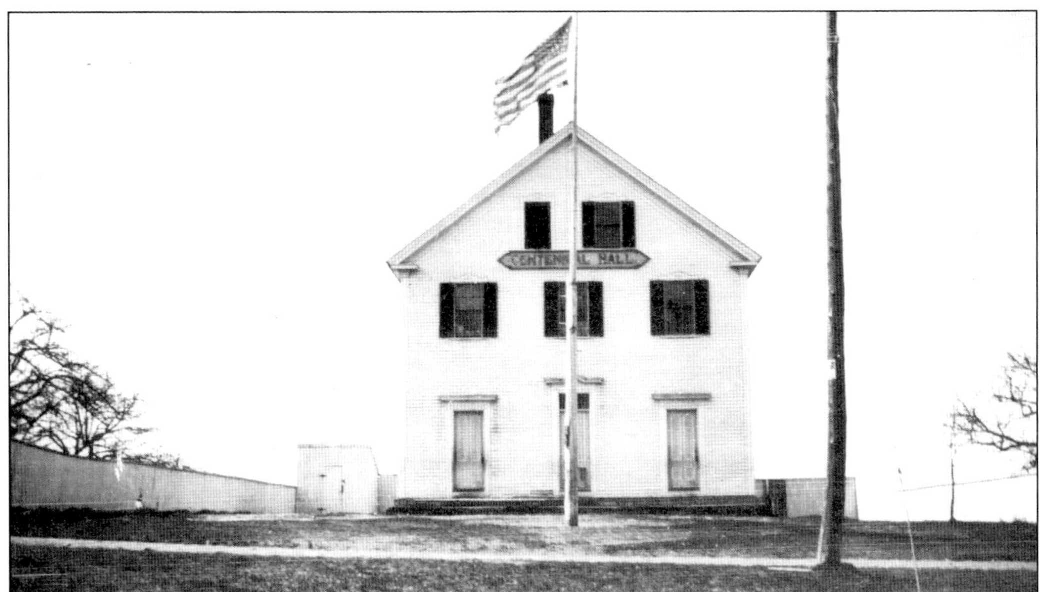

Built in 1876 during the United States' centennial, this building was named Centennial Hall. It was located on Upper Village Street behind the current Cloutier's Market. The lower floor was used for school district No. 2, while the upper floor contained a large hall. The town voted to dispose of the building in 1961. (Courtesy of the True family.)

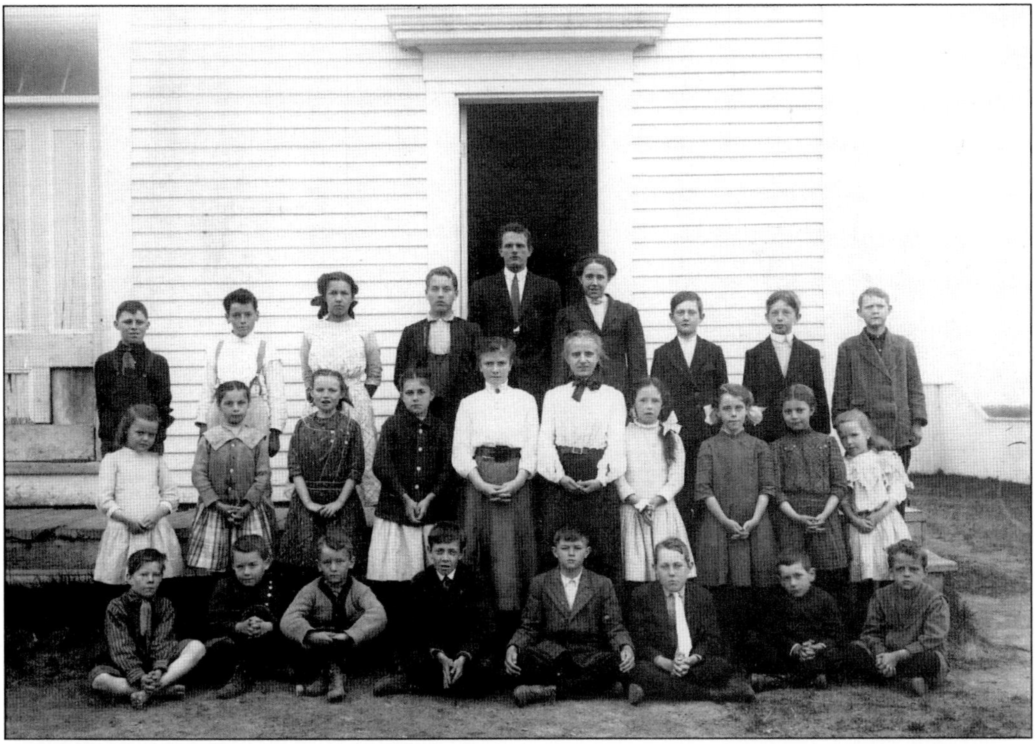

Ernest H. Hunnewell is shown with his students on the front steps of Centennial Hall. He served several years there as a teacher until 1912, when he became superintendent in charge of a dozen one-room schoolhouses and their teachers.

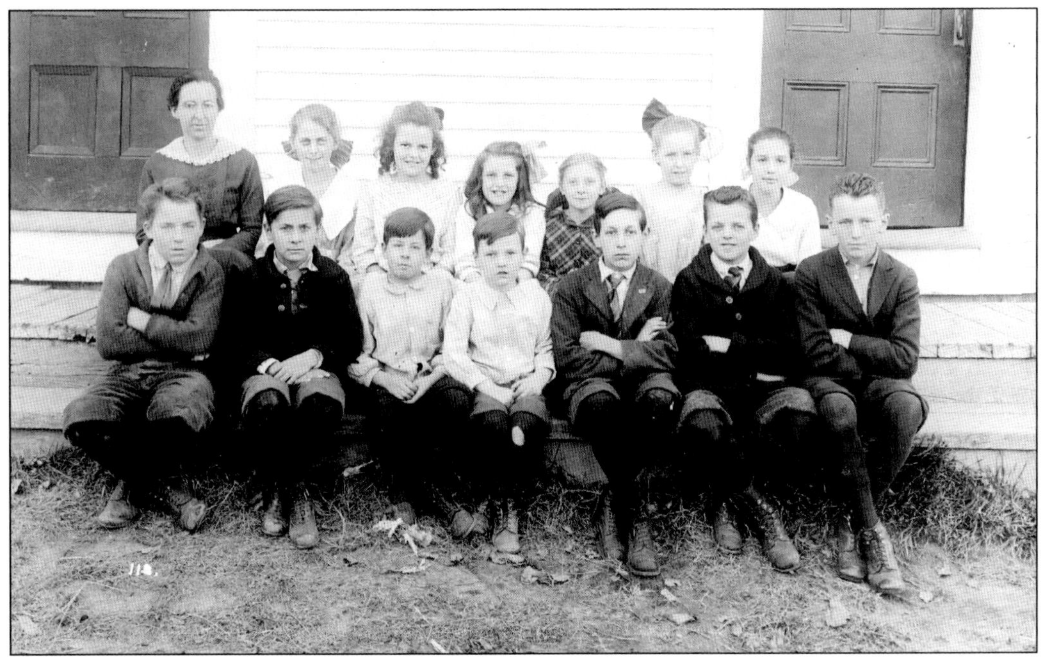

Angie Hawkes True sits with her pupils on the steps of Centennial Hall in 1919. From left to right are (first row) Merrill Peaco, Robert Eveleth, Kempton Eveleth, Herbert Chamberlain, John Lane, Norman Ray, and William Loring; (second row) Hawkes, Magdalene Gordon, Dorice Chapman, Norinne Chamberlain, Ruth Farnum, Grace Chapman, and Alice Morey.

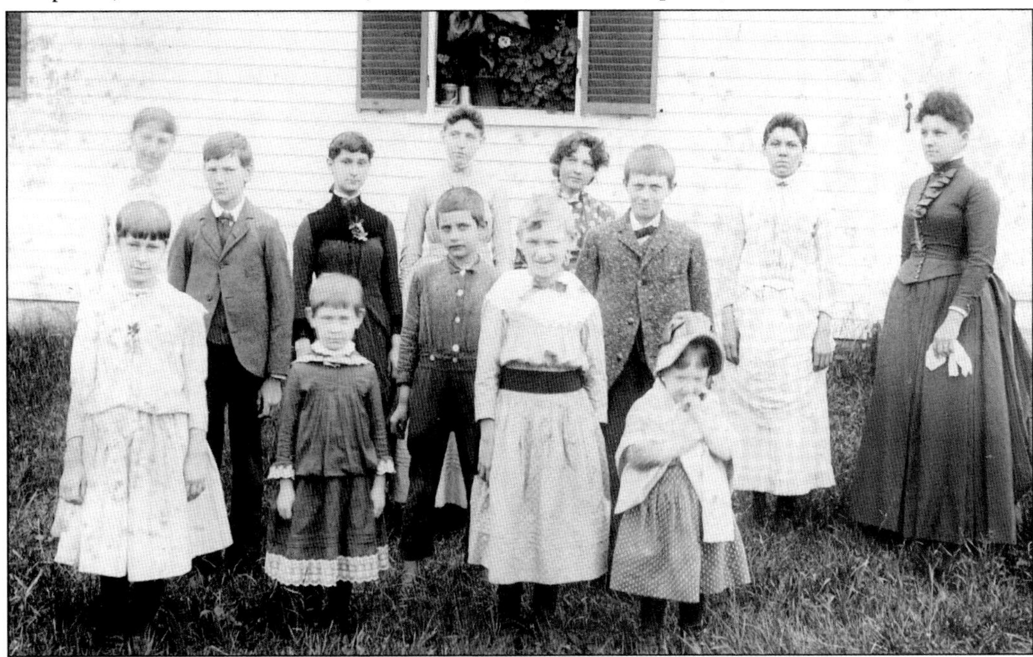

Luetta M. Wescott is shown with her students at Bald Hill Schoolhouse in district No. 3 about 1888. From left to right are (first row) Imogene Farnum, Edna King, Blanche Rowe, and Agnes Edwards; (second row) Rol Rowe, Lyman Winslow, and Nate Downing; (third row) Fanny Wells, Florence Farnum, Ethel Jordan, Sadie Davis, Ella McCann, and Wescott.

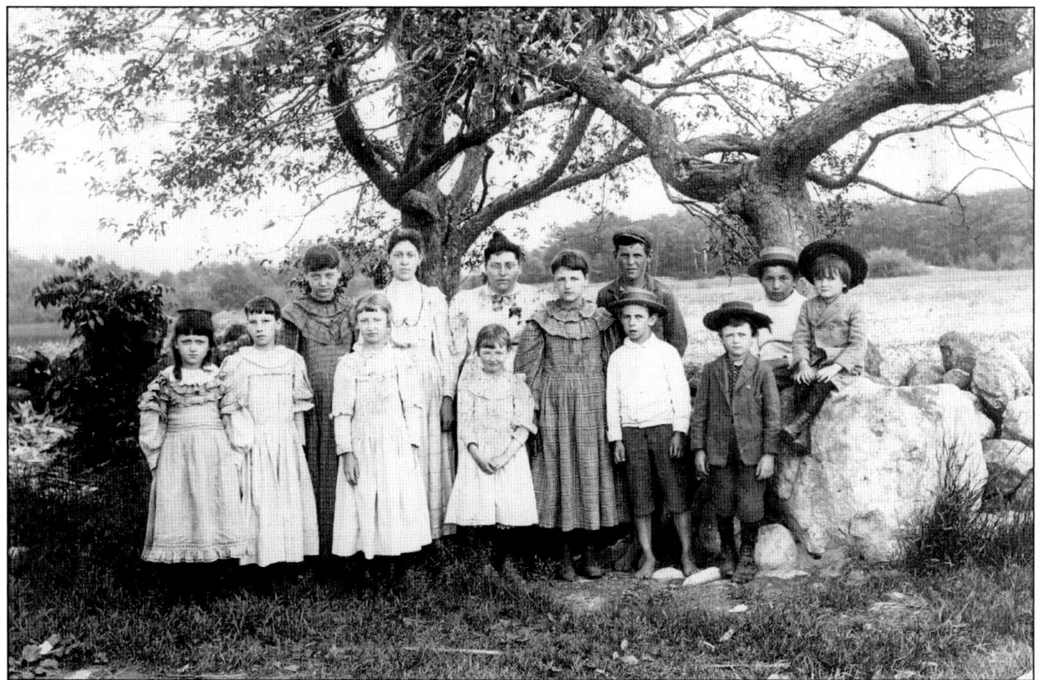

Ursula L. Wilson poses with her Bald Hill students in 1896. From left to right are (first row) Julia Nelson, Edith Pendexter, Effie Edwards, Edith Edwards, Louise Rowe, Clifton Whitney, and John Nelson; (second row) Agnes Edwards, Edna King, Wilson, Alton Farnum, Grover Winslow, and Ned Nelson. This school sat at the corner of Bald Hill Road and Tobie Road and closed in 1944.

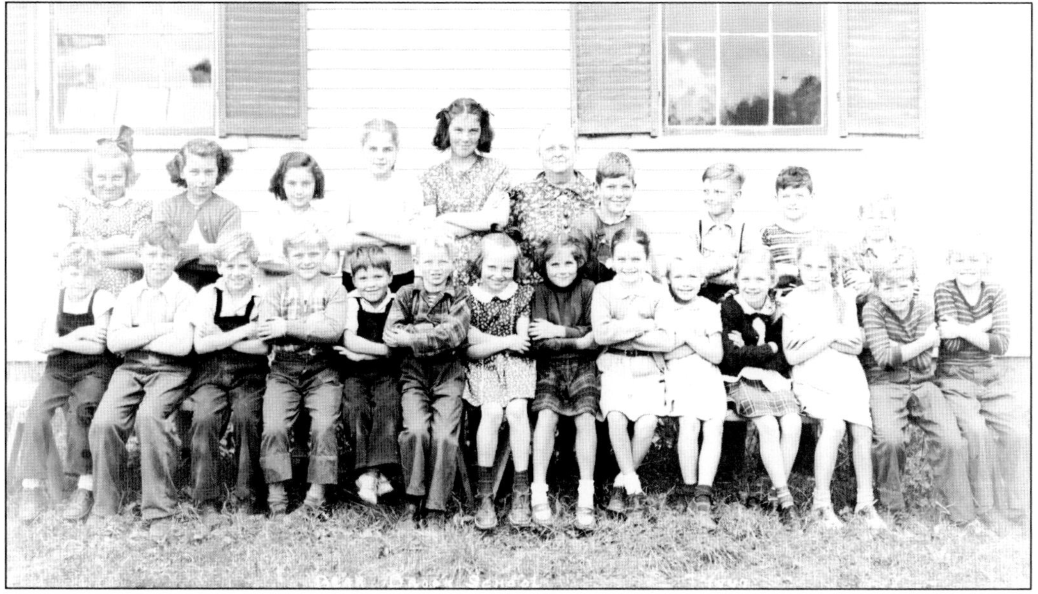

Bear Brook Schoolhouse served district No. 5 and was located at the entrance of North Pownal Road at Fogg's Corner. This replaced the previous building in 1886 on the same site. The first building was moved across the road for a Grange hall, while this one became a dwelling at 16 North Pownal Road. The 1947 class led by Mabel True Jones is shown here.

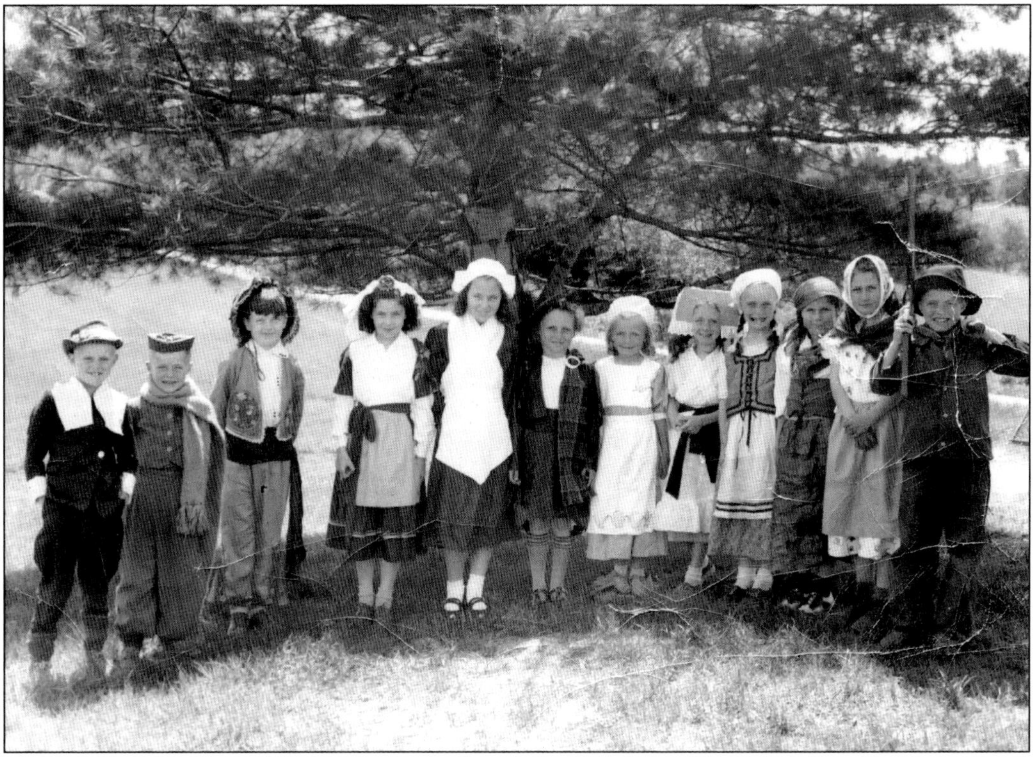

These Bear Brook Schoolhouse students dressed to represent different countries around 1947. From left to right are Bob Hill, Allan Hill, Rodney Orr, Patricia Farwell Edwards, ? Sanborn, Pauline Burns Bragdon, unidentified, Brenda Ford Bradbury, Laura Hill, Janet Babb Ray, unidentified, and Jake Hill.

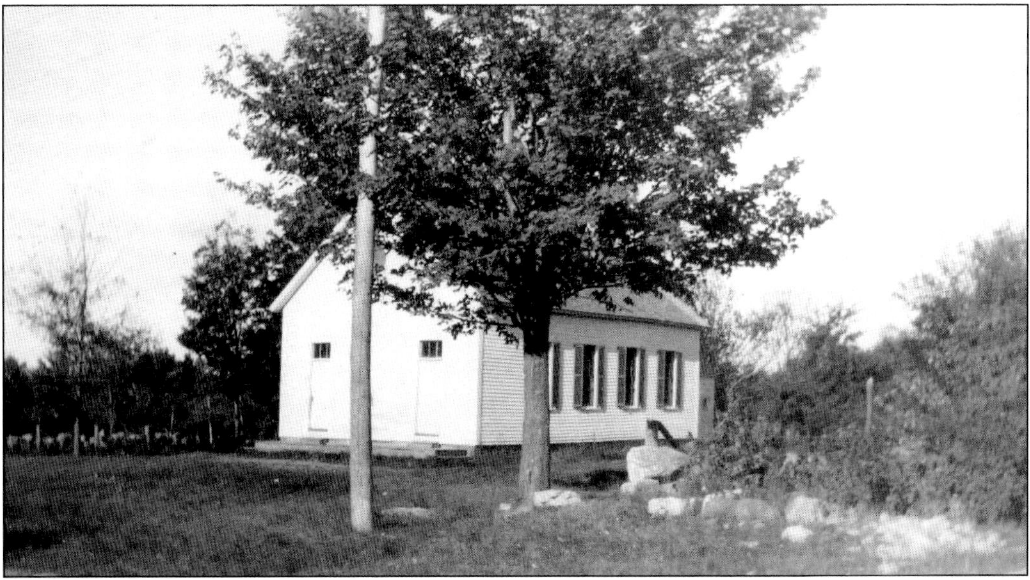

Over the Hill Schoolhouse (also called Gloucester Hill and Harris Hill) in district No. 6 is shown here in 1923 where it still remains as a summer residence at 381 Gloucester Hill Road. It was even used for apple storage by Thompson's Orchards.

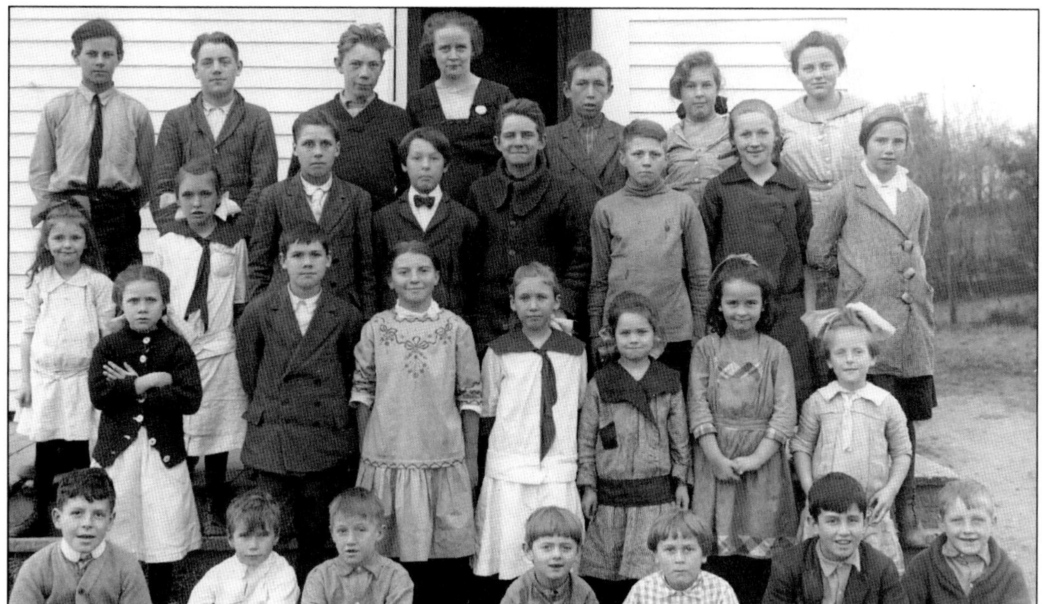

Muriel Stinchfield Blake is shown here standing with her pupils at Gloucester Hill Schoolhouse in 1914. This building was constructed in 1879. The previous schoolhouse was located on Lewiston Road opposite the entrance of Gloucester Hill Road.

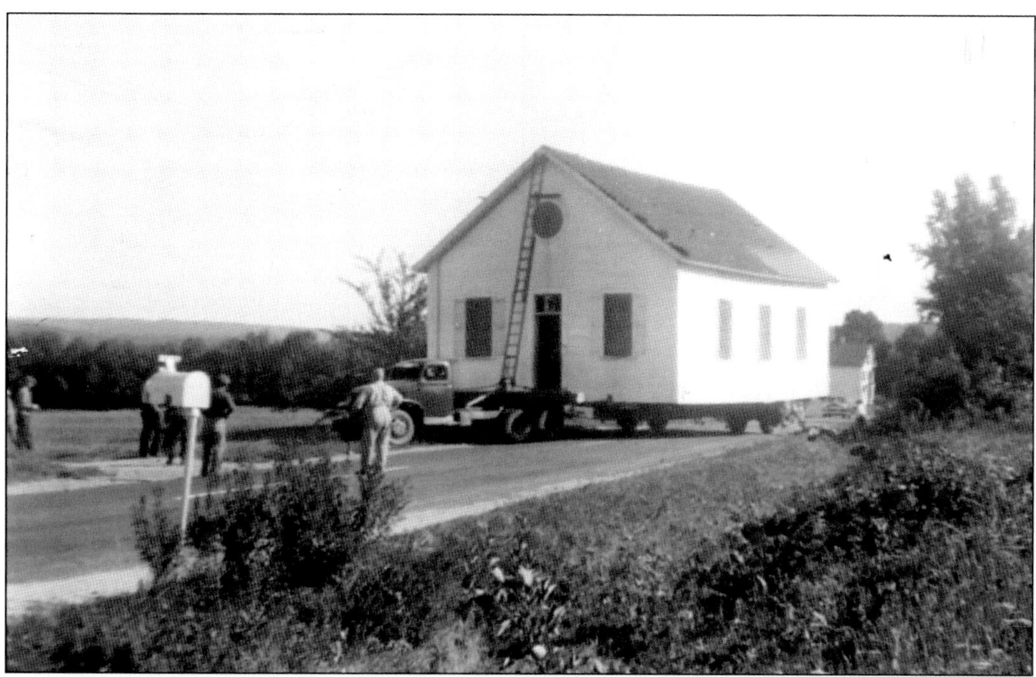

The 1878 Pond Schoolhouse, which served district No. 7, is shown here in 1947 being moved from its original spot near the Grange hall opposite Sabbathday Lake to its current location at 613 Shaker Road where it is a home. It was last used as a school in 1943.

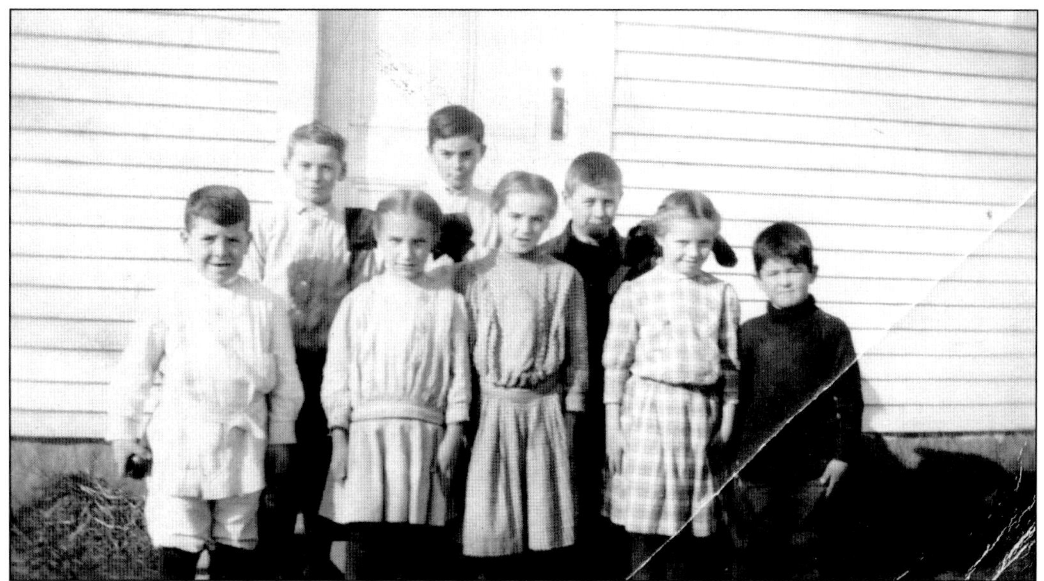

Students are shown here in 1913 posing outside Webber Schoolhouse, which served district No. 8. It sat beside Webber Cemetery on Intervale Road near Pineland. The door on the left was for the girls, and in that entry were a sink, a water pail, a tin dipper, and a tin wash basin. The door on the right was for the boys, and in that entry was the wood box for the big box stove. The schoolhouse was closed in 1918 and sold to the state to be used for a blacksmith shop at Pineland.

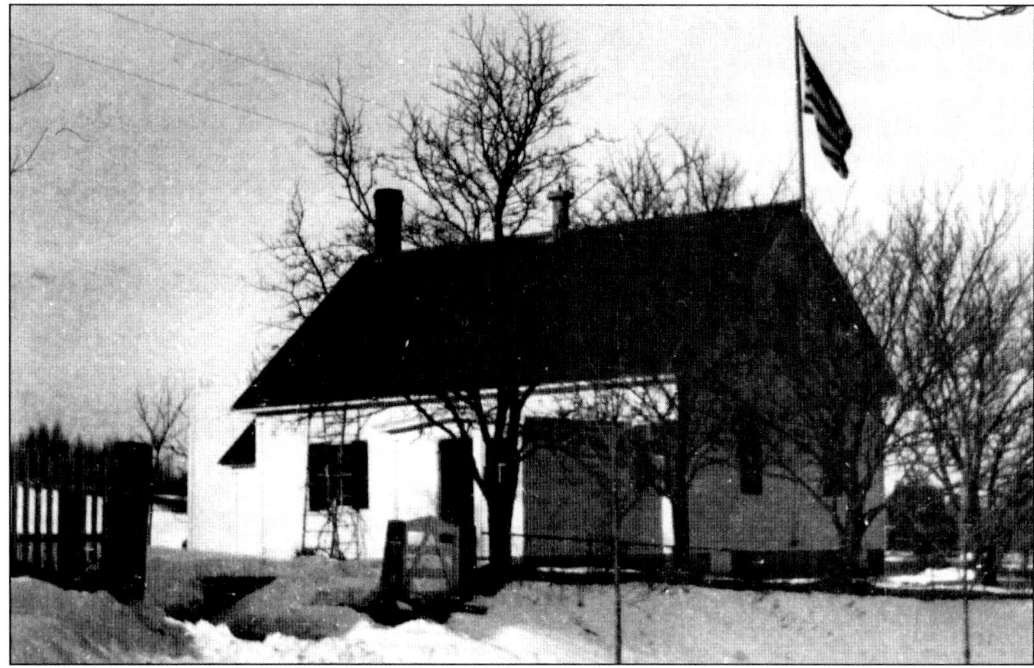

Harry Merrill bought the 1880 Shaker Schoolhouse, which served district No. 9, and moved it to his nearby property to use for apple storage. It also served as the summer home for his daughter and her family. It has since been moved back to its original location at Shaker Village and serves as the research library. (Courtesy of the True family.)

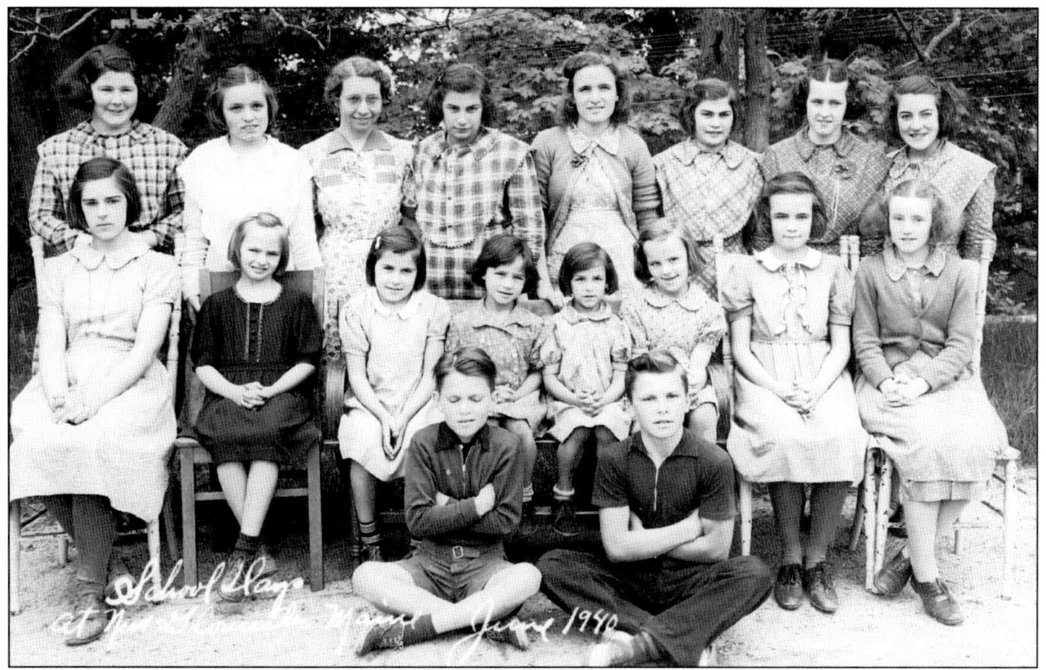

Students of Shaker Schoolhouse are pictured here in 1940 and were taught by Mildred Fickett Bennett McMullen, who was the first non-Shaker to teach there. Among those pictured are Henry and Blynn Merrill, Esther Carr, Eunice Brackett, Helene Carter, Vera May, Virginia May, Lillian May, Arlene Smith, Katherine Carr, Lorraine Smith, Patiencia Nichols (teacher), Rosalie Carter, Janet Nichols, Lucy Merrill, and Frances Carr (Sister Frances of the Shakers, seen on the far right in the third row).

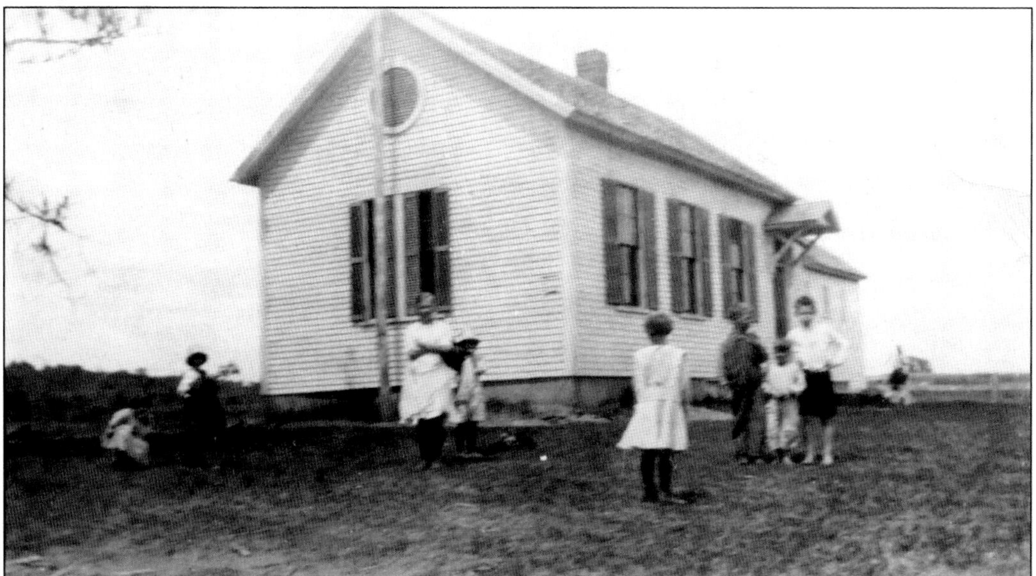

Penney Schoolhouse, which served district No. 14, is shown here during recess in the 1920s. The 1878 structure was last used as a school in 1942 and is now a dwelling at 350 Penney Road. The previous schoolhouse sat near the brick house on the opposite side of the road and was purchased by Cyrus Stinchfield, who sold the lot to the town for the replacement shown here.

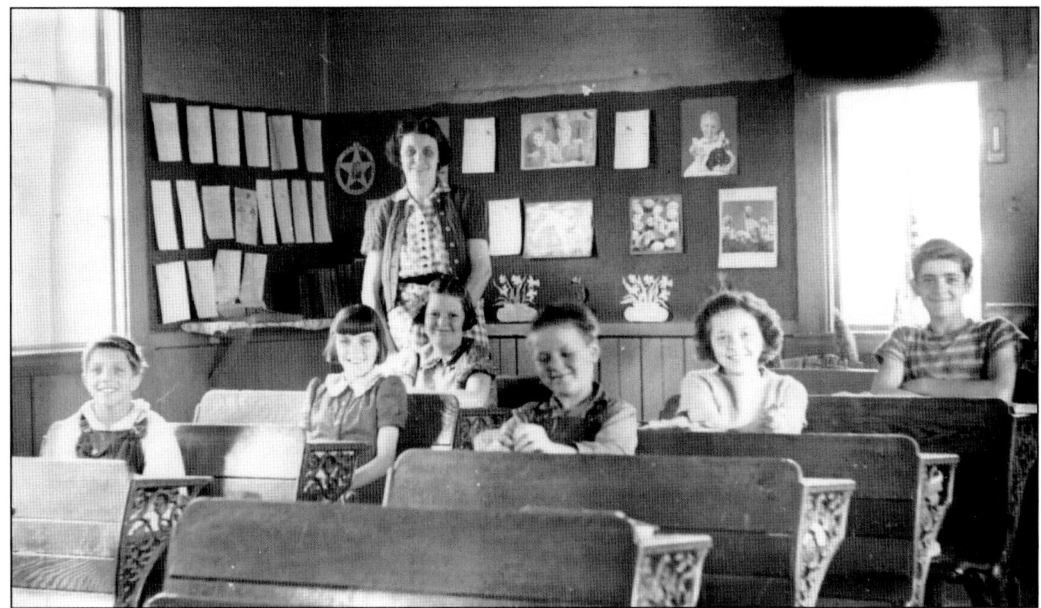

Doris Humphrey stands behind her pupils inside Penney Schoolhouse in 1940. From left to right are Melcon (Mickey) Ray, Madaline (Mannie) Blake Emerson, Jackie Martin, Herbert Blake, Leonora Ray Dixon, and Delbert Ray.

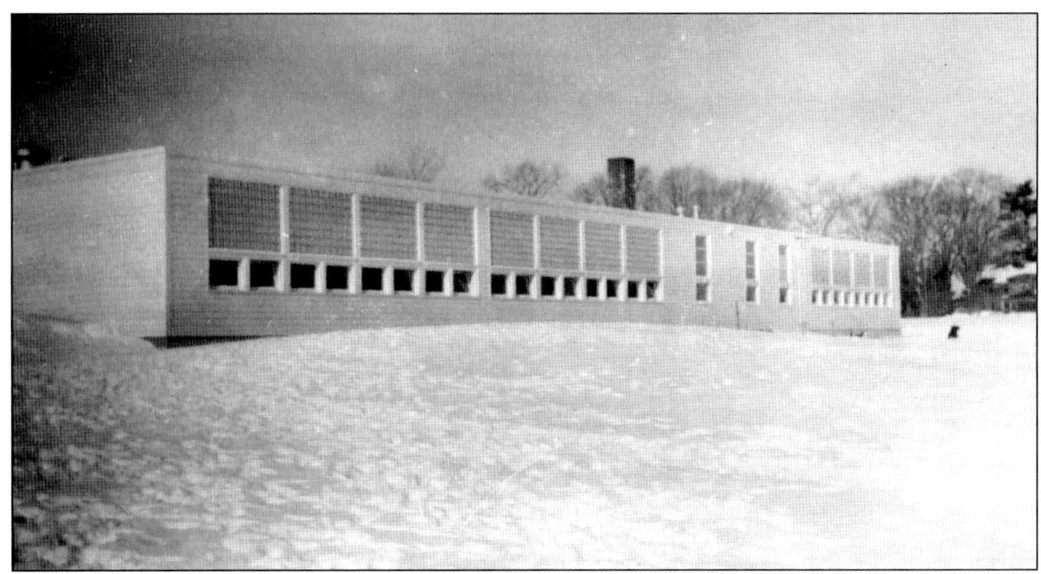

A 10-acre lot was purchased from the Eveleth farm in 1949 for the construction of Memorial School. The five remaining one-room schoolhouses were consolidated upon the opening of this school in the fall of 1950. In January 1950, a plot of land across the road was given to the school district "to insure an attractive outlook from the front of the new school building."

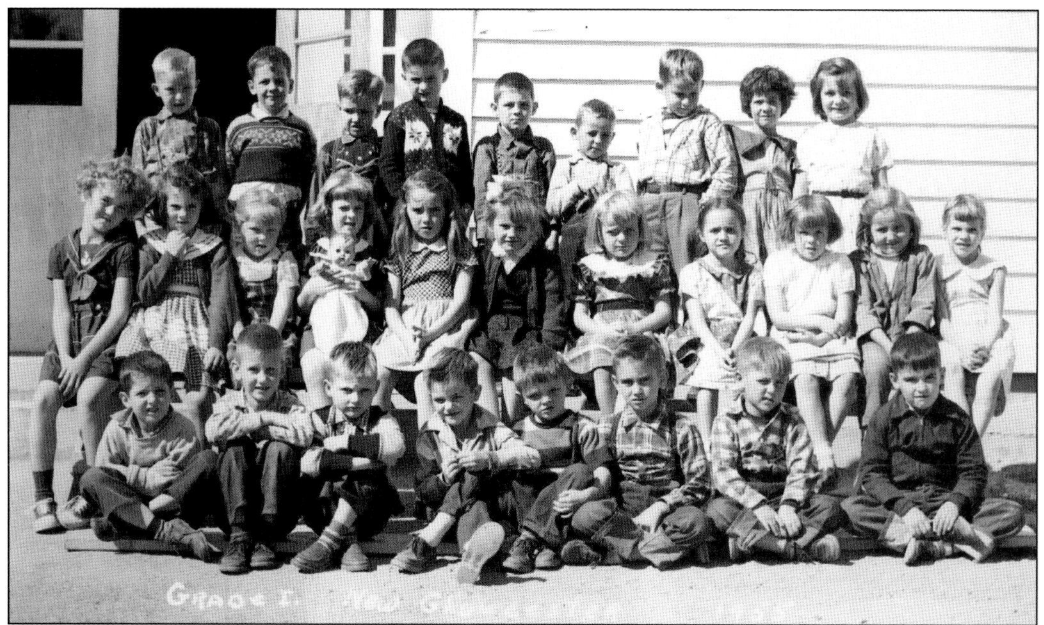

First-grade students are seen posing in front of Memorial School in 1955. The school was originally used for grades one through seven but today is used only for grades kindergarten through second. The structure was a modification of the state plan for elementary schools, being a wooden and glass block building measuring 60 by 144 feet. Ernest Ward was hired in 1950 to operate the new 48-passenger bus.

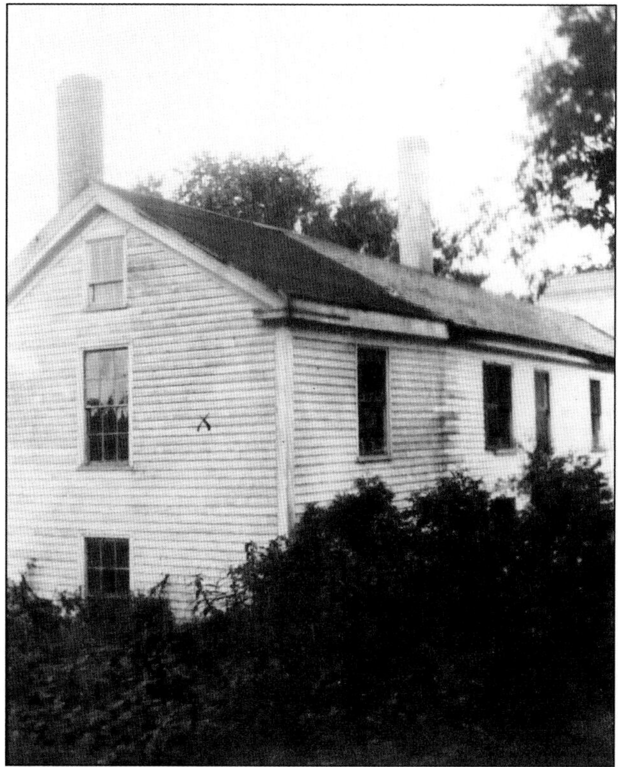

This 1919 picture shows where a classroom was at the Bailey School conducted by Joseph E. Bailey and his daughters Lizzie, Abbie, and Louie. It was a private boarding school for girls and a day school for boys and girls of New Gloucester. Prior to that, it was the home of William Pitt Fessenden, then the Yeaton School, and later the home to artist D. D. Coombs at 14 Cobb's Bridge Road.

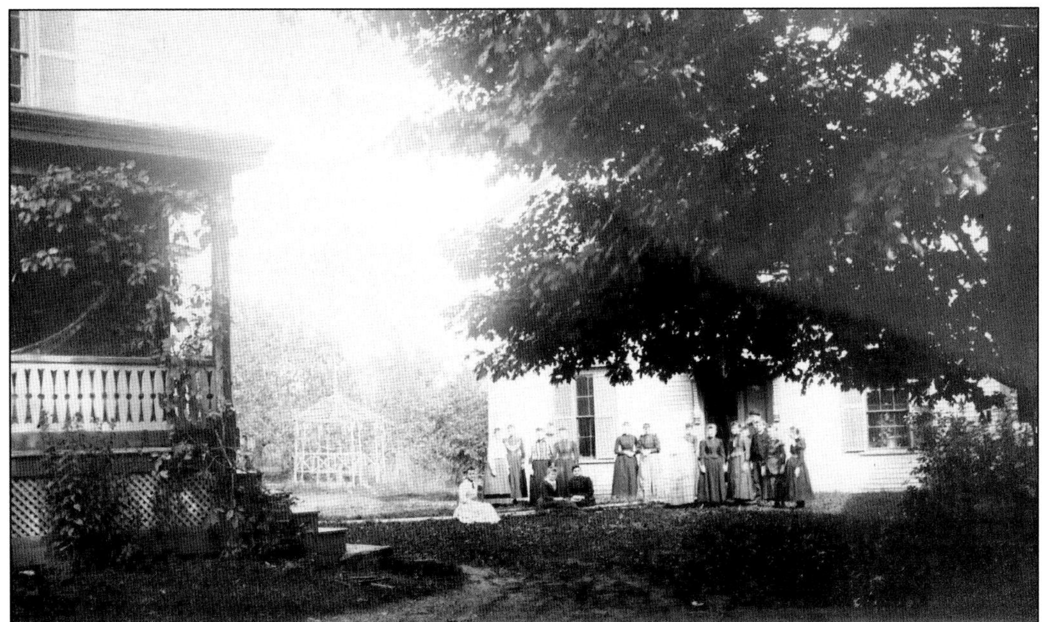

Stevens School was a private day school and boarding school run by Mary B. and Sophie P. Stevens from 1888 until Sophie's death in 1904. It consisted of three buildings. The main house (home of Dr. John P. Stevens, their father) sat across from the old library and burned in 1910, leaving the ell. It was used for living quarters and a dining room for boarding pupils. The schoolhouse sat behind and is now the barn of the Greeley residence. From the ell, a long, covered boardwalk connected it to the family living quarters in the house at 384 Intervale Road, which also served as a post office. The girls are pictured above outside the schoolhouse with the main house on the left. Below is a picture of the girls on the covered boardwalk.

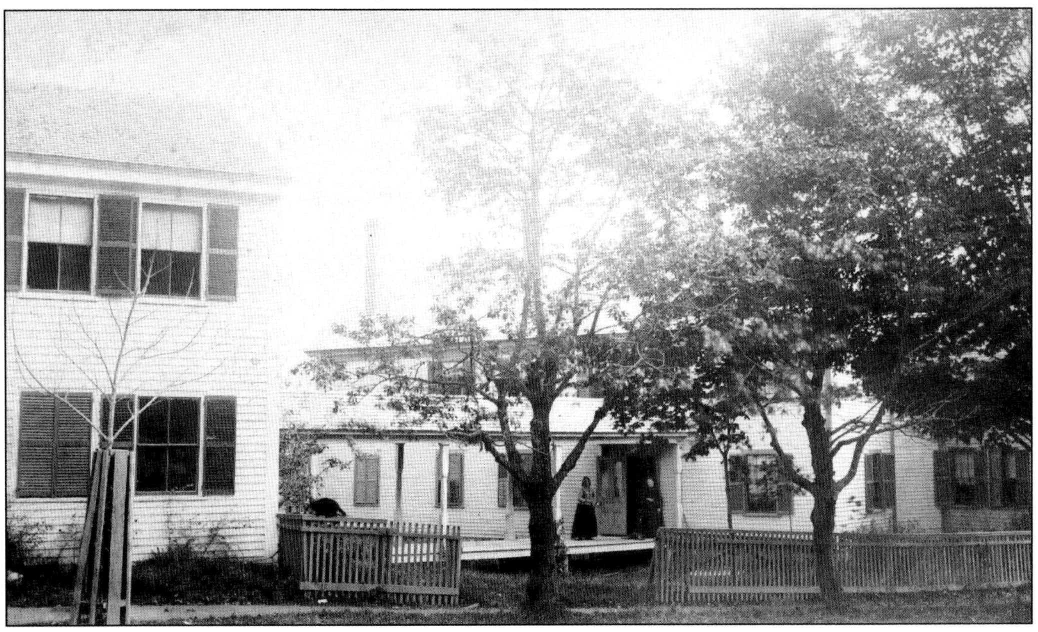

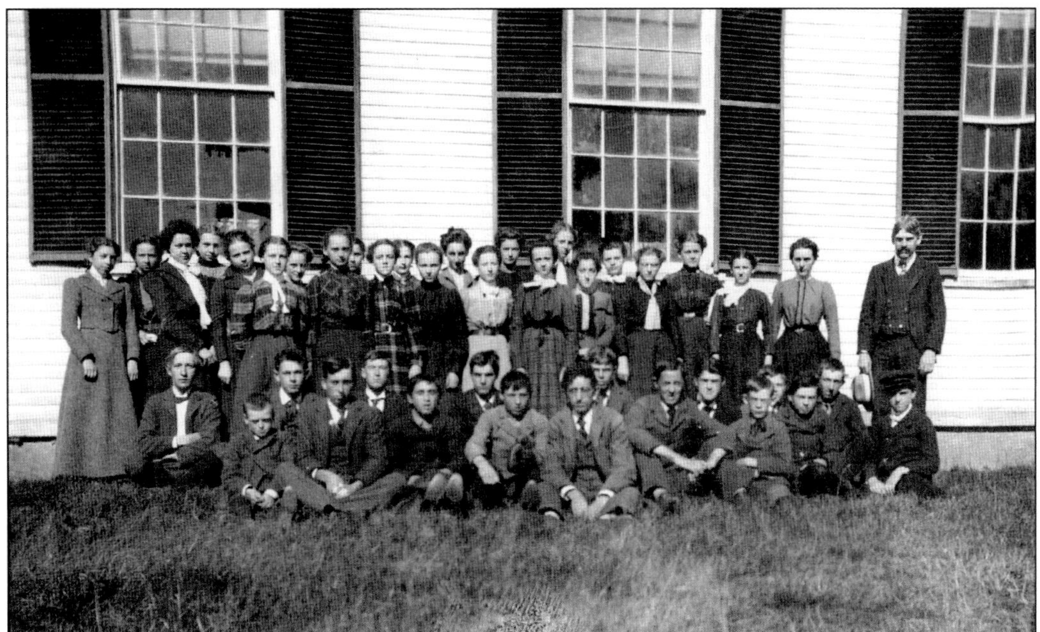

This photograph depicts students of the fall term of 1900 when high school was held at the 1838 Baptist church. The town finally established a high school in April 1900, but it was only held here from 1900 to 1902 until a new schoolhouse could be built. The building was then moved back from the road and became Charles Peleg Chandler's barn at 337 Intervale Road.

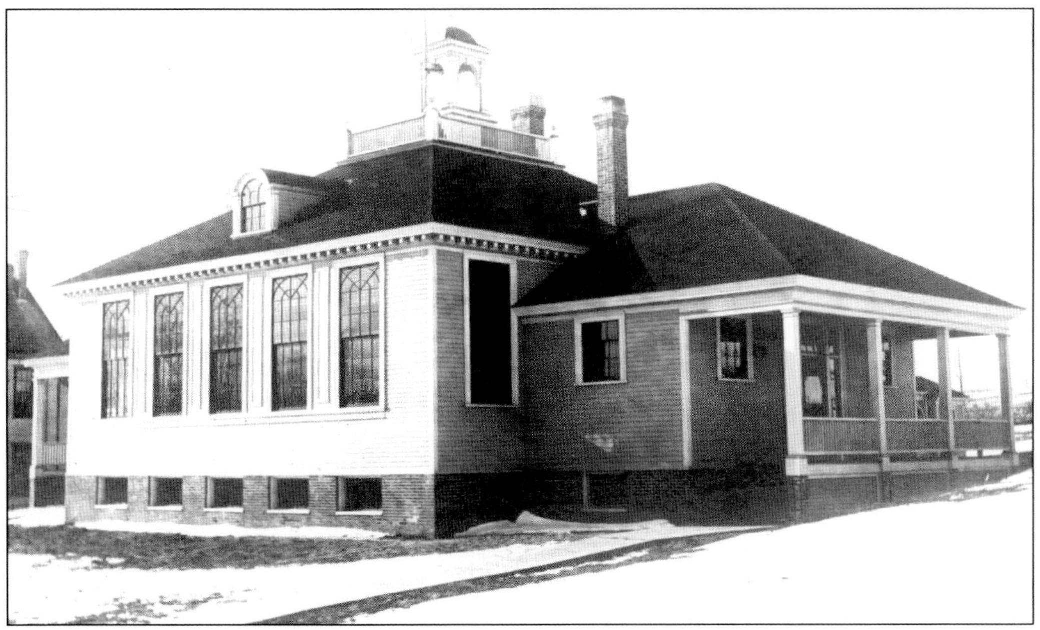

William True planned to build a home at this site beside the town hall, but "several public spirited gentlemen" purchased the lot for the town to provide a home for the new high school, which was completed in 1903. In 1962, the high school closed with the formation of School Administrative District (SAD) 15 and the opening of Gray-New Gloucester High School in Gray. It is now used for the public library. (Courtesy of the True family.)

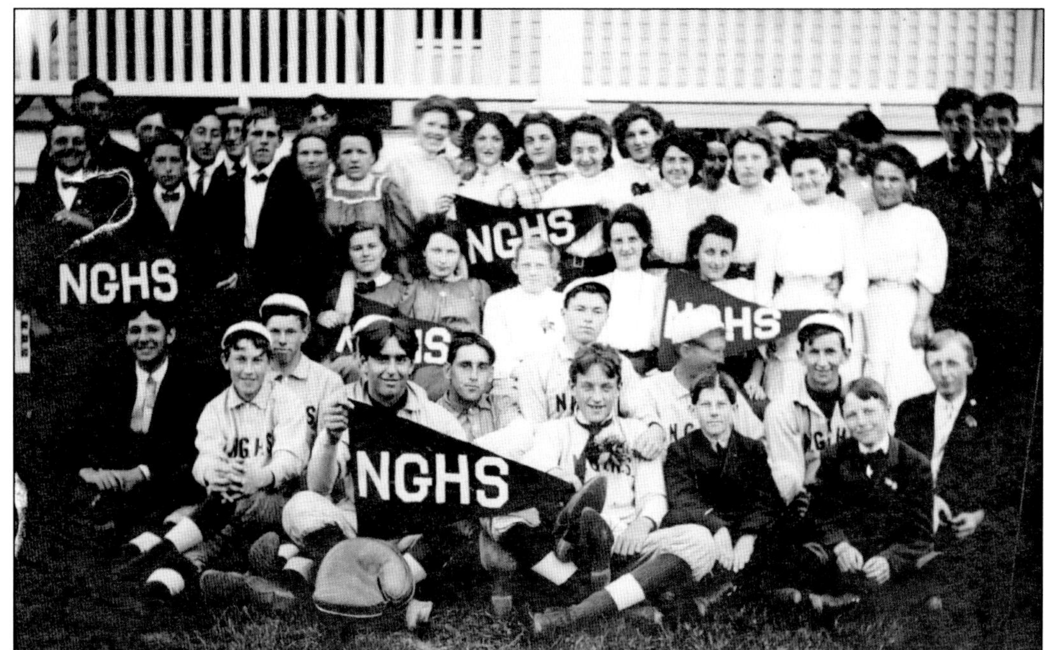

Students of New Gloucester High School are shown here in the fall of 1908. Clyde Segars (left) and Harry True of the school's baseball team hold the pennant in the front row. Notice the catcher's mitt on Segars's lap. The baseball team played on the sloping, uneven field behind the school on the old military training field.

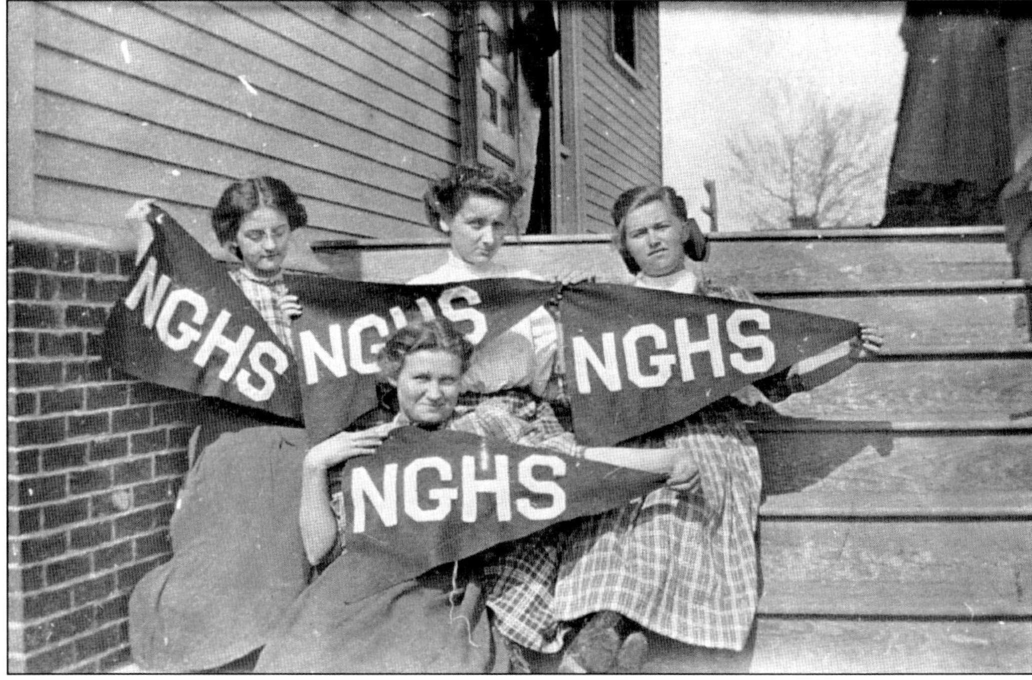

Taken sometime between September 1907 and June 1909, this photograph shows, from left to right, (first row) Nettie True Shaw; (second row) Elizabeth Woodbury Heath, Clara Edwards Plummer, and Alma Jordan Hancock cheering for their school.

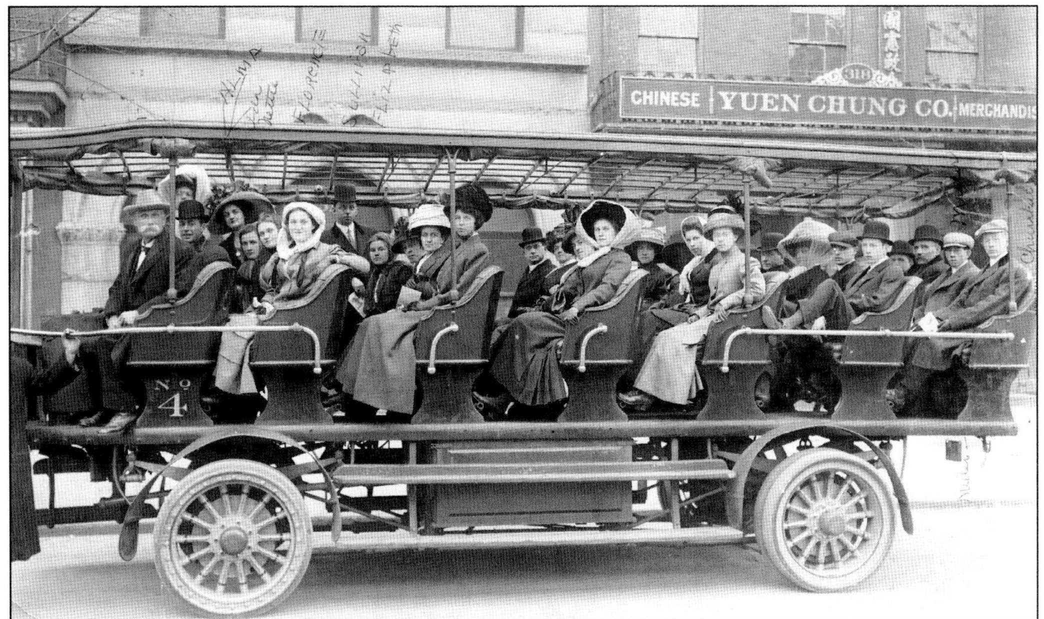

According to the high school principal's report, "The class of 1911, following the custom established by 1910, made an educational trip to Washington, using funds obtained from its entertainments. Of the class of eight, six accompanied by the principal, several of the alumni and students from other schools, took this most interesting and instructive trip of a week's length during the spring vacation."

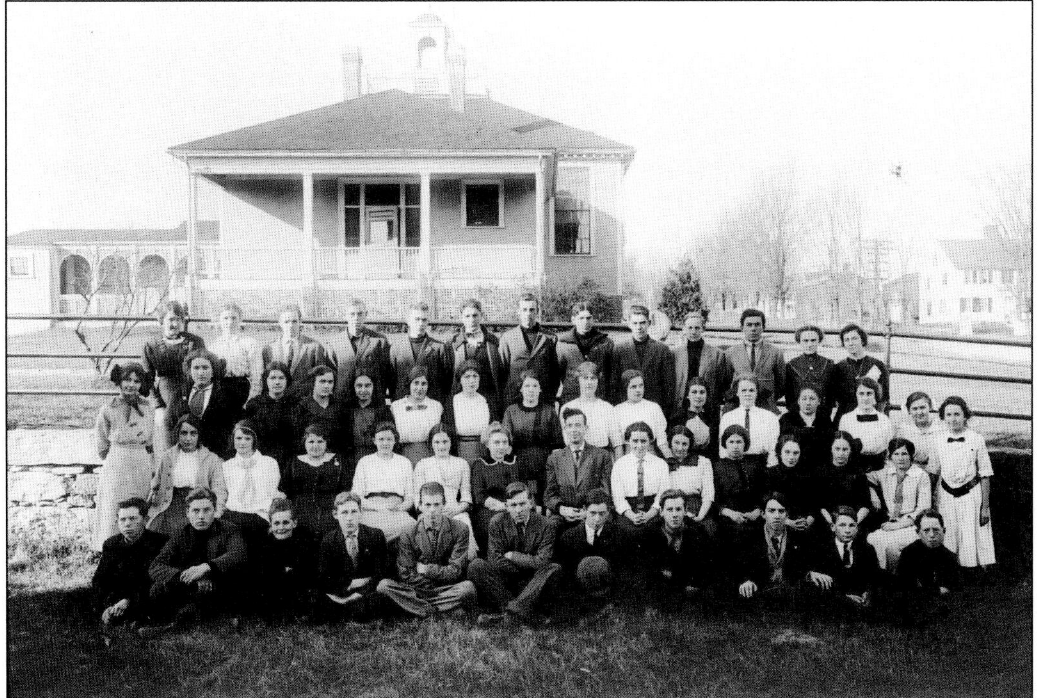

The high school students pose here outside the school in the fall of 1913. Notice that the bell tower is empty, as the class of 1915 bought a bell for the school two years later.

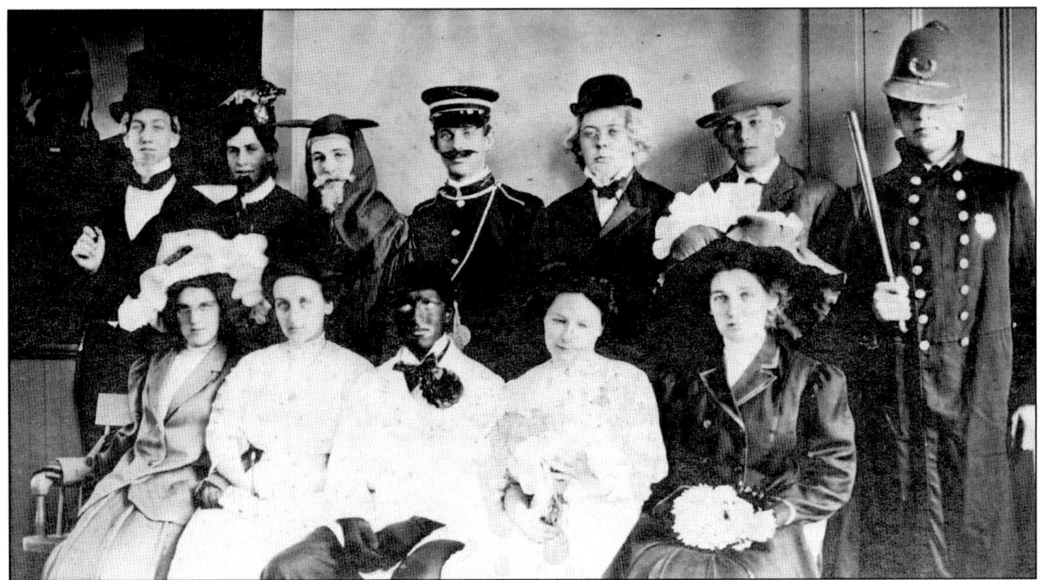

The cast of a minstrel show poses here in full costume. Plays were often followed by a sociable, with dancing at town hall and music by the New Gloucester High School orchestra and chorus.

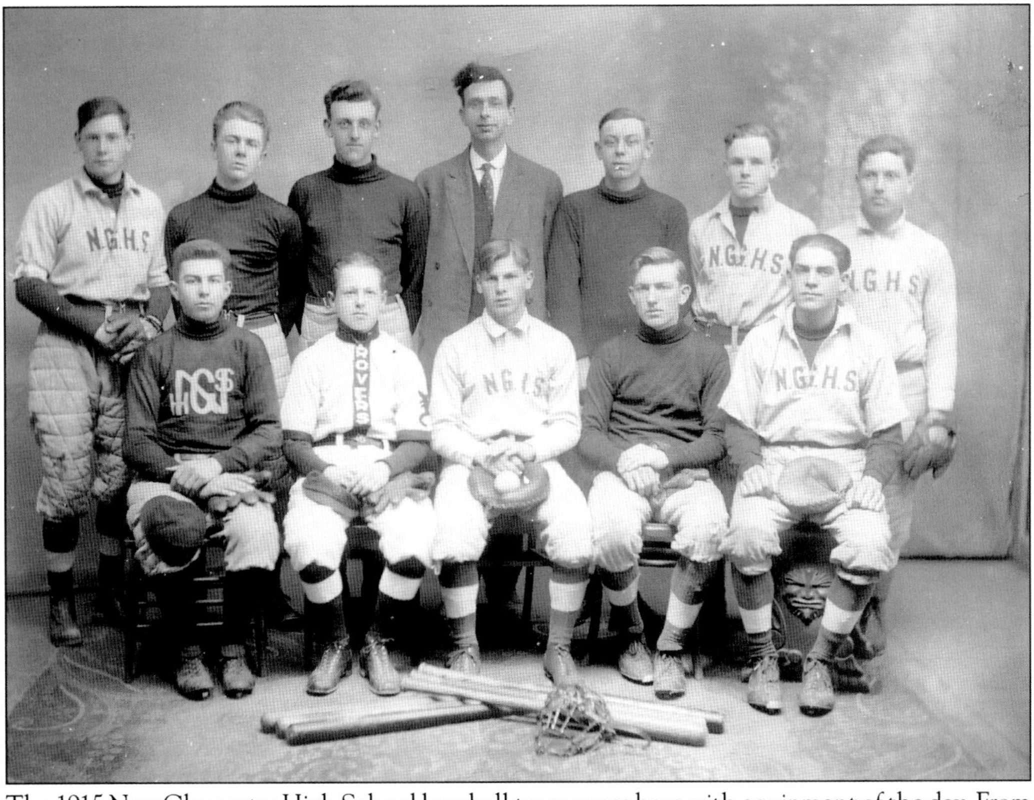

The 1915 New Gloucester High School baseball team poses here with equipment of the day. From left to right are (first row) Ernest Titcomb, Willard Berry, Pearl Johnson, George Kilpatrick, and Harvey Tufts; (second row) Frank Fickett, Herb Waterman, Arthur Edwards, Tom Gay (coach), Eugene Humphrey, Joe Johnston, and Wesley Peaco.

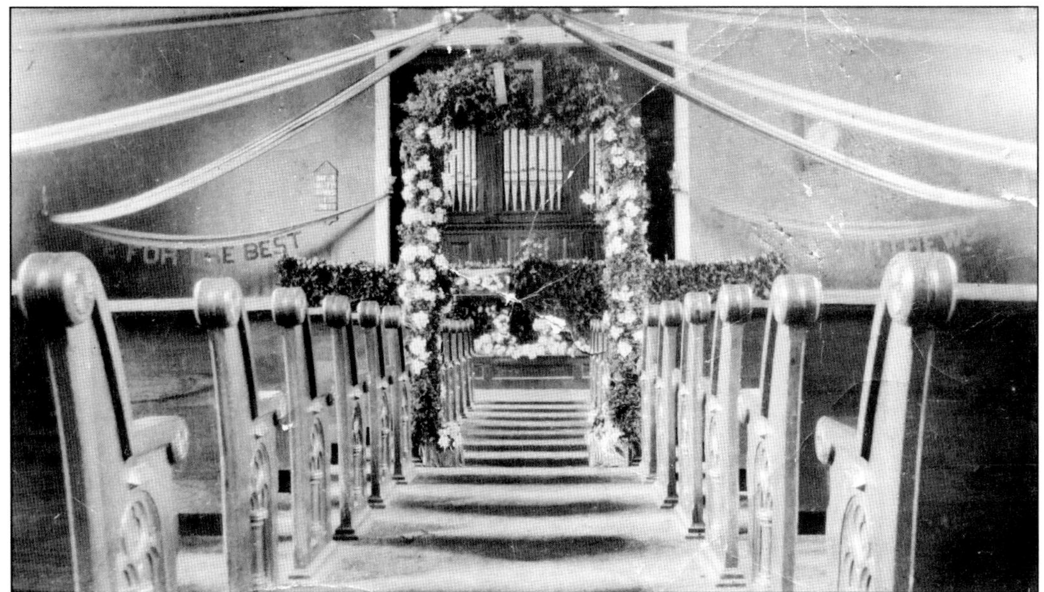

High school graduation ceremonies were typically held at the Congregational church, as can be seen decorated here in 1917. An archway was placed partway down the aisle for this service, with a 17 placed above it.

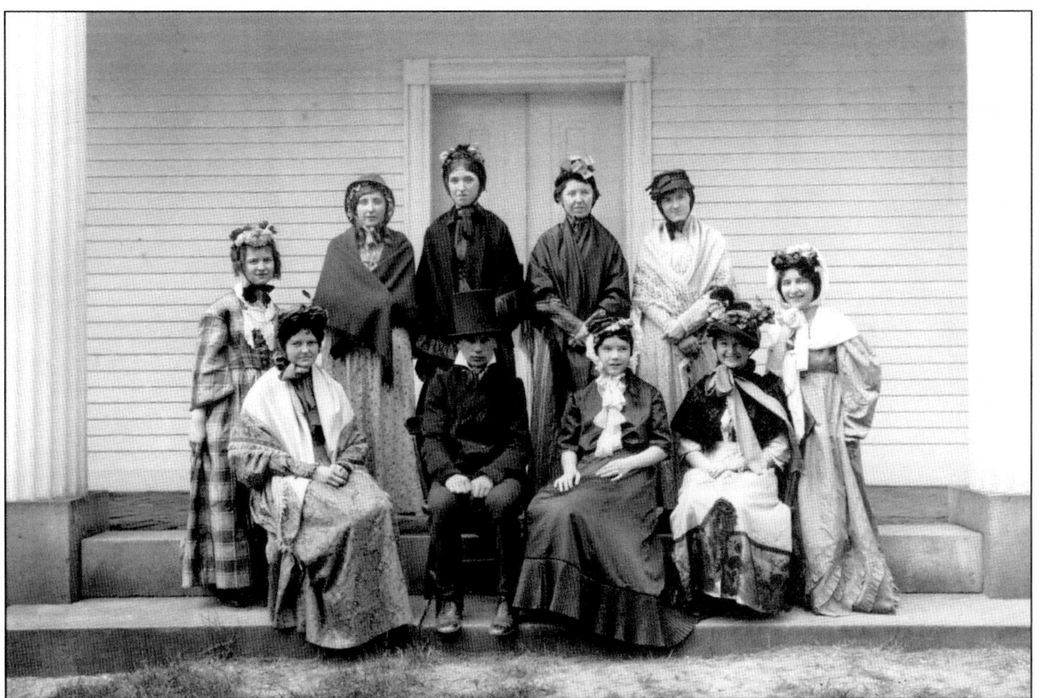

The Old Peabody Pew play was presented by the class of 1925, with the assistance of undergraduates at the Congregational church. From left to right are (first row) Doris Chapman Bearce, James Curtis, Beatrice Farwell Robbins, and Dora Colomy DeCoster; (second row) Minna Thompson, Ruth Farnum Leonard, Erma Goff Hatch, Grace Chapman Douglas, Ruth Sinclair Ayer, and Gladys Curtis.

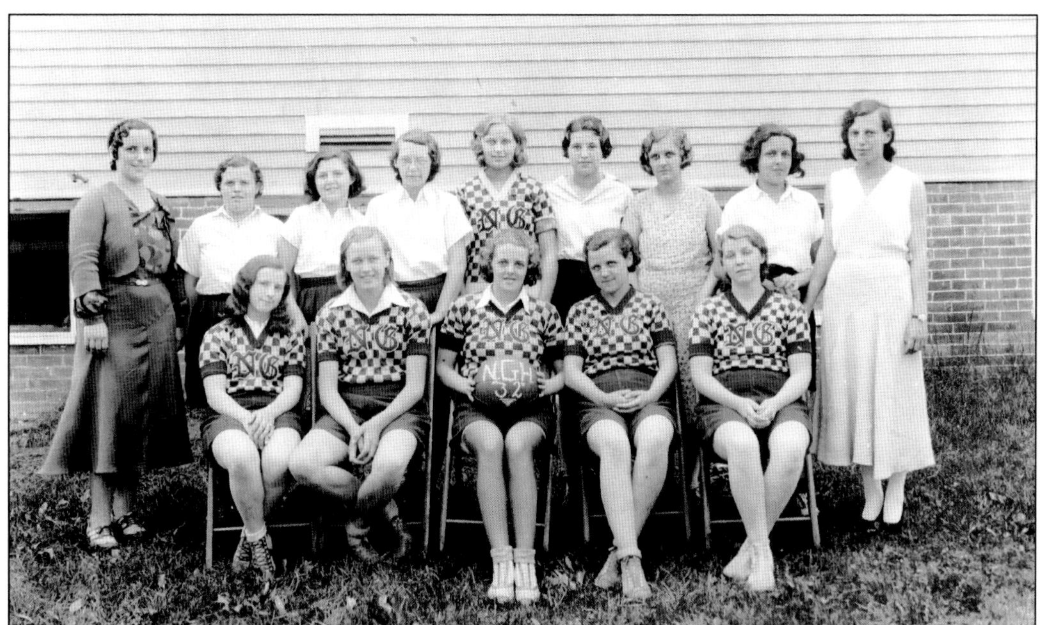

Members of the 1932 girls' basketball team shown here are, from left to right, (first row) Ruth Siebel Coleman, Hazel Blake Files, Dolly Ray Webb, Helen Kilby, and Audrey McIntire Lord; (second row) Ruth Patterson Estes (coach), Alice Burnell Andrews, Orlean Bunker Sturgis, Wilma Chapman Hachey, Thelma Fickett Fitzgerald, Phyllis Segars Snow, Irma Jones Cox, Gail Ray Franzen, and Anne Worden Hunter (manager).

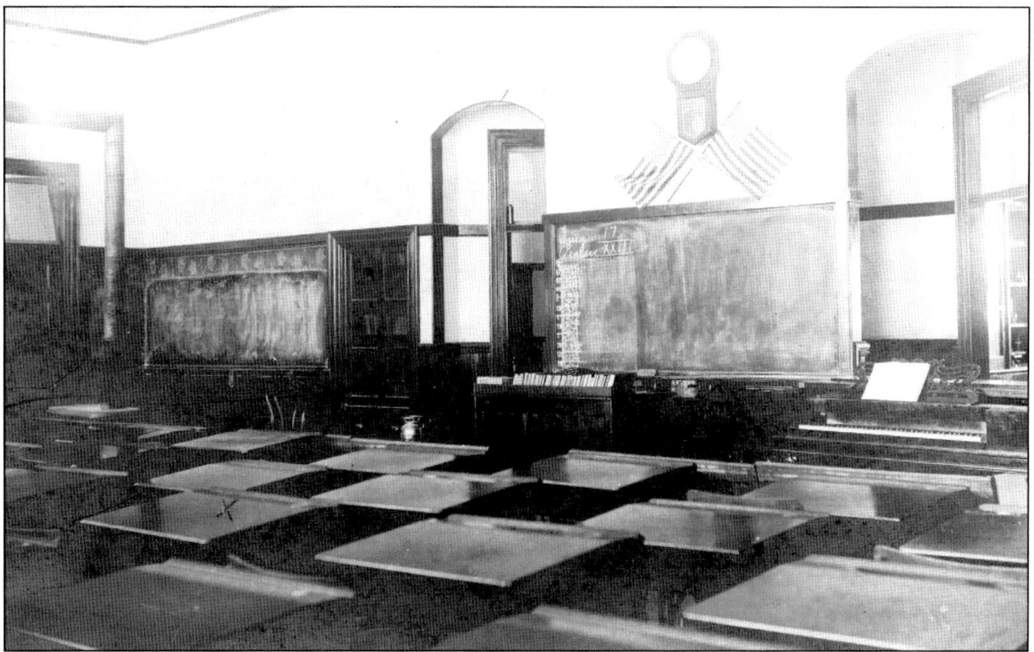

This 1939 interior view of the high school was typical of the times. Note the stovepipe in the far left corner. A teacher once asked the class how all the footprints got on the ceiling, so a couple of the teenage boys showed him—they flipped him upside down and pressed his feet to the ceiling. (Courtesy of the True family.)

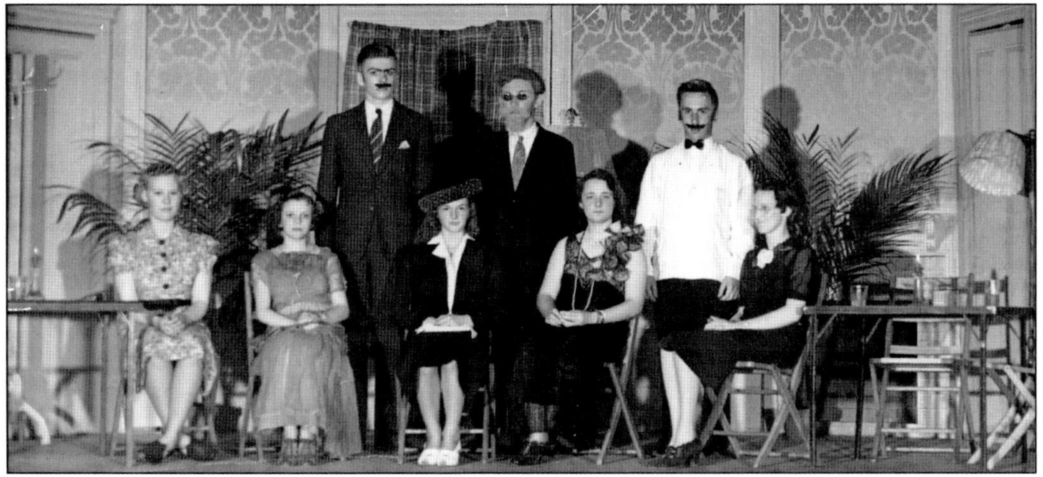

Pictured on April 29, 1939, cast members of the senior class play *Aaron Slick from Punkin Crick* are, from left to right, (first row) Marjorie Chase, Mildred Libby Wilson, Louise Chamberlain Foley, Annie Fogg Murray, and Elva Card (coach); (second row) Payson Farrar, Keith Williams, and Carroll Blaisdell.

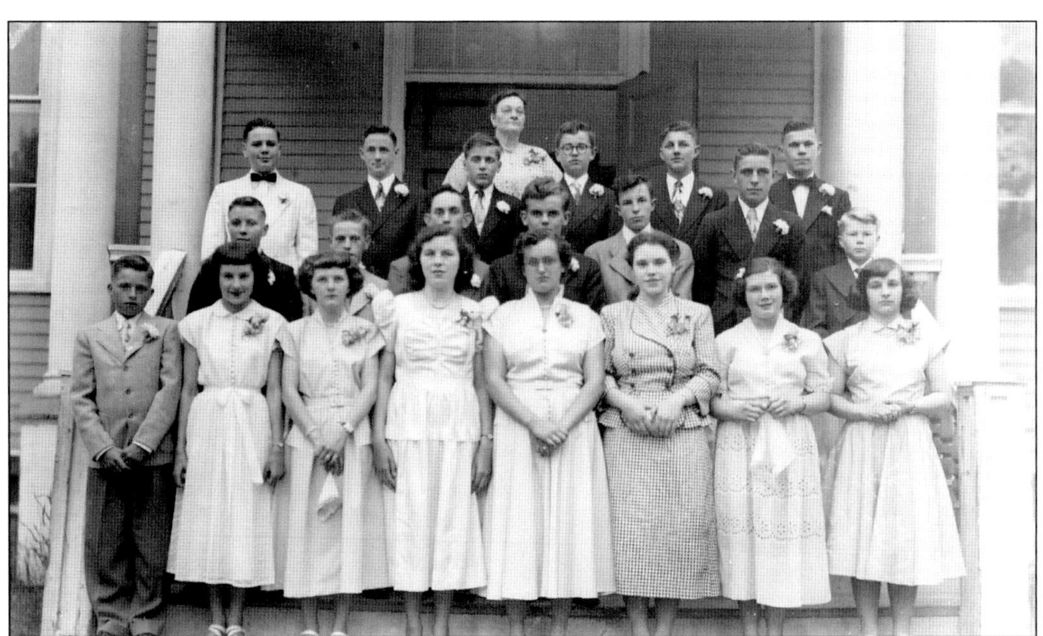

The eighth-grade class of 1951 is shown here on the steps of town hall, where classes were held for a few years due to large high school enrollments. They are watched over by teacher Thirza McConkey Waterman.

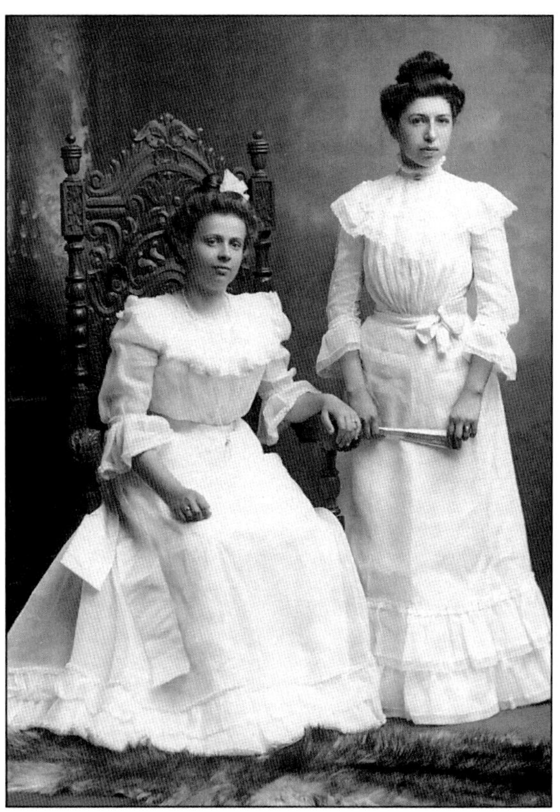

Members of the class of 1902, the first graduating class of New Gloucester High School, Bessie Corliss Ford (left) and Annie Berry never had the chance to enjoy the new high school building, as it opened in 1903. They instead spent their years at the old Baptist church building. (Courtesy of the New Gloucester Public Library.)

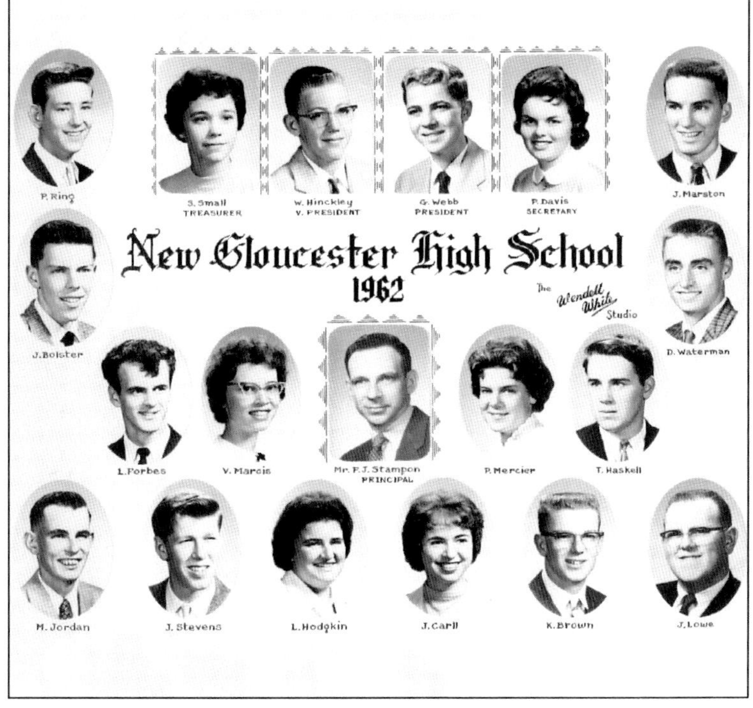

Depicted here is the final class to graduate from New Gloucester High School. It had an estimated 631 graduates over 61 years. New Gloucester students have attended Gray-New Gloucester High School in Gray since the consolidation in 1962. (Courtesy of the New Gloucester Public Library.)

Four

Lower Gloucester and Over the Hill

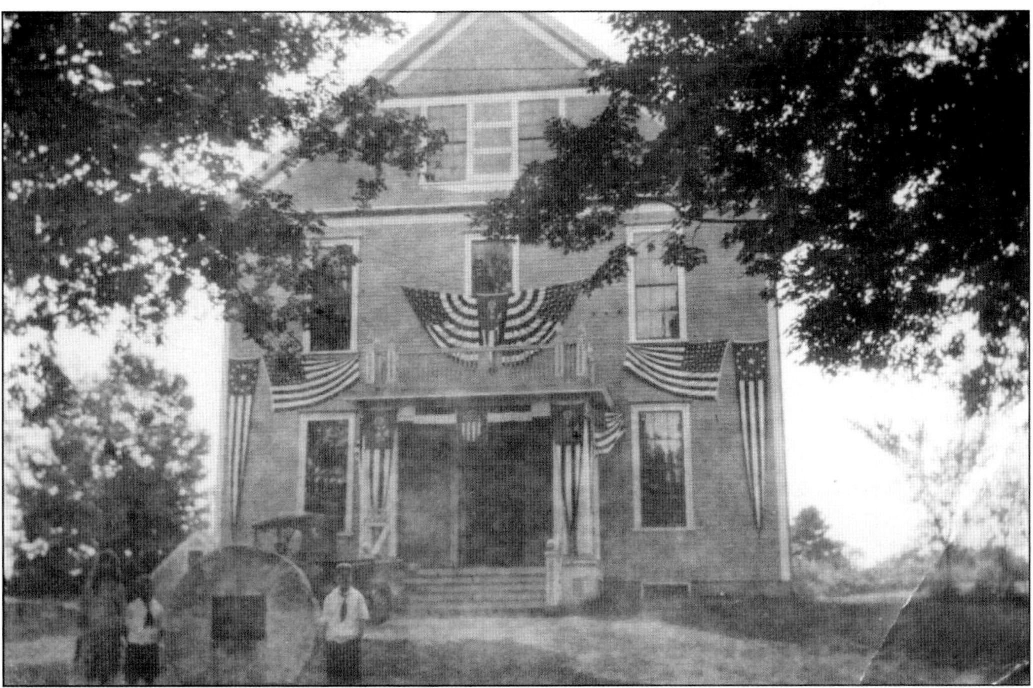

This picture, taken by William Greeley, shows the town hall decorated for the 1924 sesquicentennial. Posing by the millstone, his children are, from left to right, Marion, Bill, and John. The town hall was built in 1886 on a large tract of vacant land known as the training field, which was used for preparation during wartime. The previous town house was the first Baptist church built in 1804 below the Foxcroft house. It was sold and taken down in 1886, with the lumber used to build a barn.

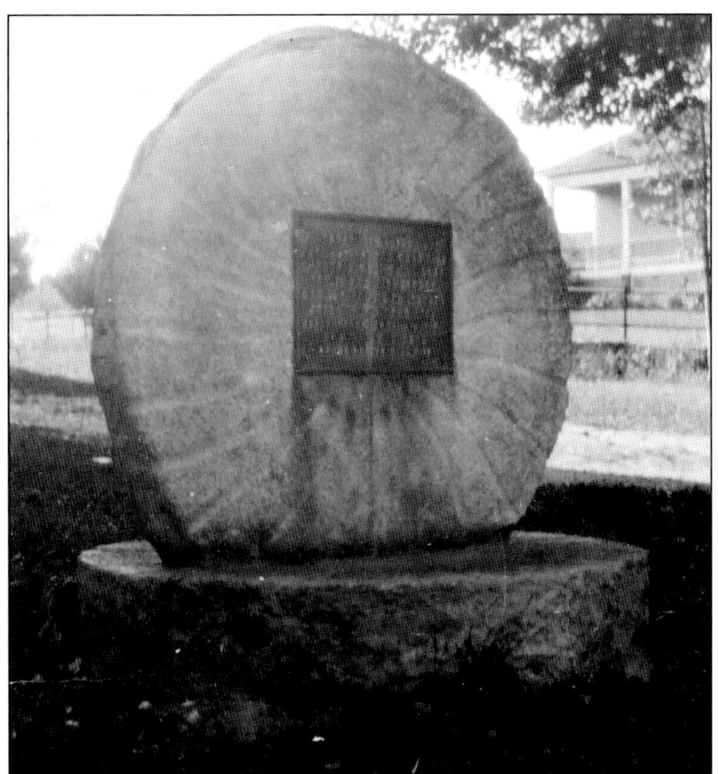

The plaque reads, "These millstones, cut from native rock, were used in the first grist mill erected by the pioneers of New Gloucester on Stevens Brook in the year 1758. Presented to the town in 1913 by William P. True, owner of the mill site." Prior to 1758, the settlers walked 12 miles with corn on their backs to have it ground in North Yarmouth and returned the same day with cornmeal.

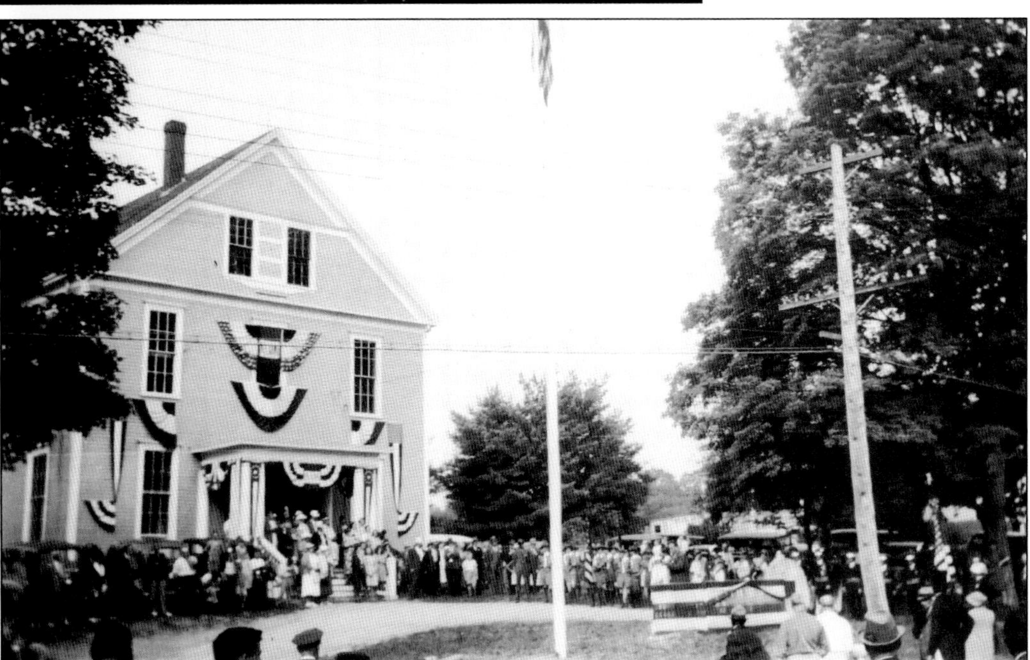

The town hall is decorated again for the bicentennial celebration of the settling of New Gloucester, held on September 3 and 4, 1939. The flagpole was contributed by Clarence L. McCann, fitted by Otis H. Campbell, and raised by the aid of Pine Tree Telephone and Telegraph Company men and equipment.

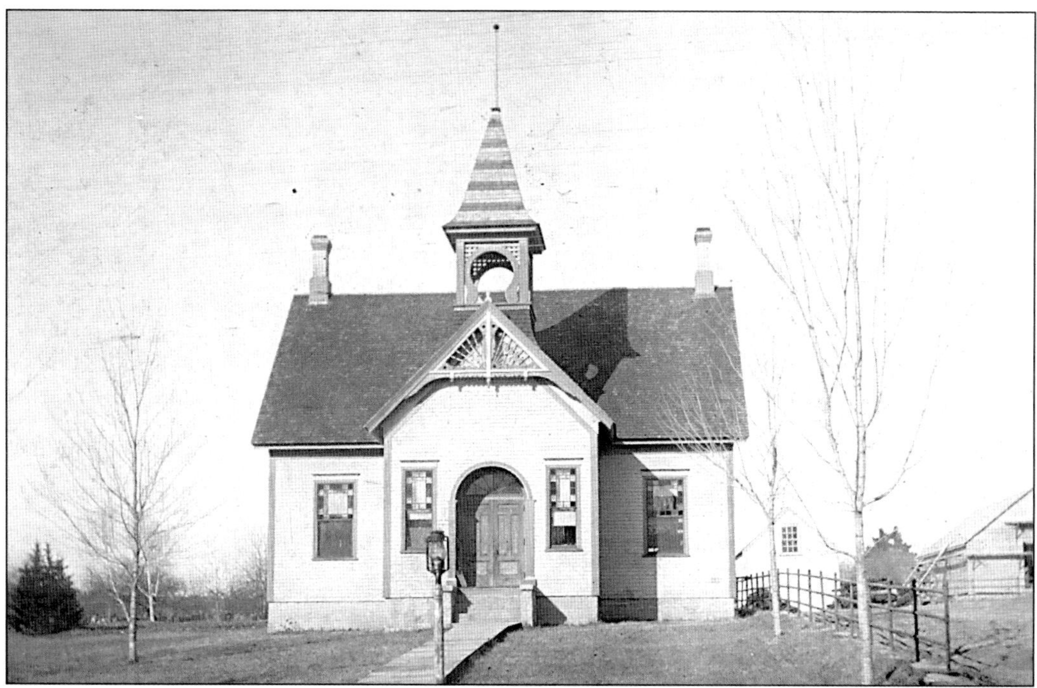

The town library was built in 1896 beside the town hall with some of its lumber from Shaker Mill. After several years of townspeople paying shares if they desired to use the "social library," the town established a public library in 1888, which was initially kept in the current office of the town manager. The first librarian was Helen A. Moseley, from 1888 to 1920. The library has since moved into the old high school. The building now serves as the meetinghouse, the home of the local cable channel studio, and the archives of the historical society. (Above, courtesy of the New Gloucester Public Library.)

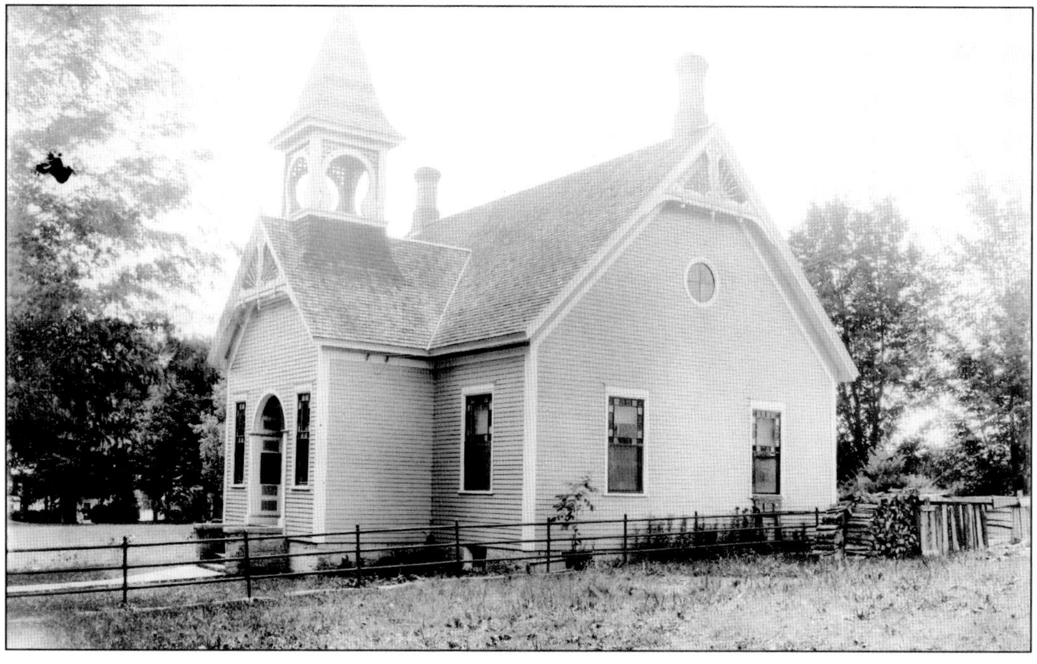

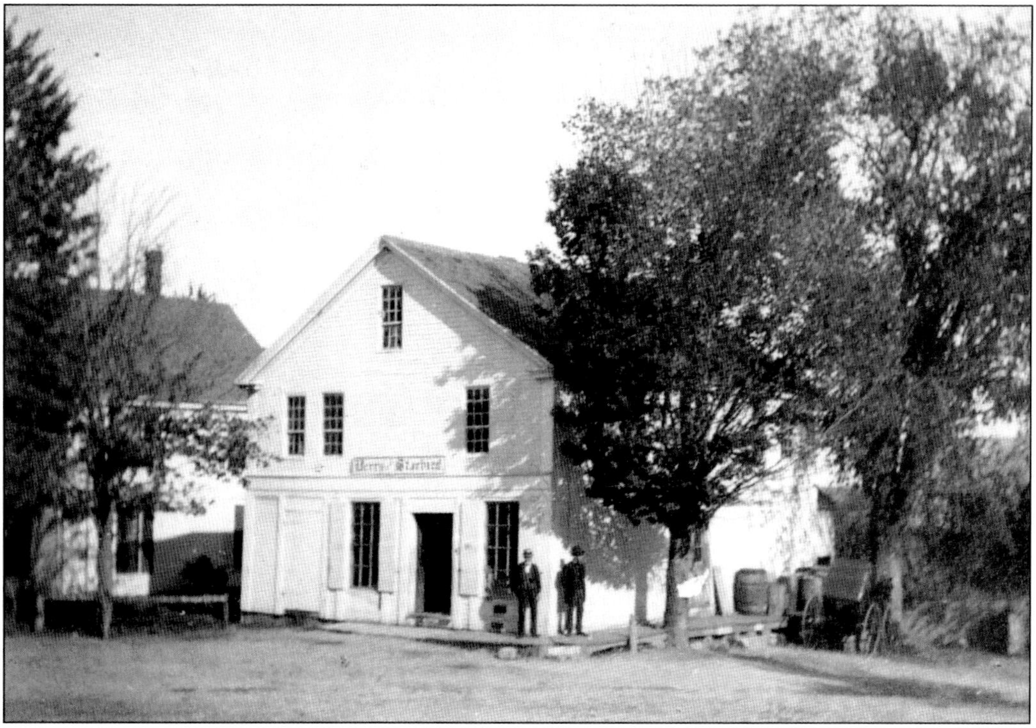

This 1892 photograph shows the old Bell Tavern being used as a store by Berry and Starbird. The building sat at the corner of Cobb's Bridge Road and Intervale Road. During the time of New Gloucester being a half-shire town with Portland (court was held here from 1792 until Oxford County formed in 1805), many jurors and witnesses boarded here.

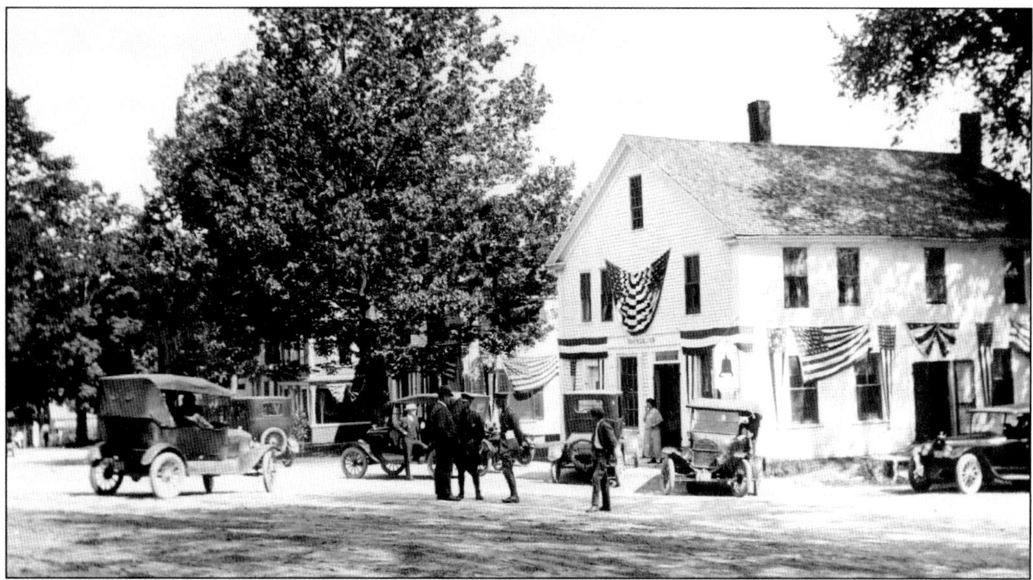

The Bell Tavern is decorated here for the 1924 celebration. It was built in 1773 by Peleg Chandler and was sold after he died in 1819. It has been used as a store, a dance hall, a post office, and a home. An ell was built for his son Peleg Jr. in 1797 but was later moved over to 5 Cobb's Bridge Road. The Bell Tavern was moved a few hundred feet down the hill in 1978 to 410 Intervale Road.

The original 1776 Bell Tavern sign was on display during the 1924 sesquicentennial. Inscribed "Entertainment for man or beast" and "Success to the friends of liberty," the sign still remains in the Chandler family.

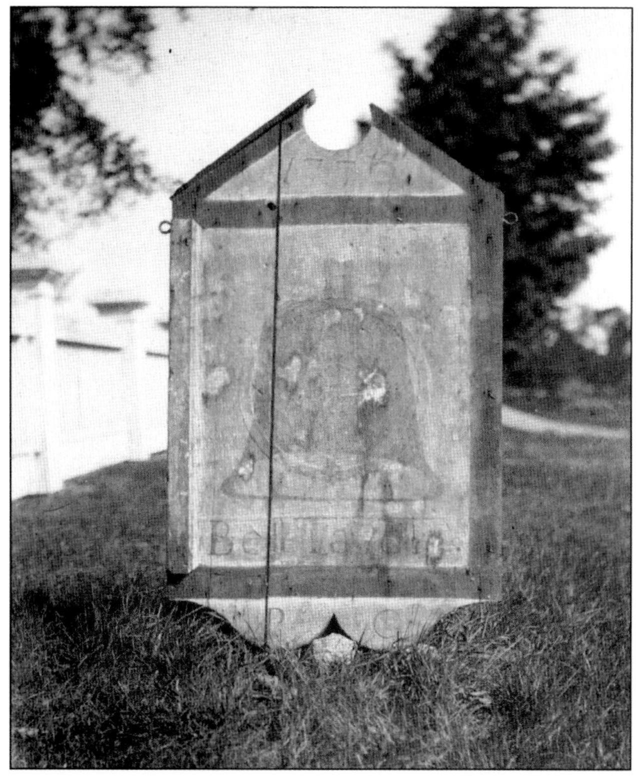

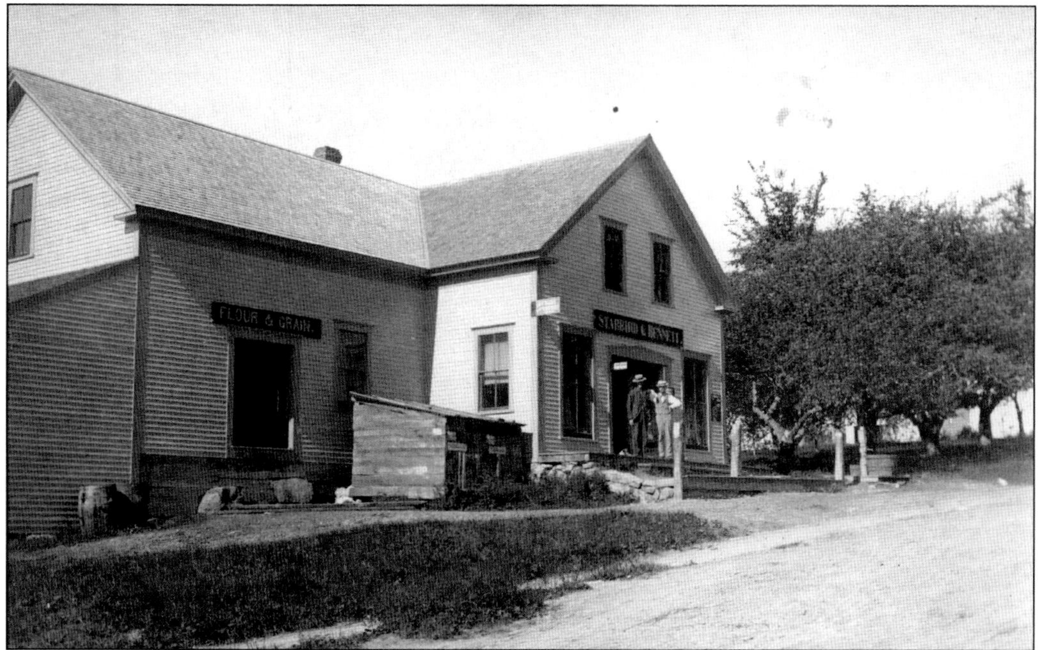

Starbird and Bennett is shown as the store name around 1898 after the owners built the structure with Charles Allen, a local carpenter. It was then sold to Charles R. Atwood in 1900, who ran it until 1919. It was the Farmer's Union for nearly 50 years, Peaco's Market, and eventually became the Village Store at 405 Intervale Road.

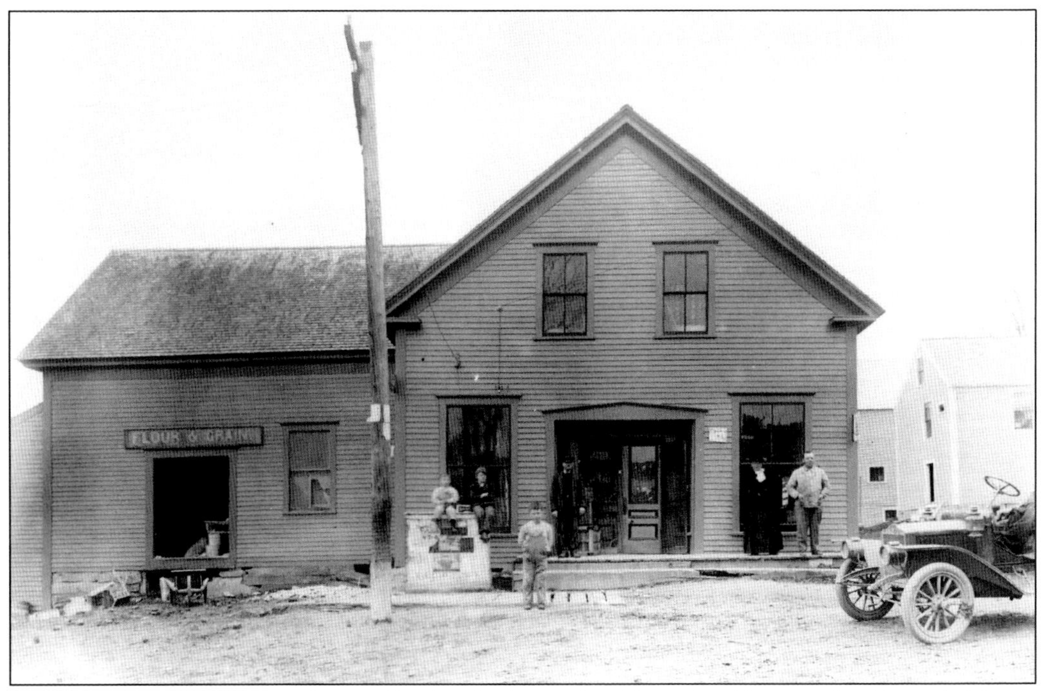

Now known as the Village Store, Charles R. Atwood sold this building to the Farmer's Union in 1919, which owned it until 1966. Shares were sold at $10 each to local farmers. There were several managers over the years, but Ronald Farwell served the longest at 31 years.

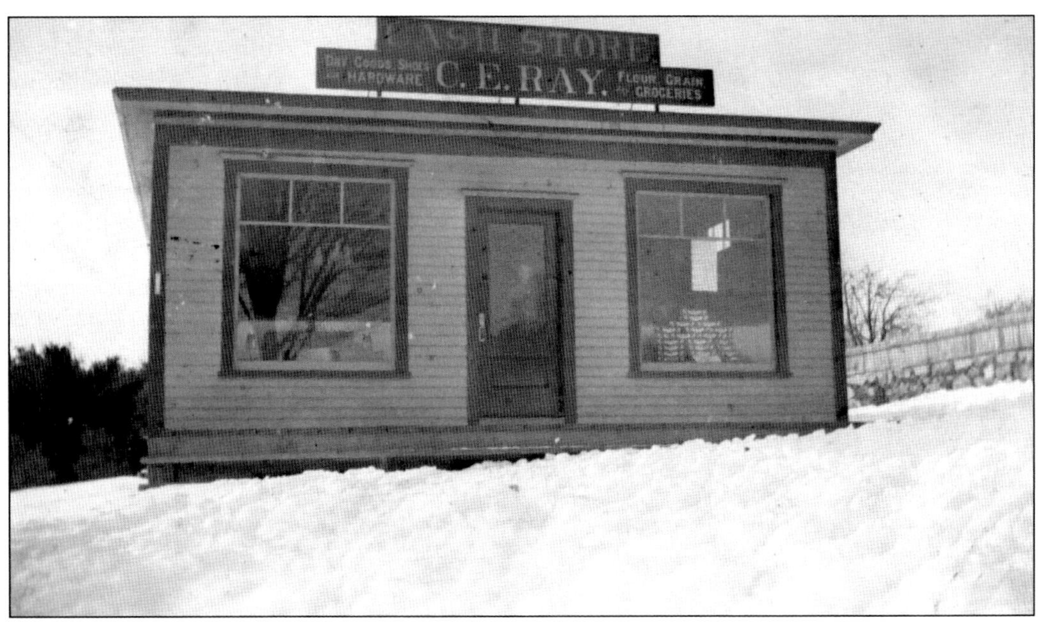

Charles Eugene Ray opened a cash store just down the hill from the Farmer's Union. He also ran a general store in Upper Gloucester. This site was later used for a warehouse for the Oliver Stores, then it was the town post office from 1968 to 1998, and it is now the location of a home at 417 Intervale Road.

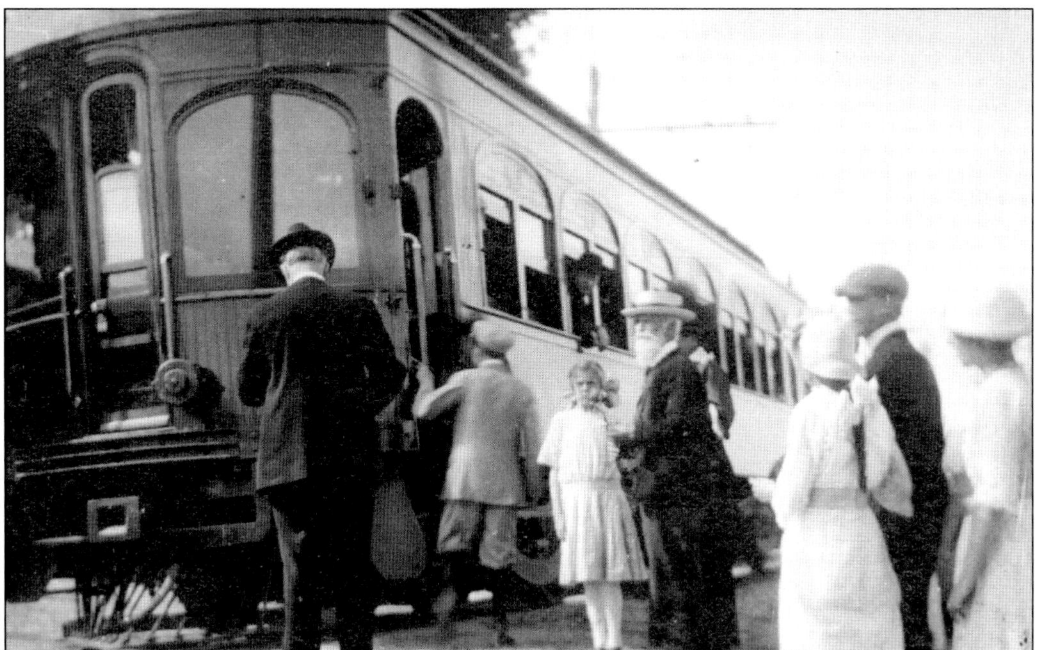

William Henry Greeley, wearing the straw hat, waits to board the Portland-Lewiston Interurban in 1917. The electric railway ran from 1914 to 1933, with stops at Upper Gloucester, Lower Gloucester, Penney Road, Town Farm Road, and Morse Road. Six cars were named for flowers and were painted a Pullman green with gray roofs and dark red doors and trim.

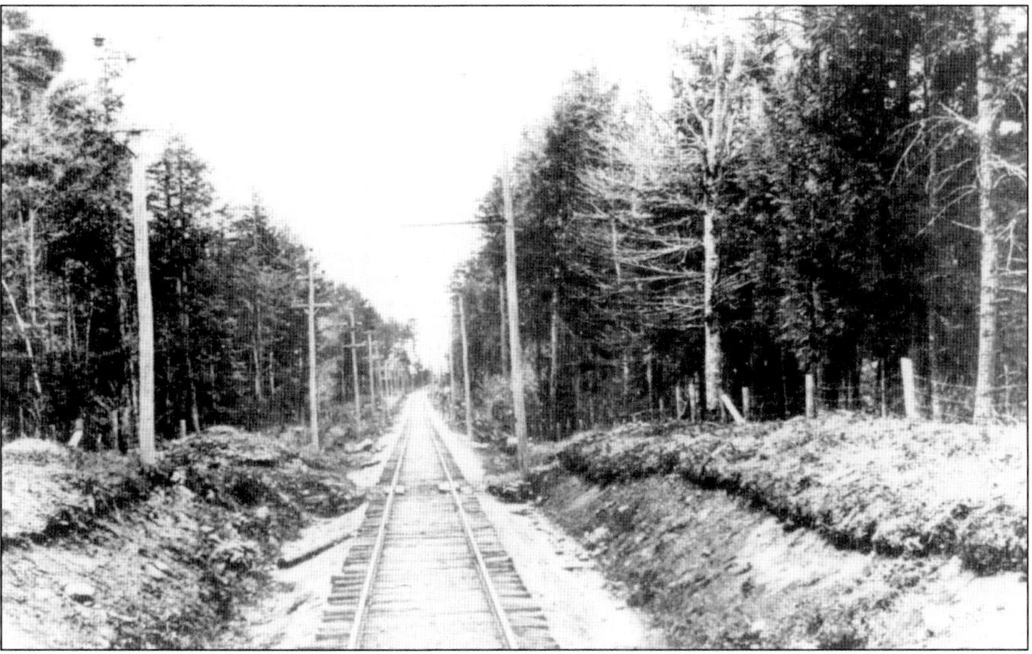

Here is a view of the railway as it passed though Chandler's Woods. Trains left Portland every hour from Monument Square and reached Lewiston in about 90 minutes. Student tickets were issued at half fare during weekdays, as many high school students would use "the finest electric railroad in all New England."

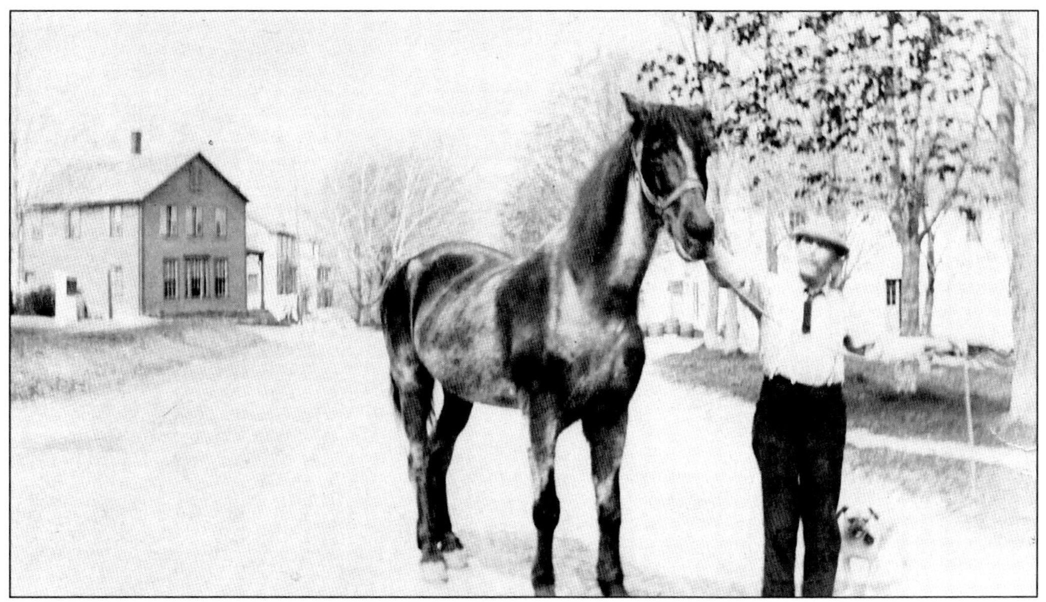

This is Samuel F. Hilton with his stallion and dog in Lower Corner at the entrance of Cobb's Bridge Road. Hilton attended 295 funerals with the town hearse from 1884 to 1897. The building to the left was the Coller house, which sat at the corner of Cobb's Bridge Road and Intervale Road. The building was dismantled in the early 1900s.

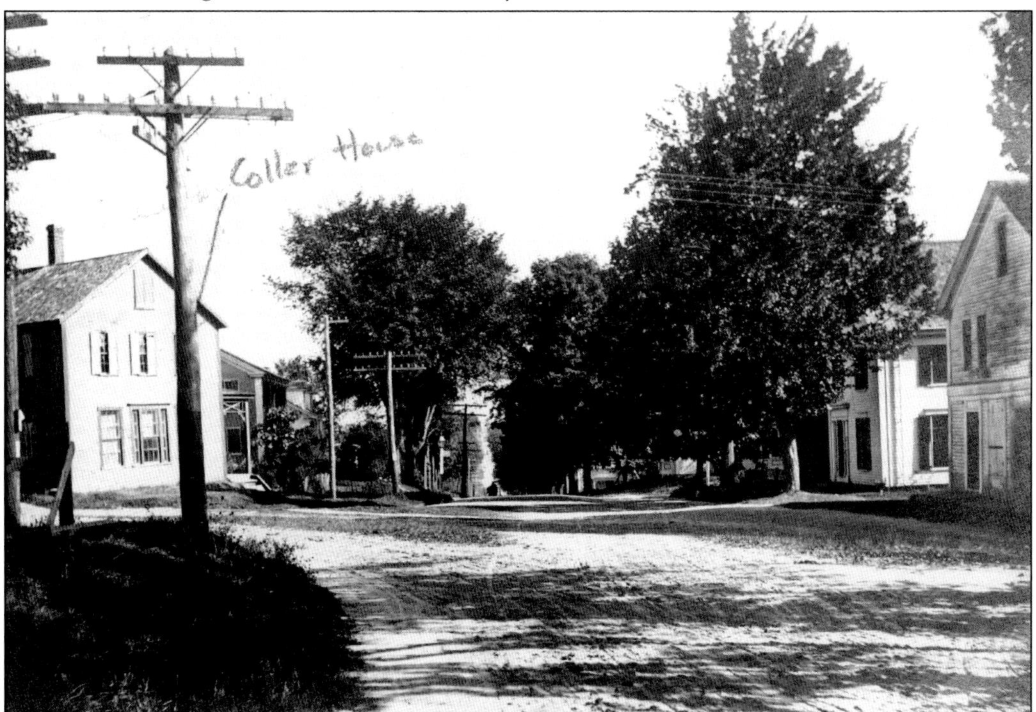

This is a similar view of Lower Corner from a picture postcard and shows the Coller house on the left and the Bell Tavern on the far right. Philip Coller owned a tin shop for several years, and Coller and Crockett manufactured Coller's Improved Creamery (patented on July 28, 1885) in New Gloucester.

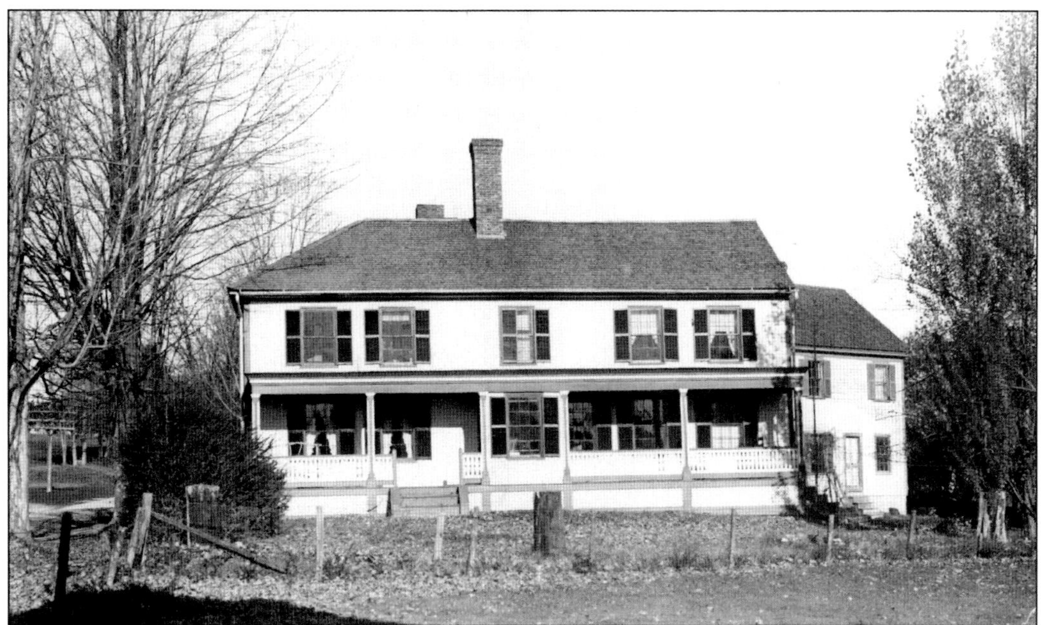

The Stevens home is shown here about 1907. This was the main building used for Stevens School until it burned down in 1910. The ell shown to the right is still there today at 388 Intervale Road. The home was formerly the Bearce Tavern, owned by Dexter Bearce from 1811 to 1827. The stable, which served as the schoolhouse, is said to have housed the first elephant ever brought into the United States when an early circus passed through town.

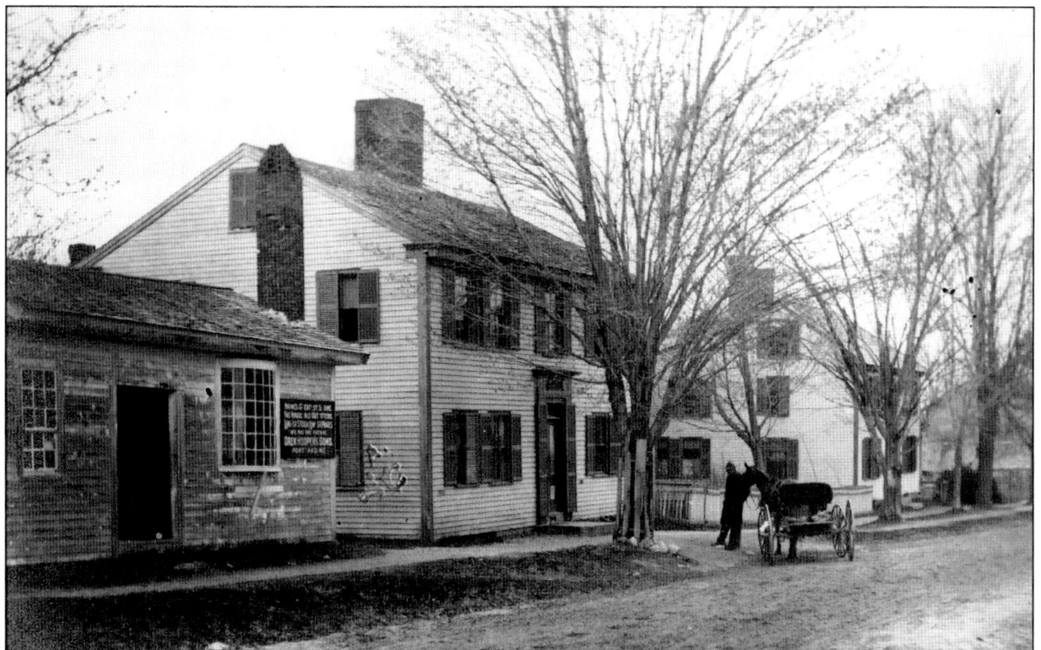

Here is an early view of the area across from town hall. From left to right are William Taylor's harness shop, the Israel Smith house (built around 1802), and the Stevens house (built around 1799). The Smith house, now at 384 Intervale Road, served as a post office, which is why the "Raymond team waiting for mail" is seen. Both houses were part of Stevens School.

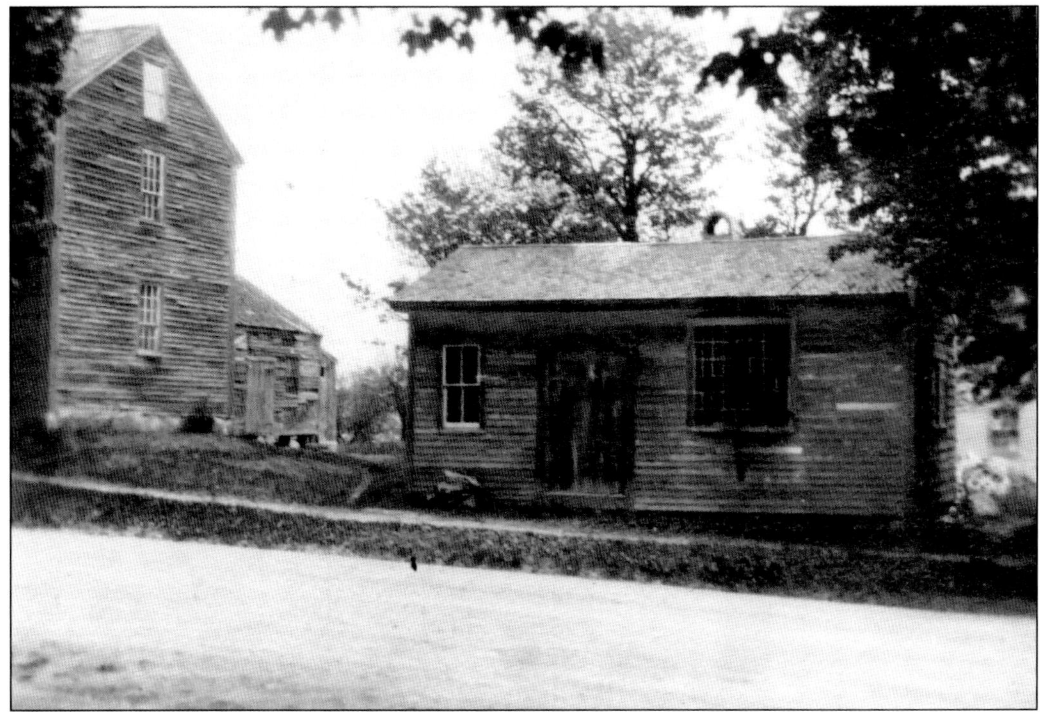

Pictured here are the William Taylor house (left) and his harness shop, which later served as a sandwich shop for high school students. Lewis True had the buildings removed in 1938. The shop was moved and made into a home at 53 Cobb's Bridge Road.

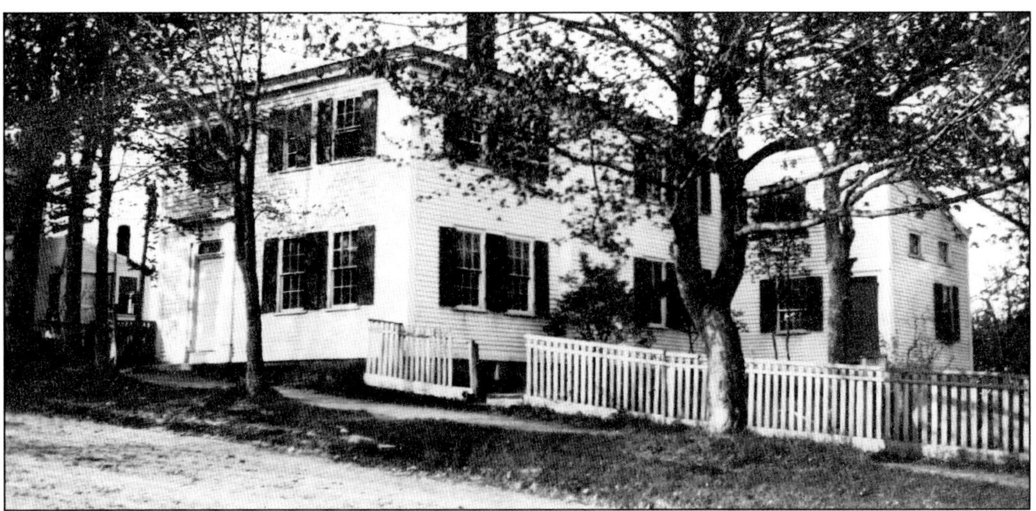

Just above the Taylor house still sits the Rev. Elisha Moseley house at 376 Intervale Road. Built between 1802 and 1805 by Moseley before the Congregational church had a parsonage, it was constructed in the fashion of homes in his native Connecticut. One room had no windows, as apparently it was used as a brewery. It was written of Moseley that his "famous beer was so well known for its curative qualities as to attract many invalids to the town."

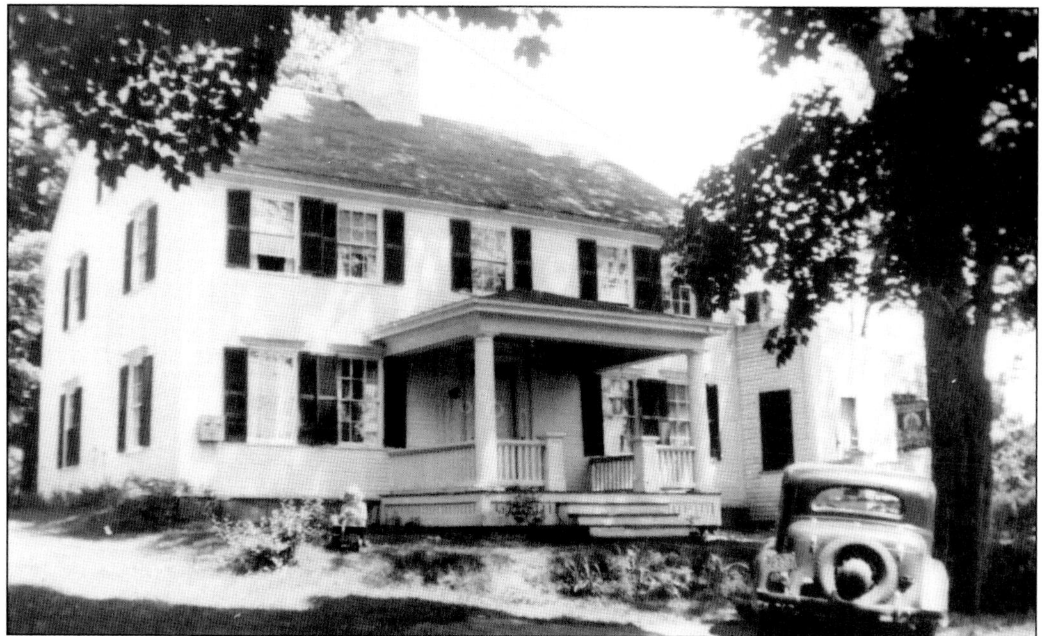

This 1947 view of the John Haskell house (built for his bride between 1792 and 1799) shows the sign for the Pine Tree Telephone and Telegraph Company office. The office and switchboard were located here for over 50 years until the conversion to dial telephones took place in 1962. Many pastors and teachers were tenants at 372 Intervale Road through the years.

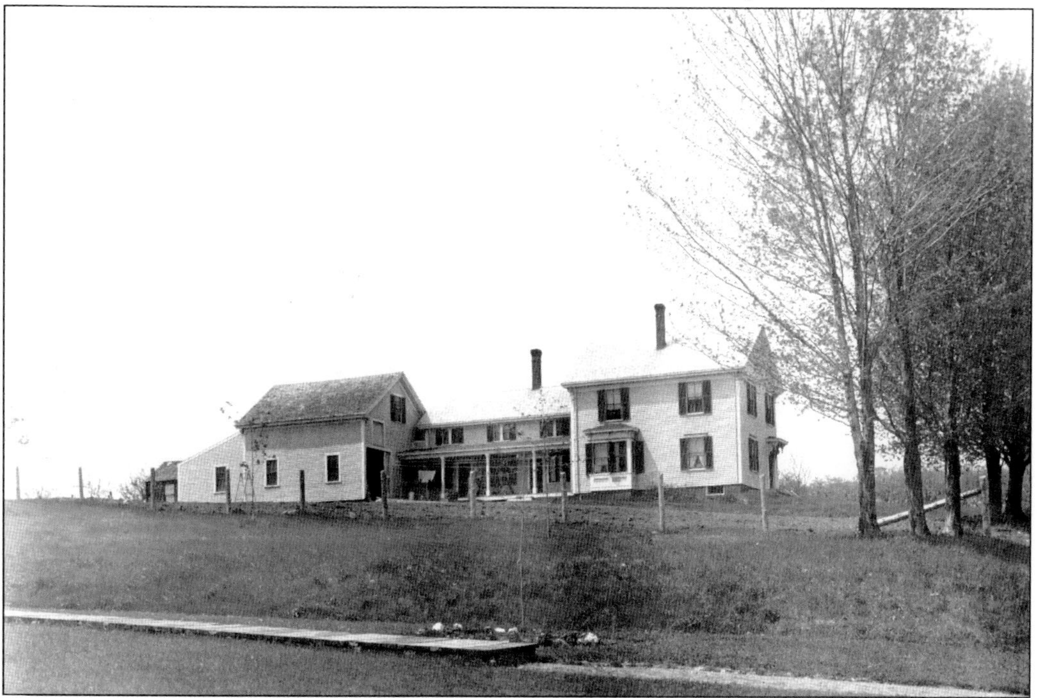

Built by Frank Merrill prior to 1885, this farmhouse still sits above the high school at 369 Intervale Road. It was home to the True family from 1897 to 1930 and has been in the Wills family since then. (Courtesy of the True family.)

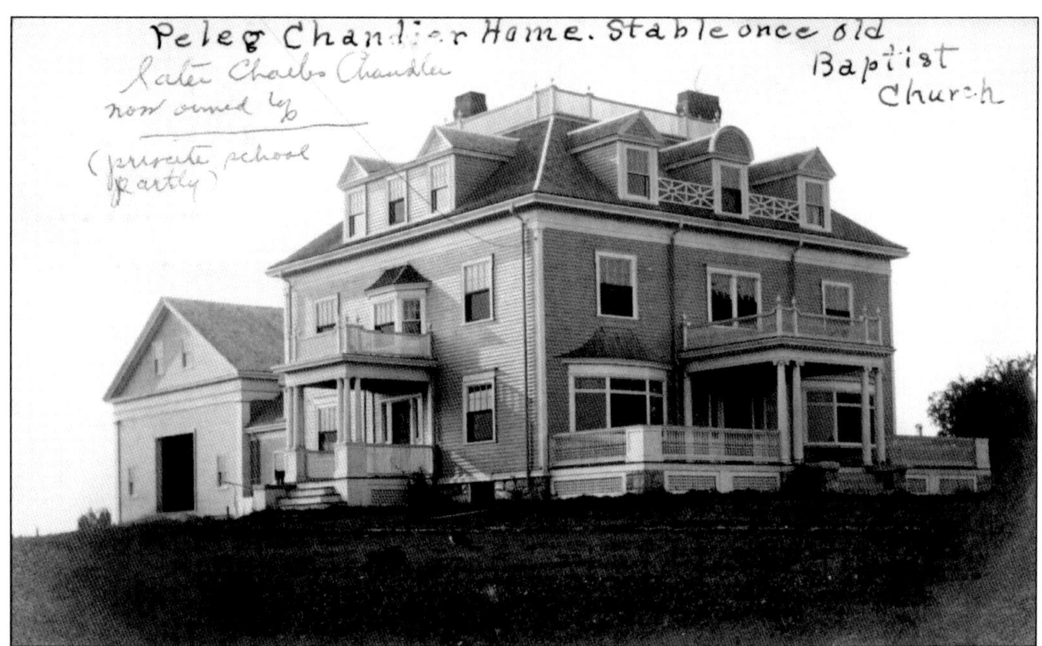

The 1903 Charles Peleg Chandler house (now the Chandler House Bed and Breakfast situated at 337 Intervale Road) is labeled on an early postcard. The barn (left) was moved to that location in 1903 after it was no longer needed as a high school building. Prior to that, it had been the Baptist church and sat closer to the road.

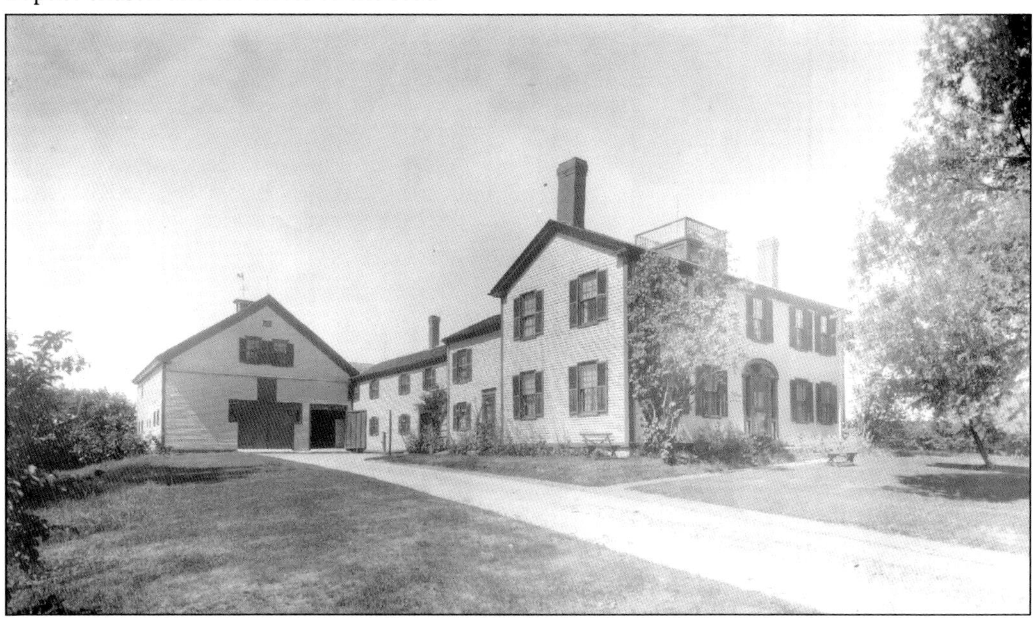

The Capt. A. Greeley Cutter house can still be found at 327 Intervale Road. Built by Peleg Chandler Jr. in 1820, the house later became the property of a retired ship captain who came from Portland in 1866 after that city's great fire. Herbert L. Berry, a graduate of Gorham Normal School, earned the money to attend school by assisting Cutter around the house and gardens. Berry eventually purchased the property in 1908, residing there until his death in 1930. (Courtesy of the True family.)

Capt. A. Greeley Cutter designed the gardens pictured here. He imported rare shrubs, flowers, and trees, as well as intricate items, for his house. In 1877, there were 100 apple, 80 pear, and 20 cherry and plum trees. The gardens were a showplace in town for years. (Courtesy of the Maine Historic Preservation Commission.)

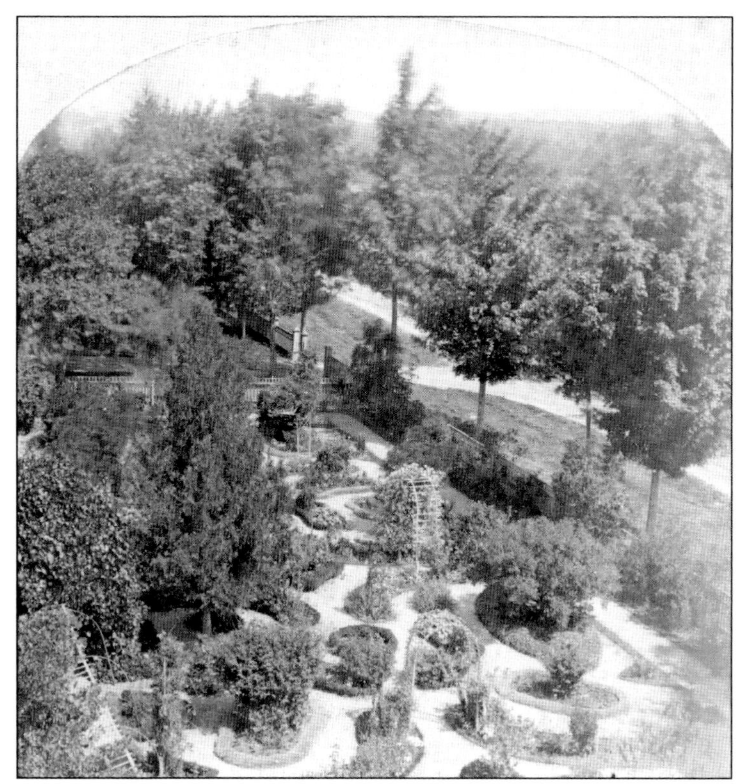

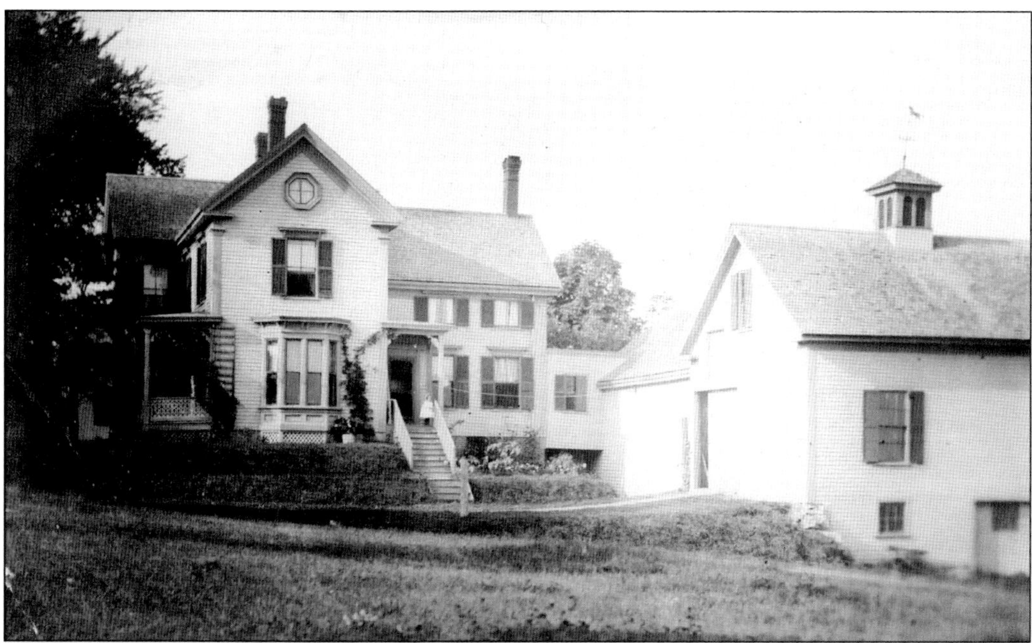

This picture postcard depicts the Charles Thompson house, built around 1880. There was a paint shop or woodworking shop on the property, which was moved and is presumed to be the shed between the house and barn. The buildings can be found at 336 Intervale Road.

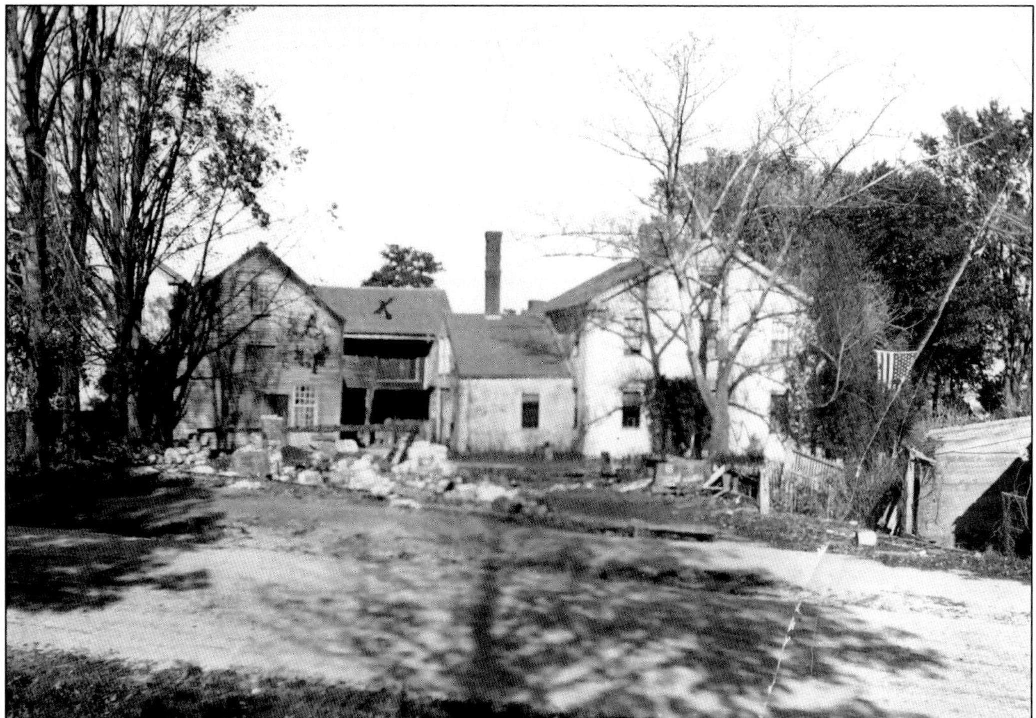

Since 1872, 10 Cobb's Bridge Road has served as the Greeley residence. It is believed to have been built around 1800 by Thomas Johnson, who used it as a tavern. The hall over the shed was an early Masons hall, used from 1804 to 1809 and 1814 to 1819, but was torn down in 1918. The barn served as the schoolhouse for Stevens School.

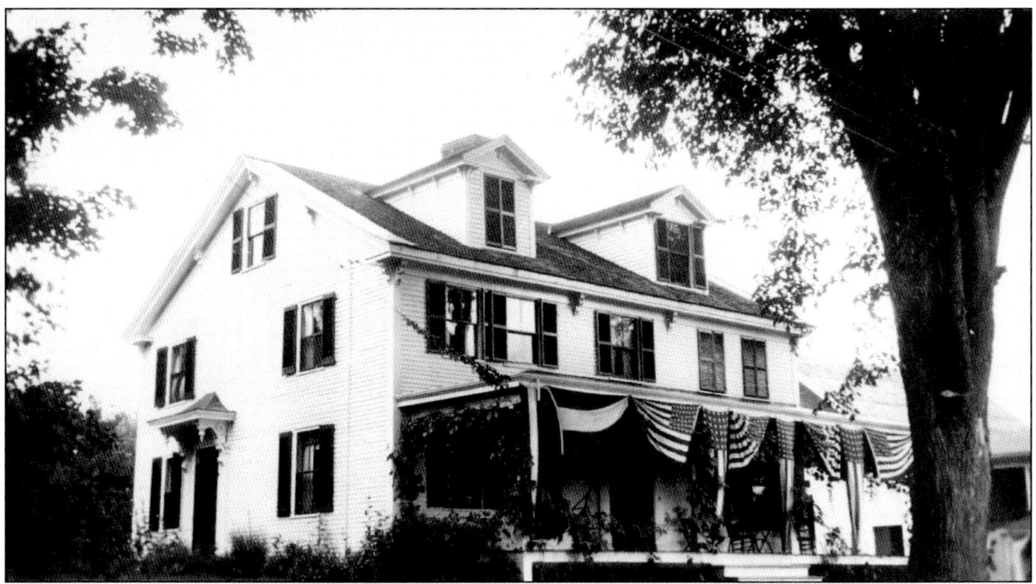

The William Pitt Fessenden house at 14 Cobb's Bridge Road is shown here decorated for the 1924 sesquicentennial. Built by Obadiah Whitman in the early 1800s, it was home to the Yeaton School and later the Bailey School. Artist D. D. Coombs not only went to school here but also lived here.

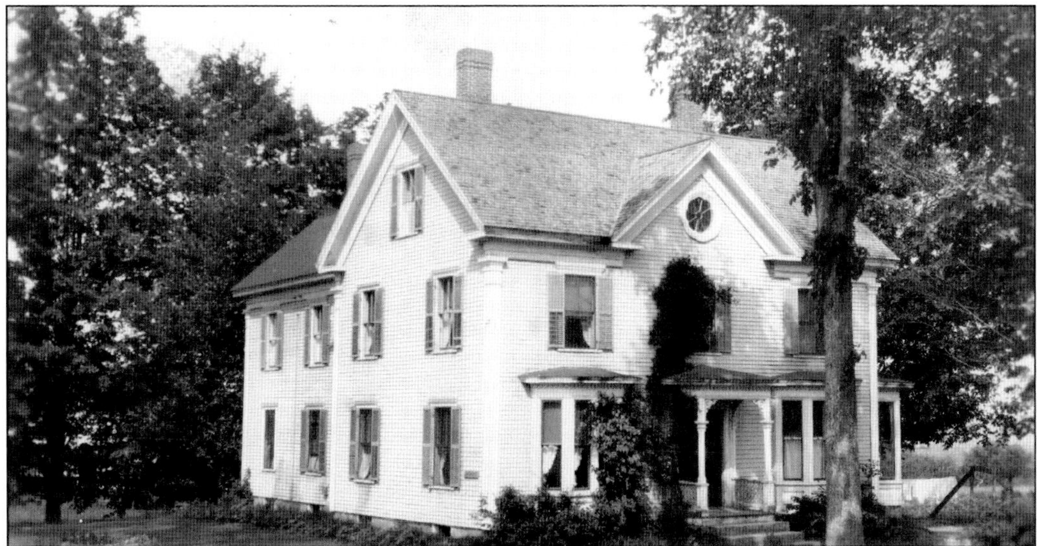

The home at 31 Cobb's Bridge Road was started by Caleb Haskell in 1891, but he had not finished it when he sold it to Dr. John I. Sturgis. The doctor completed the house and built a stable. It was later the residence of Dr. Linwood Sweatt, who operated a small hospital and operating room there from 1925 to 1935.

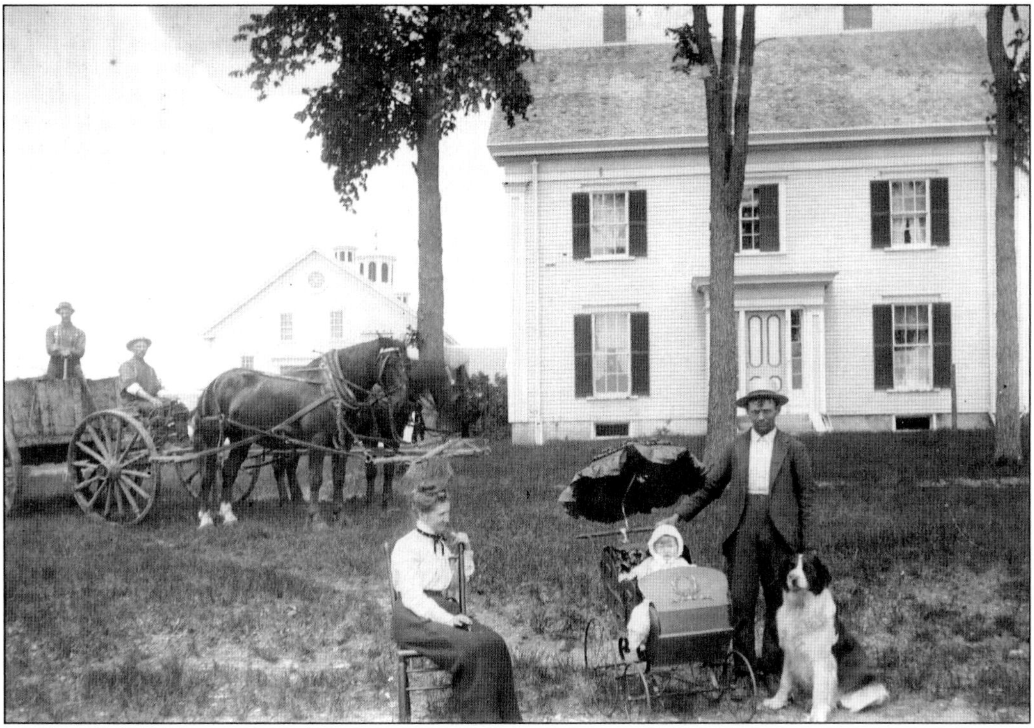

Andrew C. Chandler Sr. built this home in 1860 on the same lot that his great-grandfather Peleg Chandler had built a small house in 1762. Apparently wanting the longest barn in town, Andrew C. Chandler measured the longest one and built his 1 foot longer (110 feet). It became home to Eastgate Fellowship in 1977 and is now Eastgate Christian School at 68 Cobb's Bridge Road.

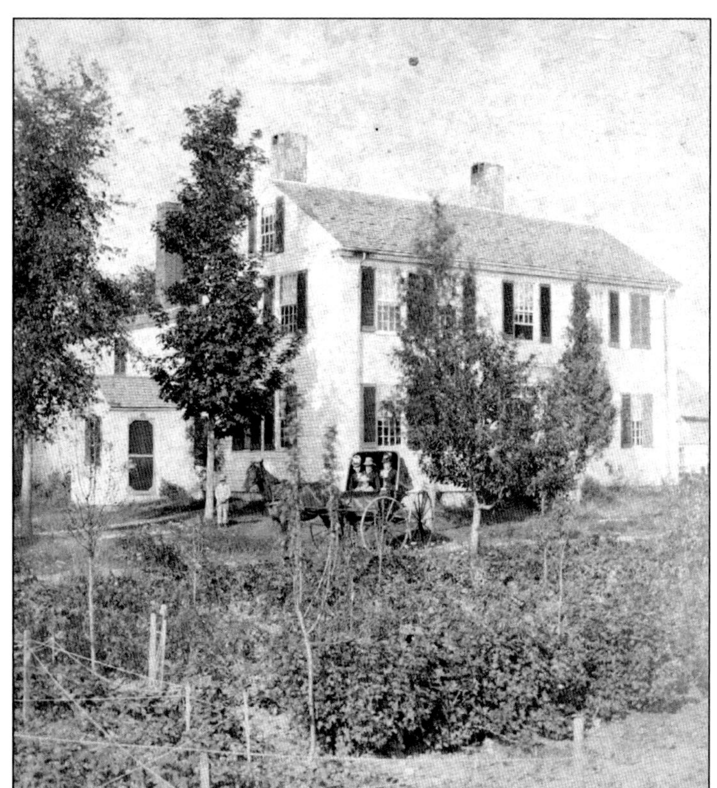

This view from about 1880 of the John W. True farm at 97 Cobb's Bridge Road shows Carrie True and friends in the family carriage drawn by Old Boss, with Albert True standing by the horse. The main house was built in 1812 by the Tuckers, with John W. True adding a new barn in 1885 and a new ell in 1904 after this picture was taken. It has long been known as Shady Lane Farm.

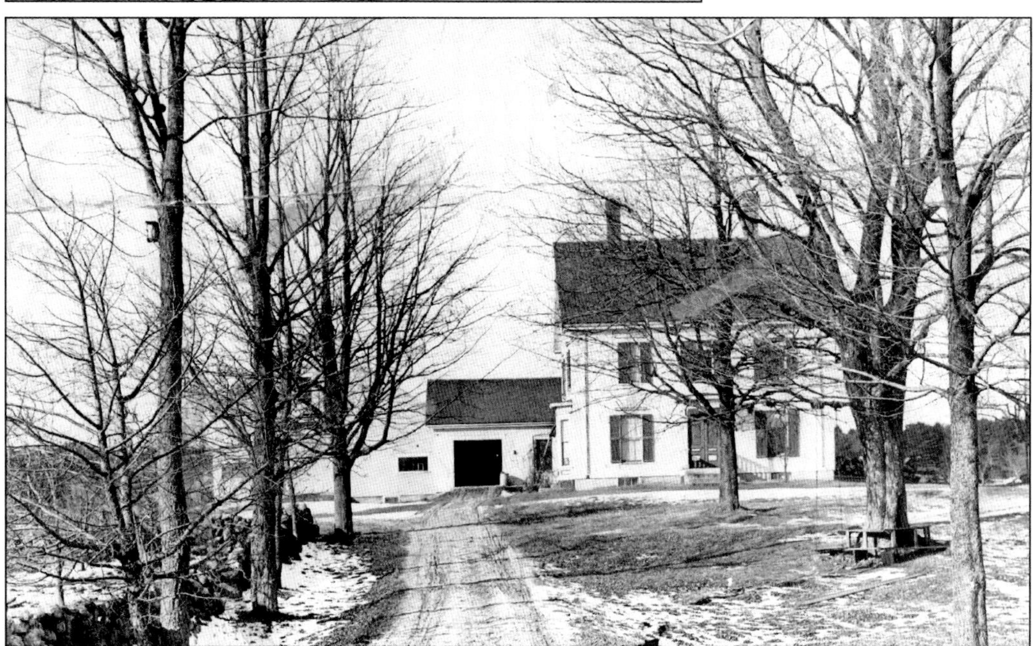

A 1910 picture postcard shows the Andrew C. Chandler Jr. farm at 120 Cobb's Bridge Road. The carriage house, the original home on the site, was owned and probably built by Obadiah Whitman. Andrew C. Chandler Sr. bought the property and built the present house and barn to give to his son as a wedding present on Christmas day in 1878.

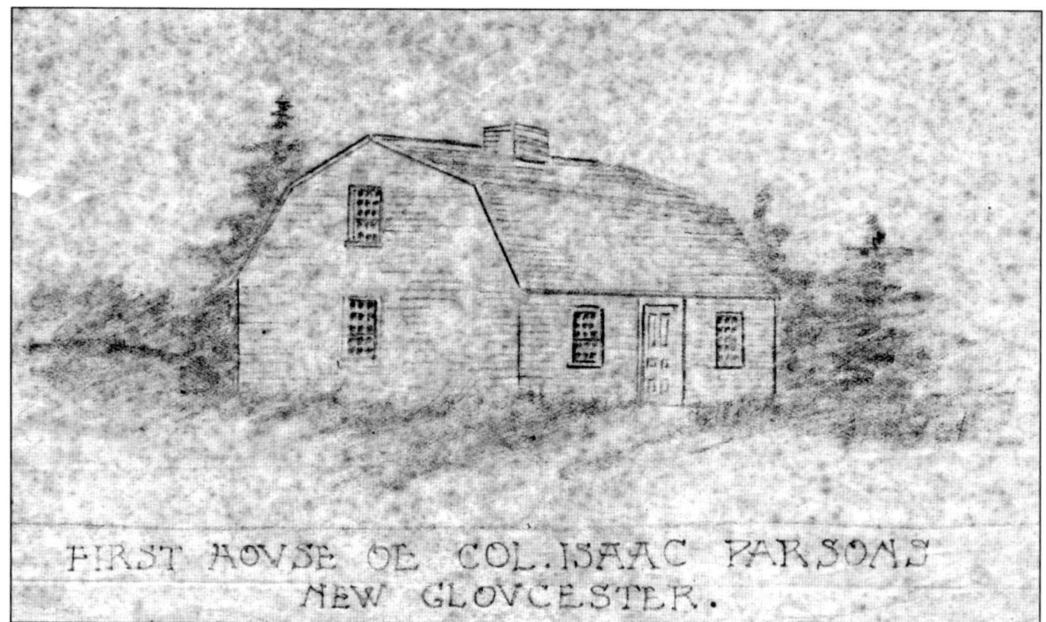

An 1836 sketch depicts the oldest frame house in New Gloucester, built in 1762. The house now at 143 Cobb's Bridge Road was built by Col. Isaac Parsons after he arrived here from Gloucester, Massachusetts, in June 1761. The gambrel originally sat across the road on the highest point of land behind Parsons's second house, built in 1782, and for many years was used as a shed connecting the big house with its ell to the garage.

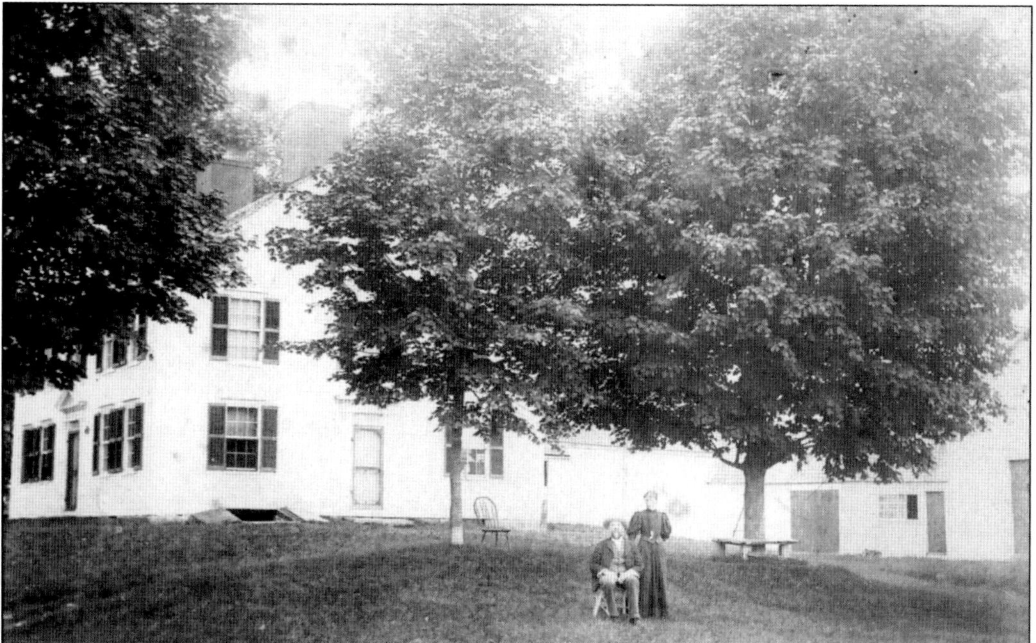

Charles P. Haskell and his wife, Helen, are shown at their residence at 146 Cobb's Bridge Road. The second house built by Parsons is thought to have been started in 1780 and completed in 1782 after his marriage to the wealthy widow Deborah Hewitt. The farm stayed in the family until Thomas Moser purchased the property and moved the 1762 gambrel "shed" across the road.

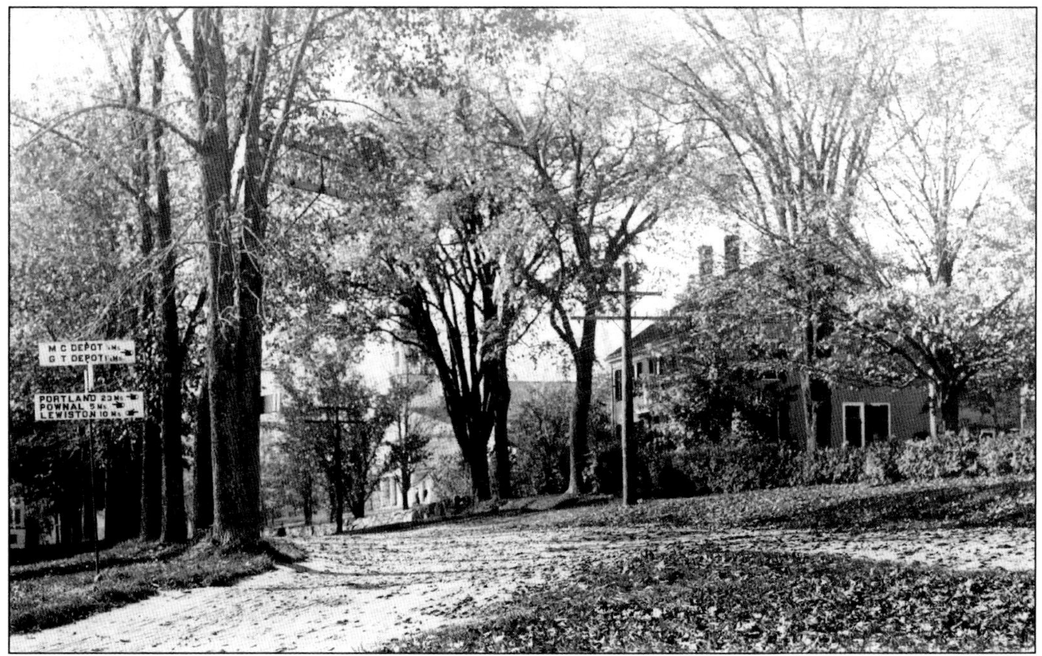

The Allen house can be seen on the right at the entrance of Gloucester Hill Road. Maj. William Coit Allen wanted his house to be the finest in town and hired a master builder to construct it in 1793. He owned land from Lower Corner to Estes Road and settled the question of whether Bowdoin College was to be located there: "I shan't let them have any land, the boys would steal all my apples."

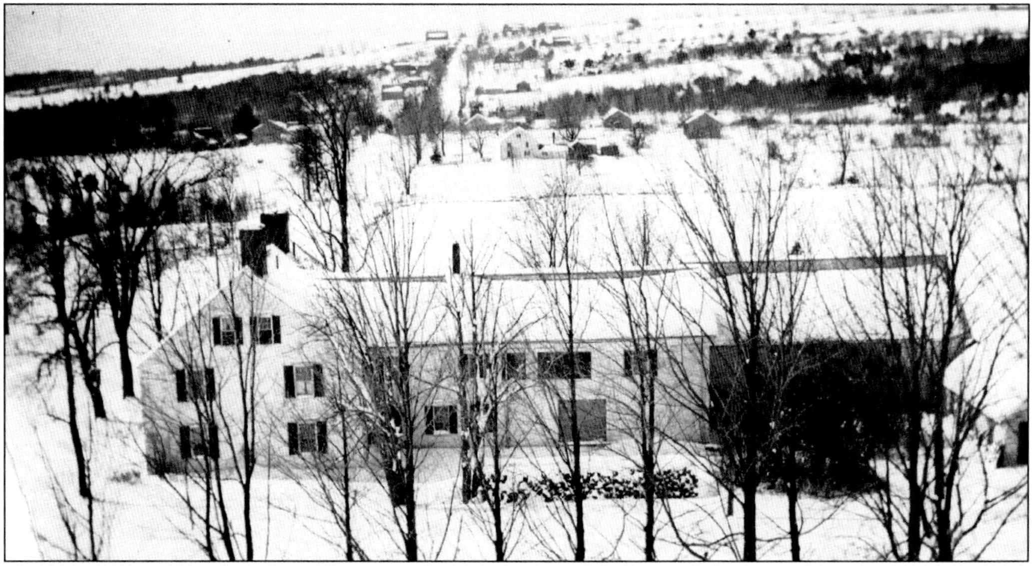

This view of the Foxcroft house was taken from the Congregational church bell tower, with every building visible to the top of Harris Hill. The house at 29 Gloucester Hill Road was built in 1765 by Harvard graduate Rev. Samuel Foxcroft, the first minister in the town. It remained in the family until 1915.

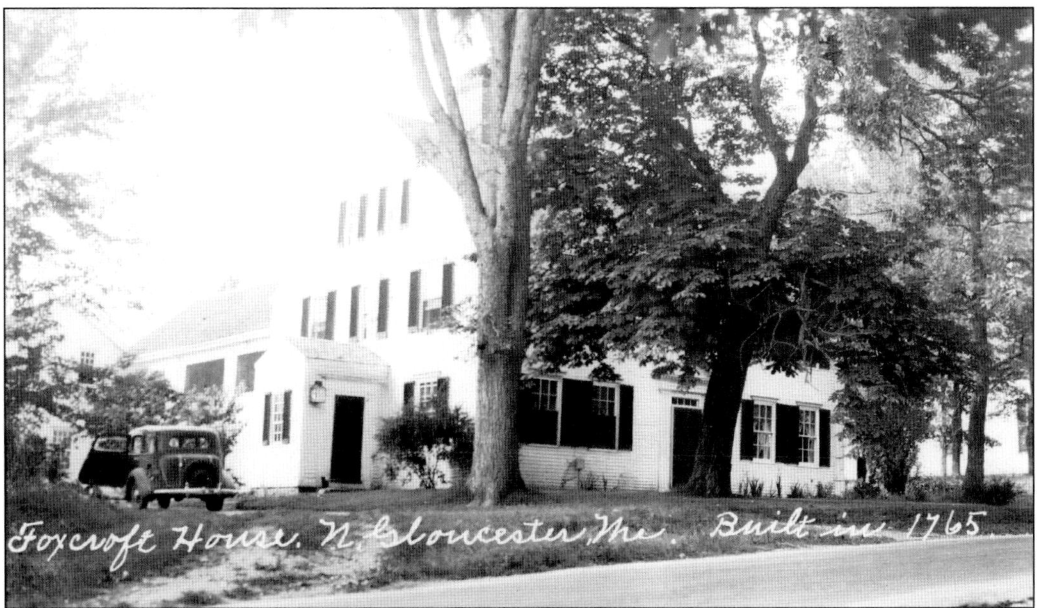

The front of the Foxcroft house is shown on this picture postcard. Foxcroft's son Joseph had a store that sat just to the left of this view that later became the carriage house (now workshop). Joseph purchased 17,950 acres in Piscataquis County and founded the town of Foxcroft.

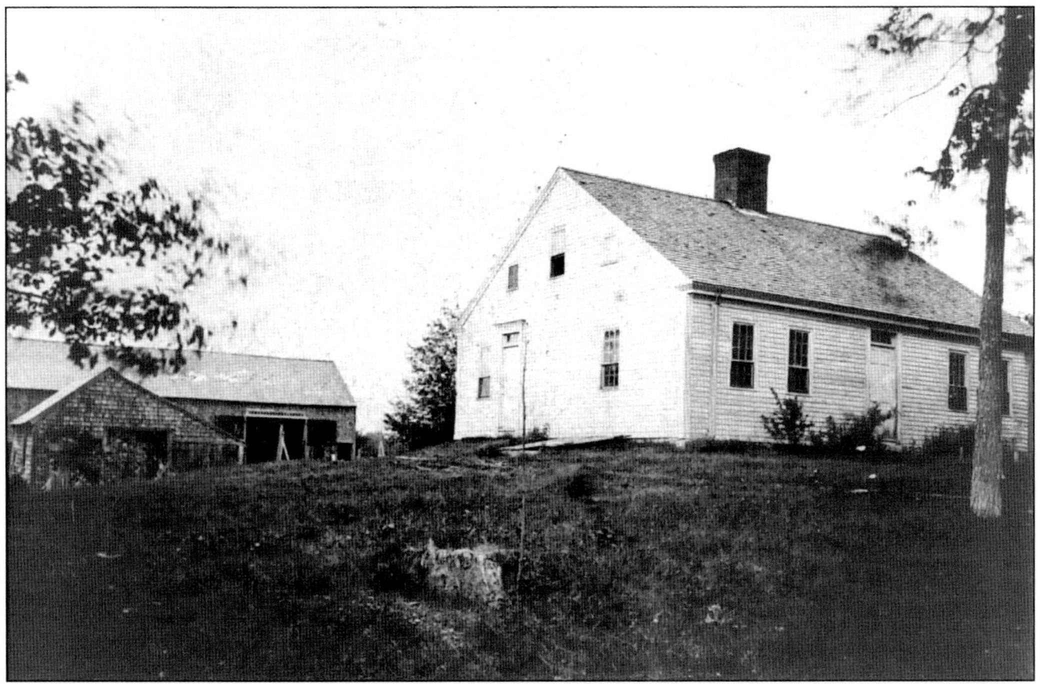

The James Winslow house (built around 1819) at 85 Gloucester Hill Road is pictured above. Grandson Charles A. Winslow resided here during the 1924 sesquicentennial and provided drinking water for the celebration from his "Purity Spring" located here, which was famous with the Native Americans and early settlers. (Courtesy of Beverly Cadigan.)

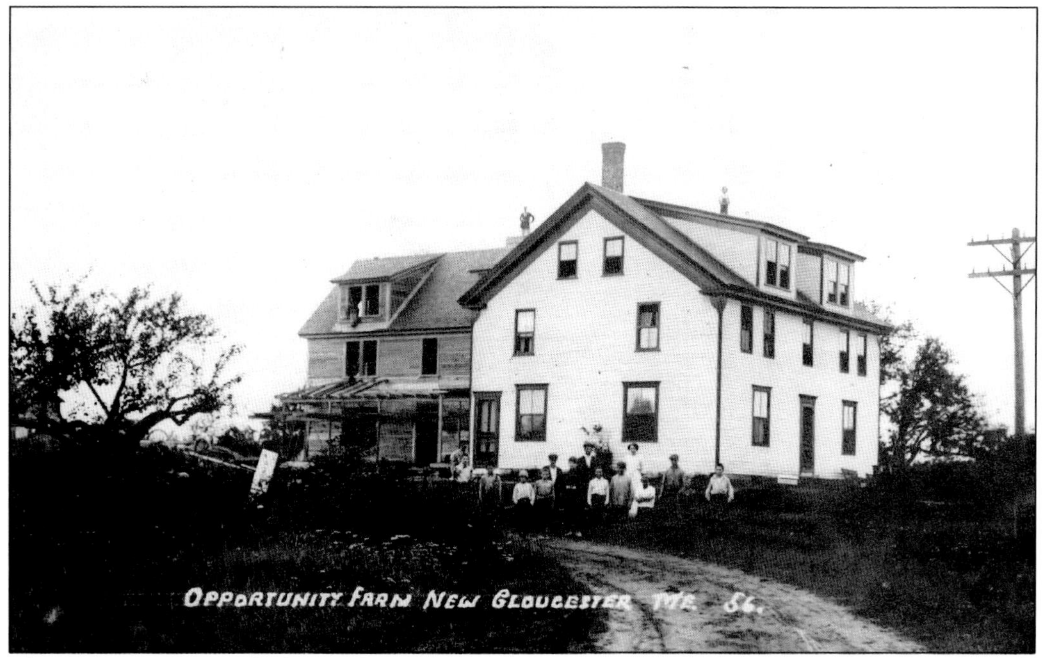

These picture postcards depict the early days of Opportunity Farm on top of Gloucester Hill (formerly named Harris Hill for Capt. William Harris who settled there). F. Forrest Pease, with the aid of Ida Newell, founded the home for homeless boys in 1910. They incorporated on June 14, 1912, as the Opportunity Farm Association. Two farms were purchased, with one known as the lower farm (above) and the other being the Charles Bennett place in 1914 (below). They operated their own school for boys, ages 9 to 16, until consolidation in 1950.

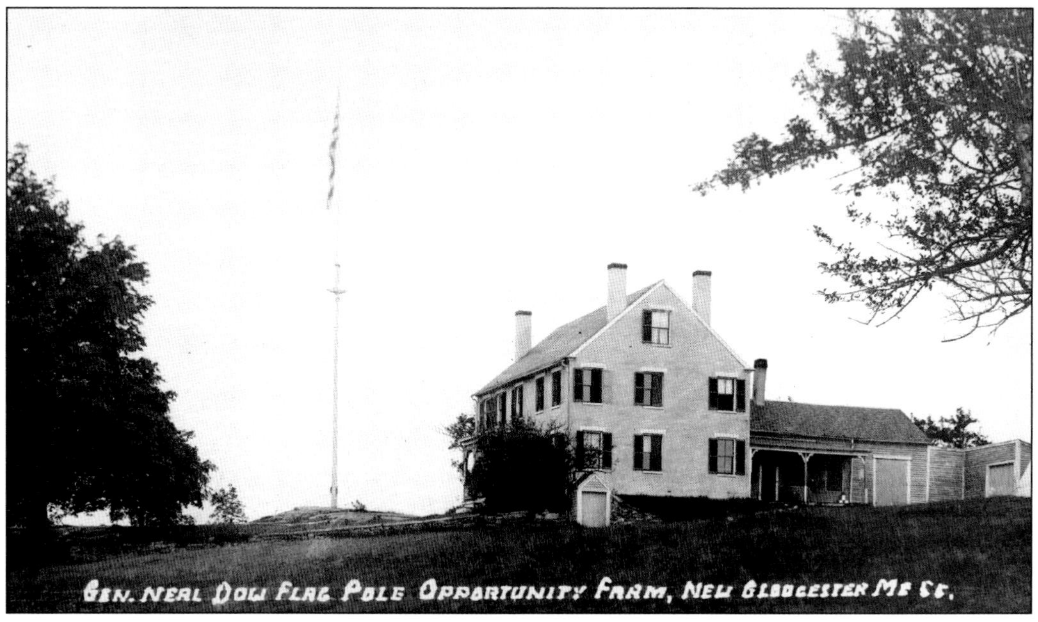

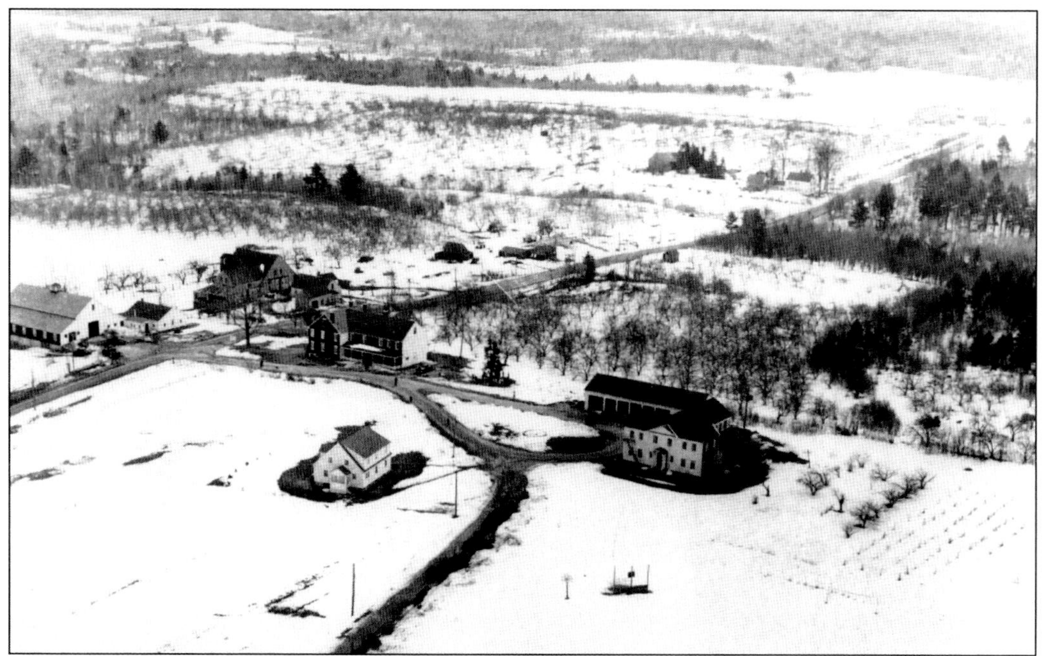

This 1950 aerial view of Opportunity Farm for Boys is from above the 1942 fire tower. The 1923 barn (left) can be seen across the road, as well as the old Bailey farm to its right and Thompson's Orchards in the distance. The house at the lower farm burned in 1925. Two dormitories were added at the corner of Bennett Road in 2001 when it became Opportunity Farm for Boys and Girls.

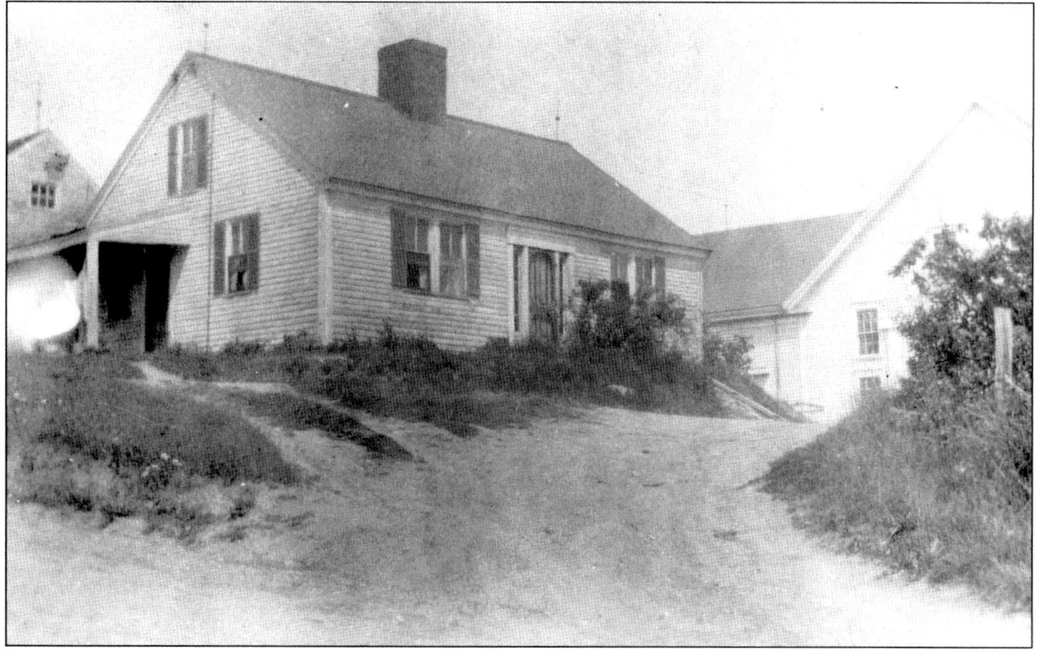

The John Bailey farm is shown here in 1927. The barn was torn down in 1973, and the house was moved back from the road. It can be found at 224 Gloucester Hill Road near the Opportunity Farm barn.

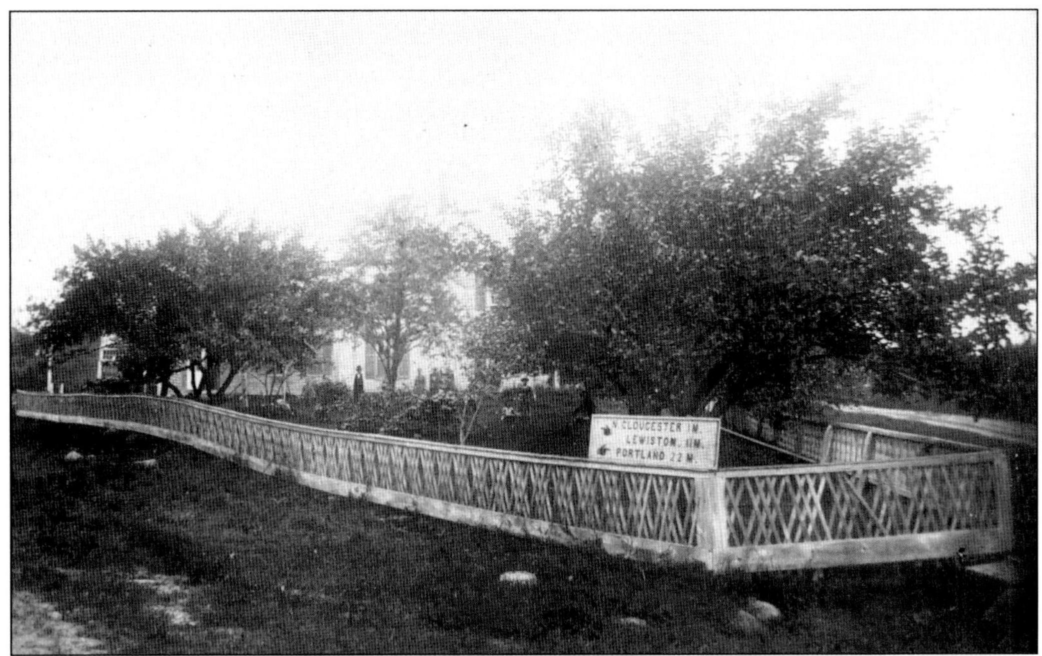

This was the view at White's Corner around 1881 at the junction of Lewiston Road and Gloucester Hill Road. Members of the Morrill family can be seen in the yard of their home at 263 Lewiston Road. White's Corner is the site of the supposed first shoe factory in Maine. It was started by Albion P. White in 1844 with 17 employees and then moved to Auburn in 1856.

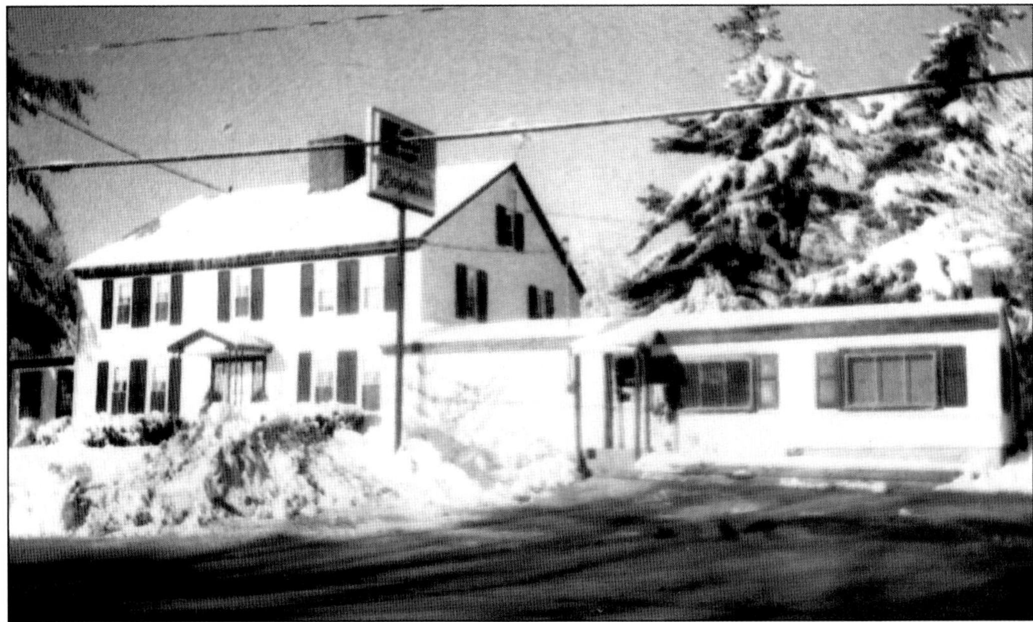

The Thomas Stinchfield house at 160 Lewiston Road was built in the 1770s. The pine boards upstairs are 23.5 inches wide, so the builders could not be accused of using the king's pine, which was greater than 24 inches and shipped to England for masts. The Leighton family purchased the home in 1942 and started a store. This picture was taken in January 1988 when the store closed.

Five

UPPER GLOUCESTER AND BALD HILL

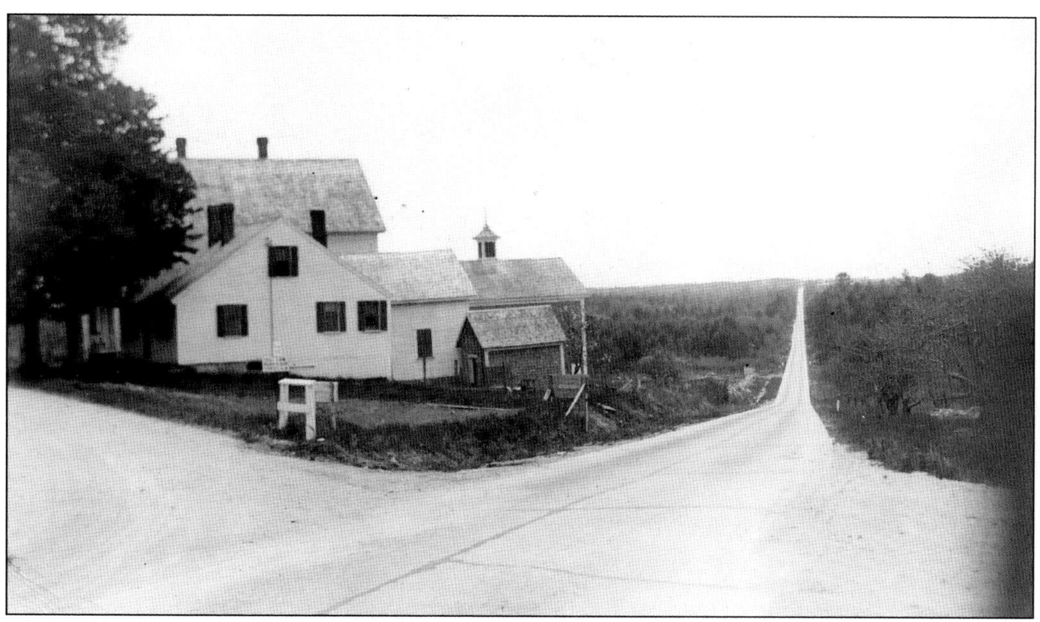

This view of the cement highway is from the location of the one traffic light currently in town. The Portland–Lewiston concrete road was opened for travel in New Gloucester on October 26, 1923. These buildings at the junction of Intervale Road and Lewiston Road burned around 1930 on what is now the site of Bicentennial Park.

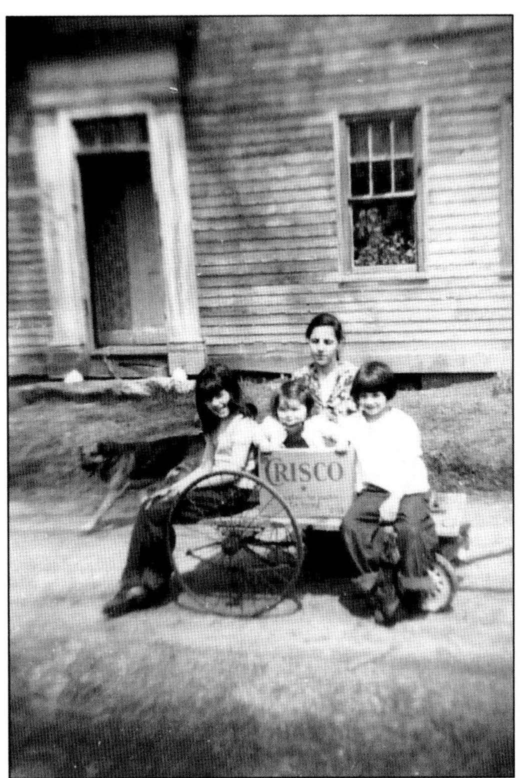

Pearl Berry Eveleth is seated behind her daughters, from left to right, Ethel, Louise, and Elizabeth Grace, with Tucker, at their homestead at 66 Intervale Road. The c. 1795 house was the site of the Nathaniel Eveleth Tavern, which had a dance hall on the second floor. Capt. Nathaniel Eveleth served as the first town clerk for 42 consecutive years, from 1774 to 1816.

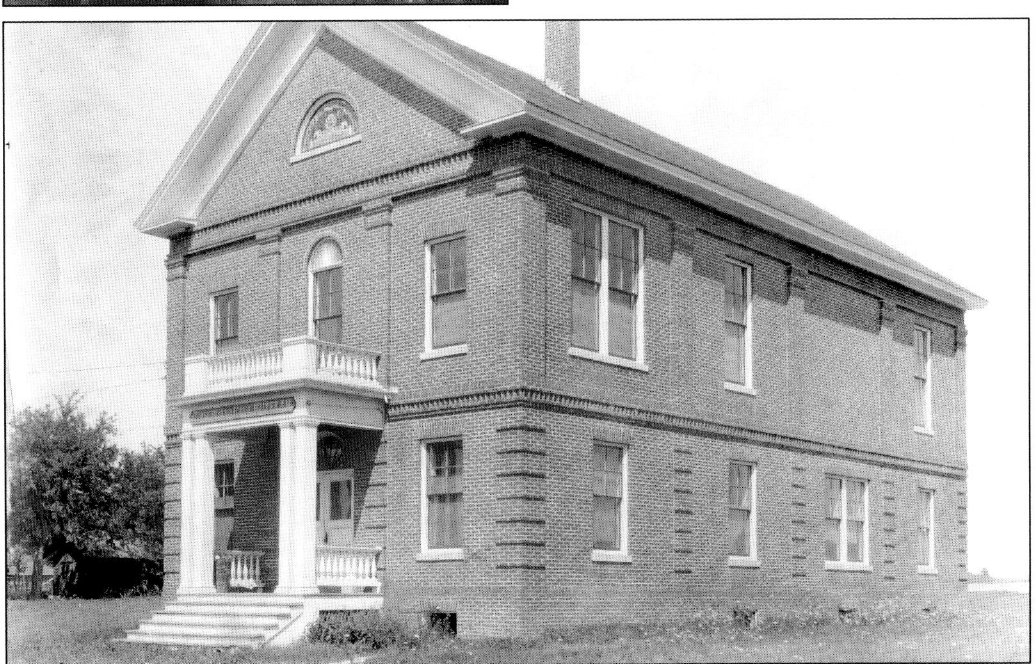

The Masonic hall was constructed and dedicated in 1903 to celebrate 100 years of Cumberland Lodge No. 12. The 34-by-60-foot brick building was constructed by Brother Silas Foster of Gray. The Masons had been using a hall dedicated 50 years earlier at 27 Upper Village Street. (Courtesy of the True family.)

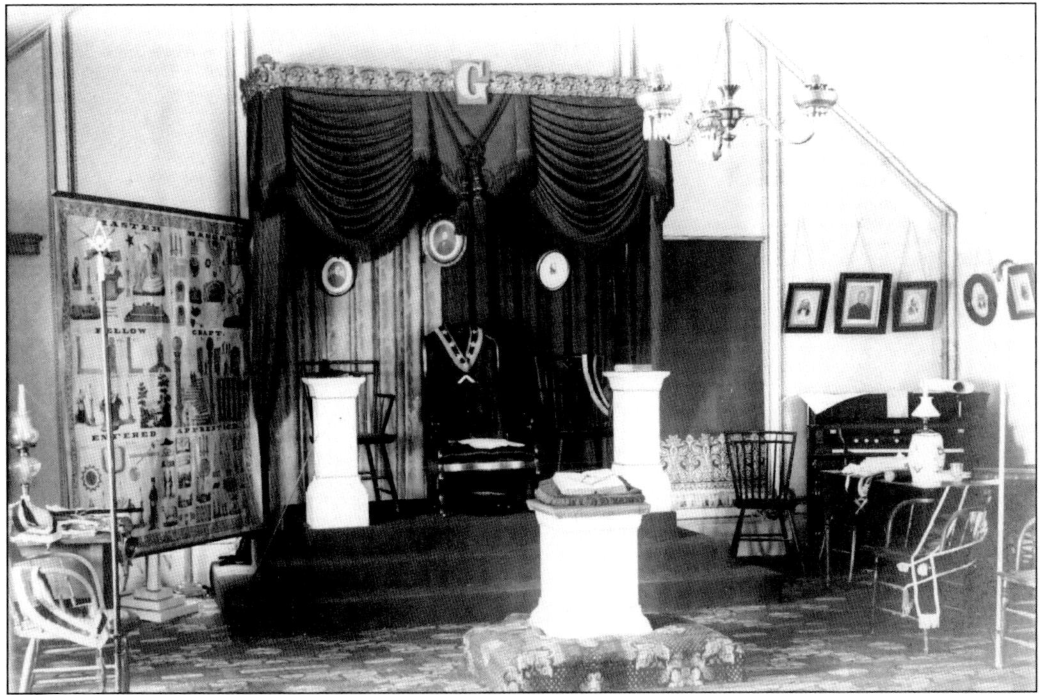

This picture postcard depicts the interior of the Masonic hall. The Masons met in several private halls during their first 50 years. The first meeting of the Masons was held in 1803 in Brother Nathaniel Jenks's hall (now 26–34 Bald Hill Road). Other early members included Ezekiel Whitman (chief justice of the Maine Supreme Court), Joseph E. Foxcroft, and abolitionist Samuel Fessenden.

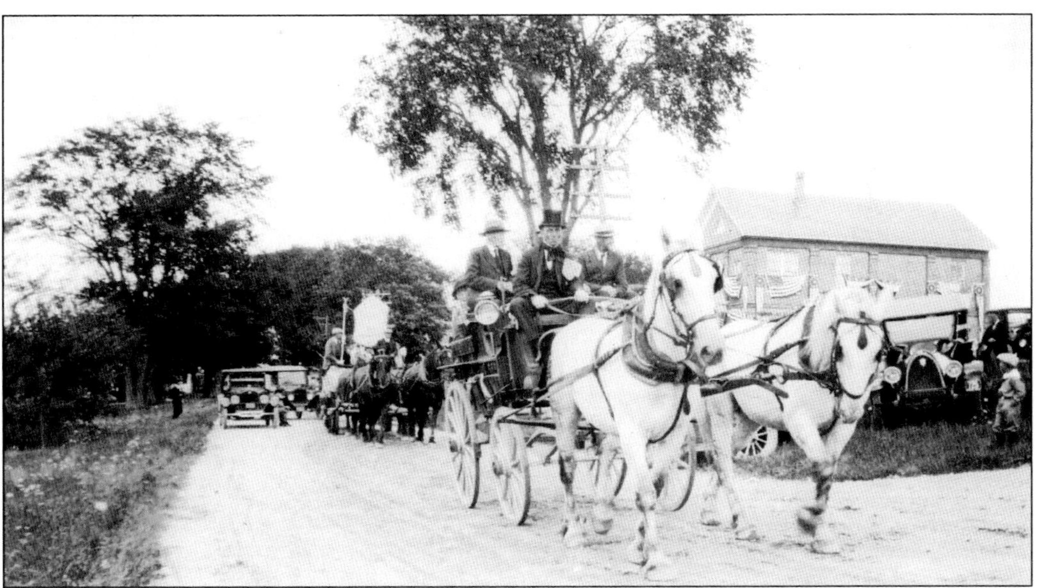

The Masonic hall can be seen at 11 Bald Hill Road in this photograph of the 1924 parade taken by Elsie Megquier. The old stagecoach is in the foreground approaching Lewiston Road and was used for mail delivery during the summer months.

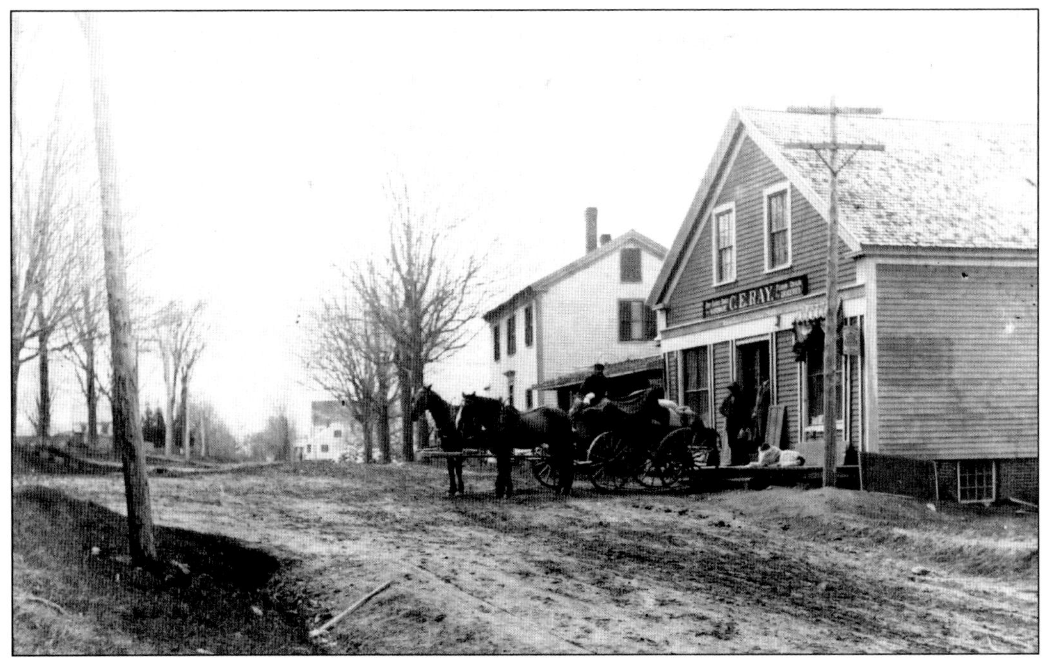

A crowd is gathered at the C. E. Ray Store in this 1905 postcard. The store was later home to Hathaway Woodworking Company, which burned down on November 19, 1947, taking the adjacent Tripp house with it. The road seen on the left is Upper Village Street, and the view is of Bald Hill Road facing Lewiston Road.

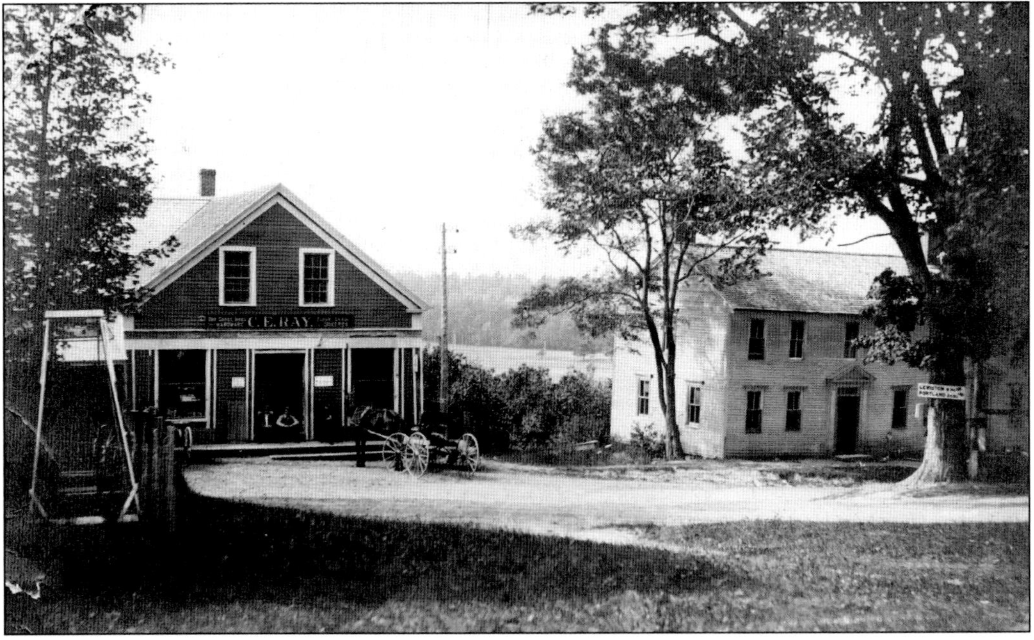

Here is a view of the same intersection taken from Upper Village Street. Charles Eugene Ray operated the store for several years after George Blake (and later his son Herbert E. Blake) ran it. The house on the right is the Hathaway house (built around 1783), which was split into two homes at 26 and 34 Bald Hill Road in 1980. Note the field seen in the background.

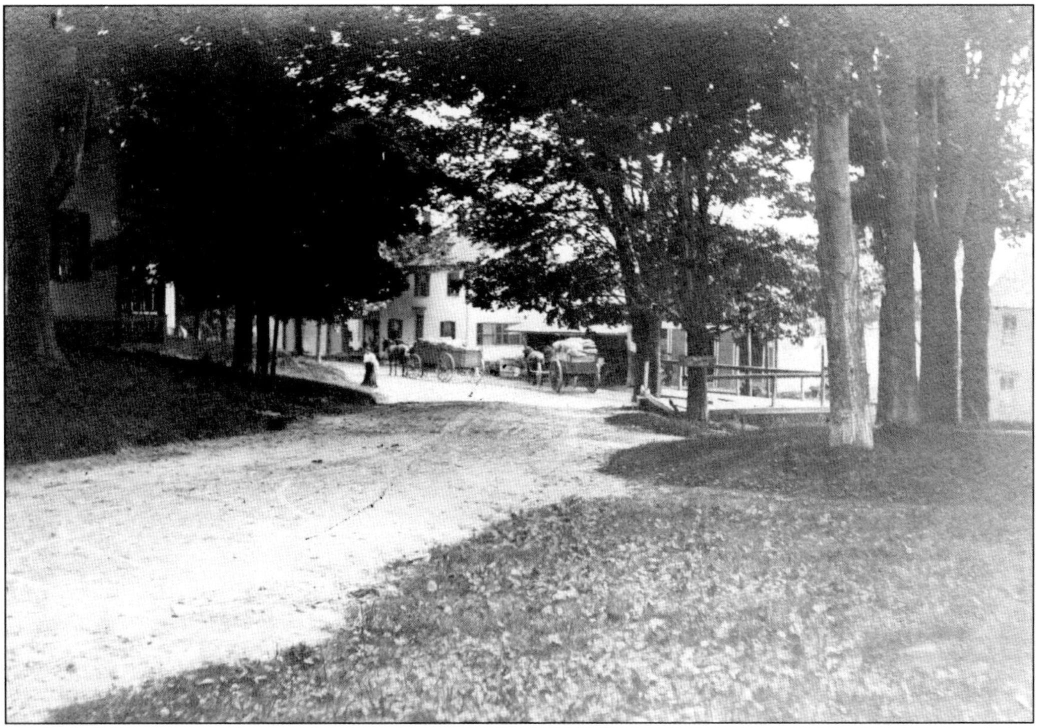

This view looking along Upper Village Street shows the bandstand that stood at the intersection with Bald Hill Road. This was the site of many concerts by the New Gloucester Cornet Band, among others. The C. E. Ray Store can be seen behind it.

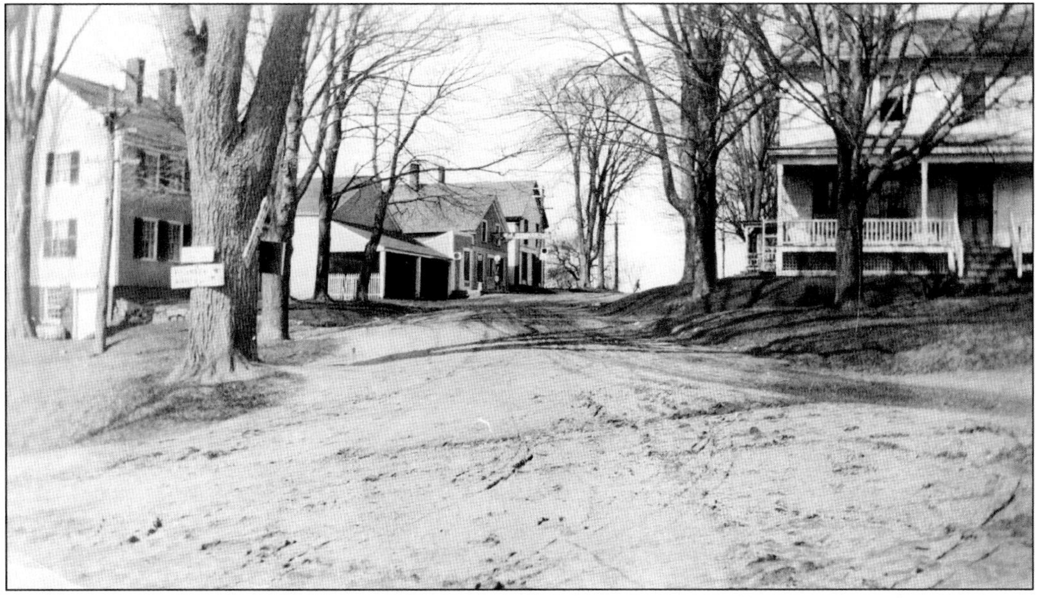

Several historic homes are seen in this photograph of Upper Village Street taken from its junction with Bald Hill Road. The old Lot Nelson Tavern (built around 1780) is partially seen on the right. This was the main road before the cement highway bypassed it in 1923 to the dismay of local businesses.

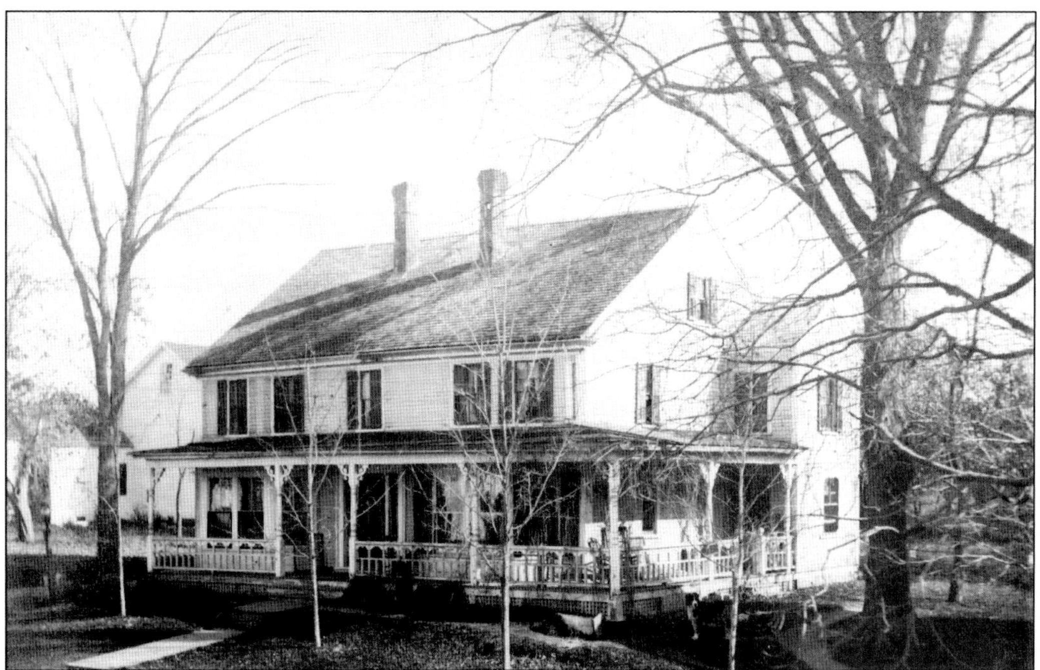

This 1905 postcard depicts the Blake house that sat just north of the Lot Nelson Tavern on Upper Village Street. This house served as a tavern, a post office, and a meeting place for the Masons prior to their hall being built across the road in 1852.

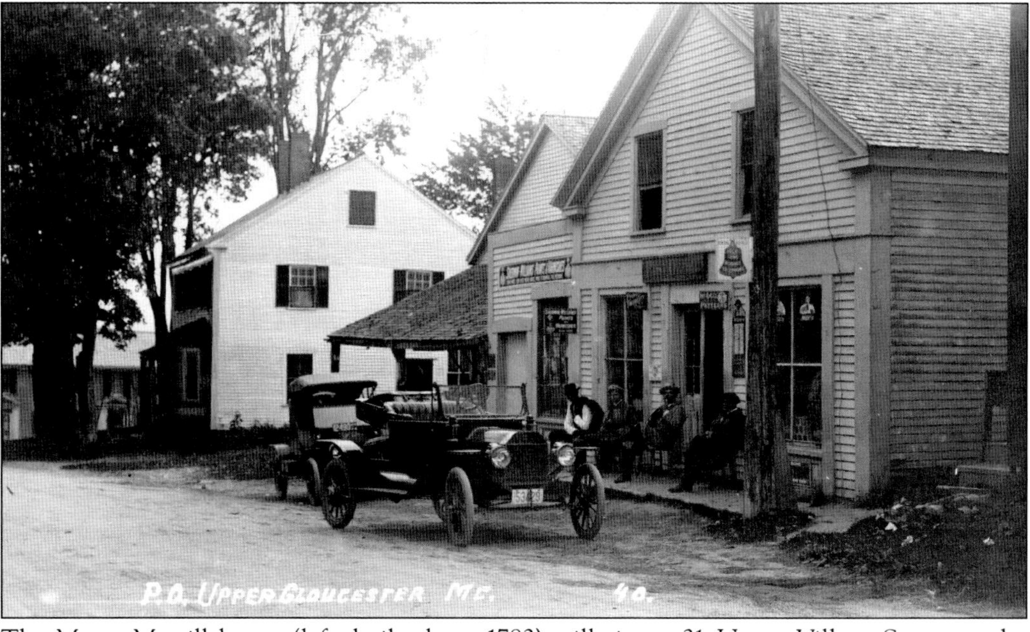

The Moses Merrill house (left, built about 1783) still sits at 31 Upper Village Street at the intersection with Bald Hill Road. It originally consisted of a dwelling with a large barn and ell attached on the north and a store with a post office (center). There was a long, large hall on the second floor that held dances and entertainment, and the tavern was below. Patrons often left their carriages here and slept at the Hathaway House across the road.

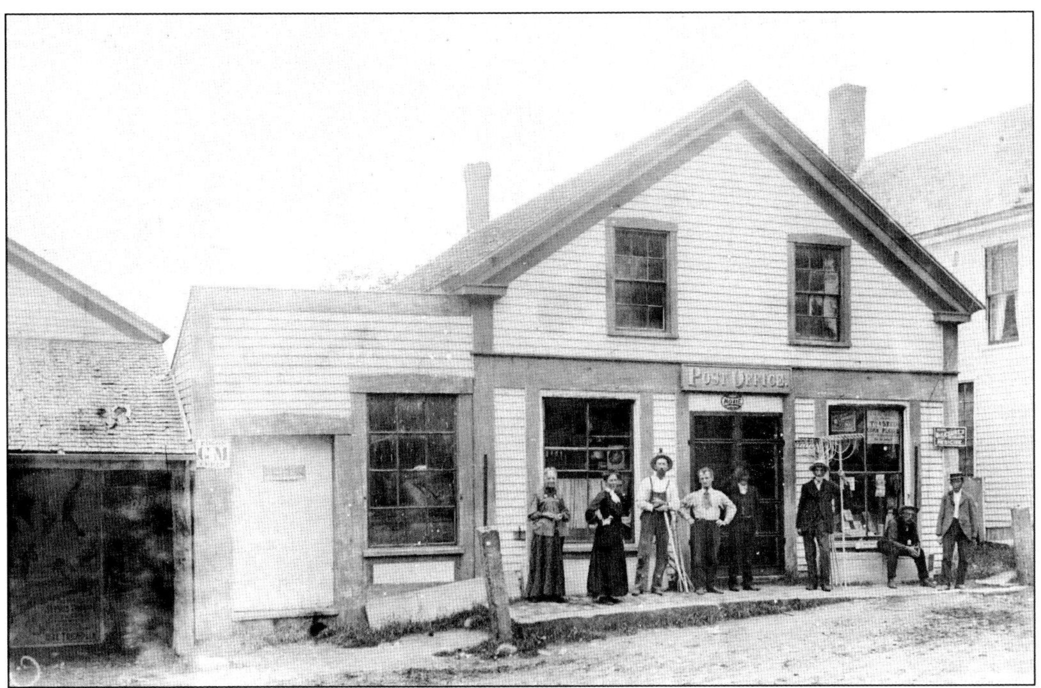

The Upper Gloucester Post Office and general store is shown here around 1903. From left to right are Sarah Foss, Mary Bickford Chipman (postmistress), Fred M. Nevins, Herbert E. Blake, unidentified, John Whitman, William Pitt Stevens, and Willie Pierce.

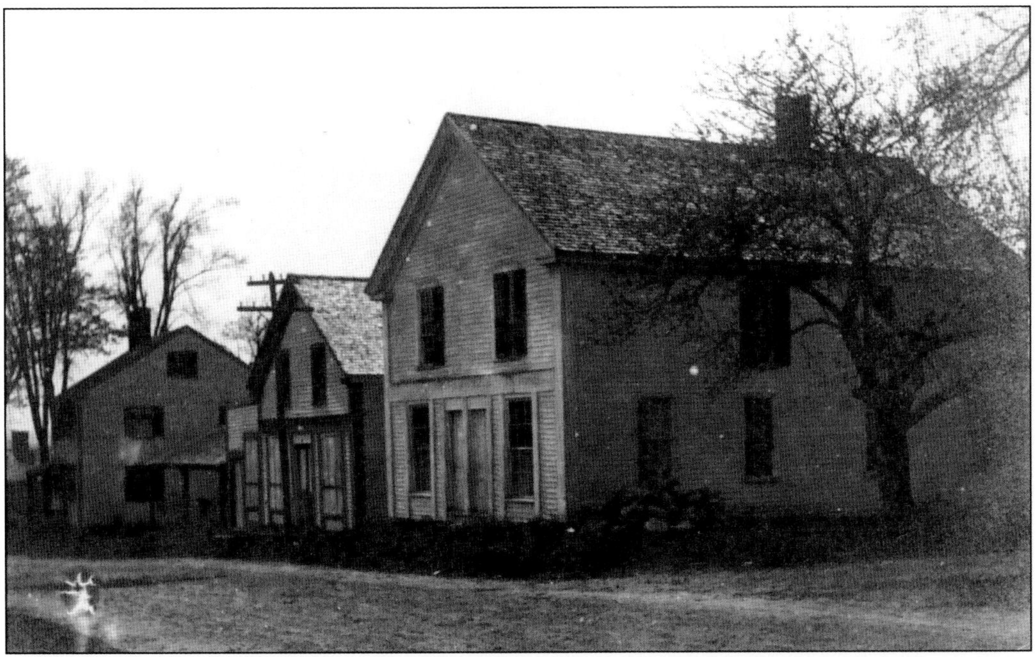

The old Masonic hall (right) at 27 Upper Village Street had its final meeting on June 9, 1903. Construction began in 1852, and it was dedicated on June 24, 1853. The first floor was used as a school in the 1890s for younger kids, while the older ones attended Centennial Hall. At an October 1903 meeting, it was voted to sell the old hall to Brother Charles Eugene Ray for $300.

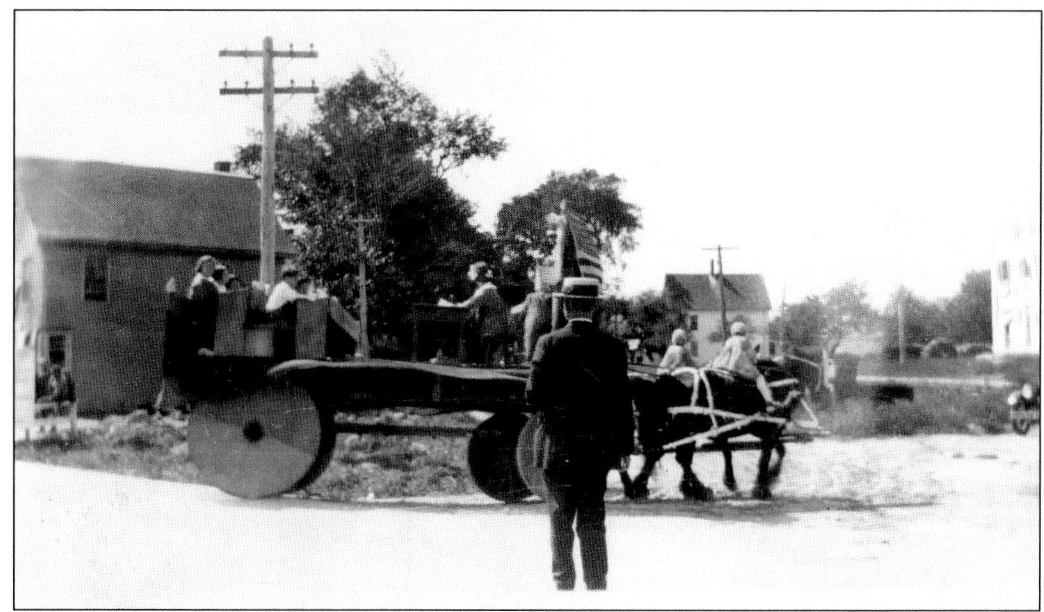

E. F. Elwell took this picture of the "old school days" float in the 1924 sesquicentennial parade. Centennial Hall is on the far right, while the old Masonic hall on Upper Village Street can be seen above the horses. The building on the left is the current home of Cloutier's Market and was the final location of the Upper Gloucester Post Office when it ceased in 1956.

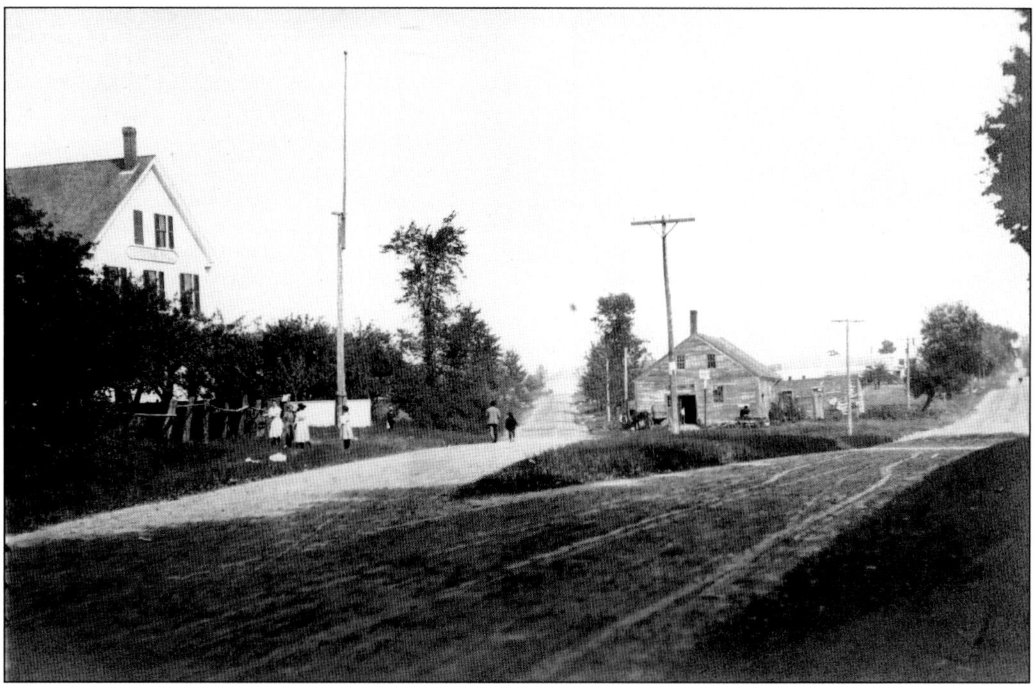

This 1907 postcard depicts the intersection of Lewiston Road and Peacock Hill Road. Centennial Hall (left) served as the schoolhouse for Upper Gloucester. Alvin Brown's blacksmith shop at the fork is in the area of the current town garage parking lot.

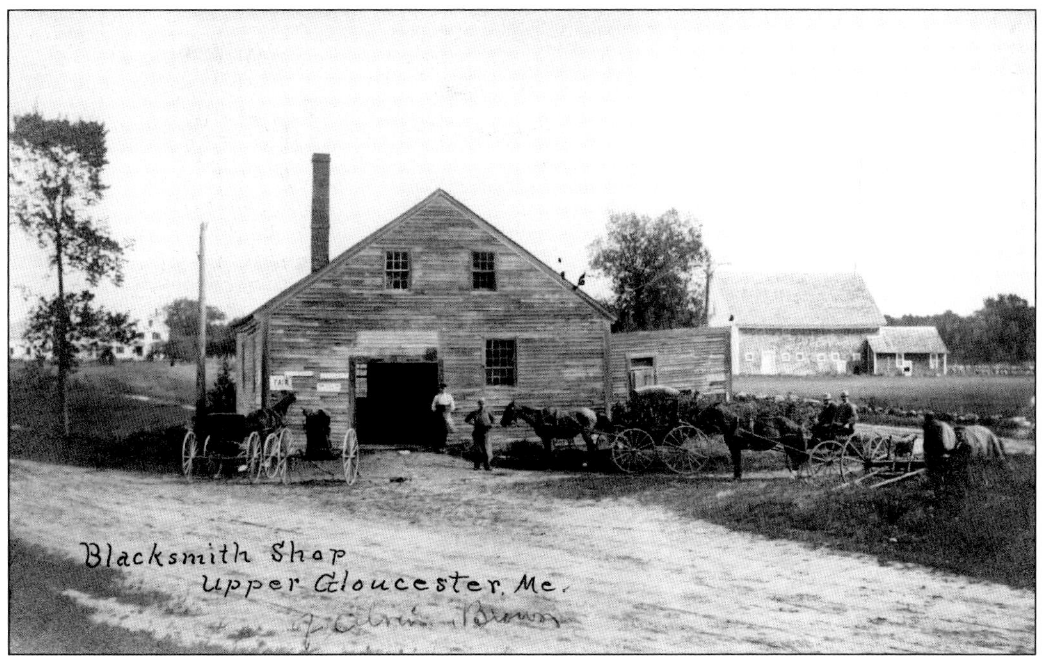

Quite a crowd is gathered in front of Alvin Brown's blacksmith shop. These shops were the garages of their time, before the days of automobiles. They shoed horses and oxen and also repaired carriages and sleighs.

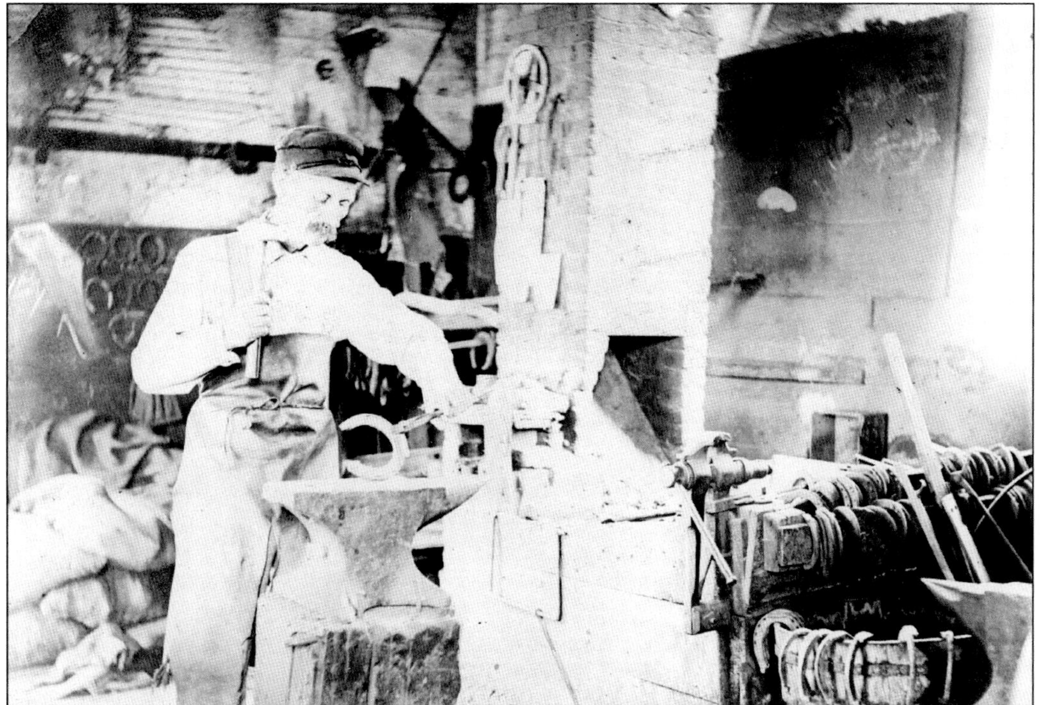

This early postcard shows Alvin Brown hard at work in his old blacksmith shop. The first blacksmith shop in town is believed to have been owned and operated by Peleg Chandler near his Bell Tavern. There have been many blacksmith shops in New Gloucester through the years.

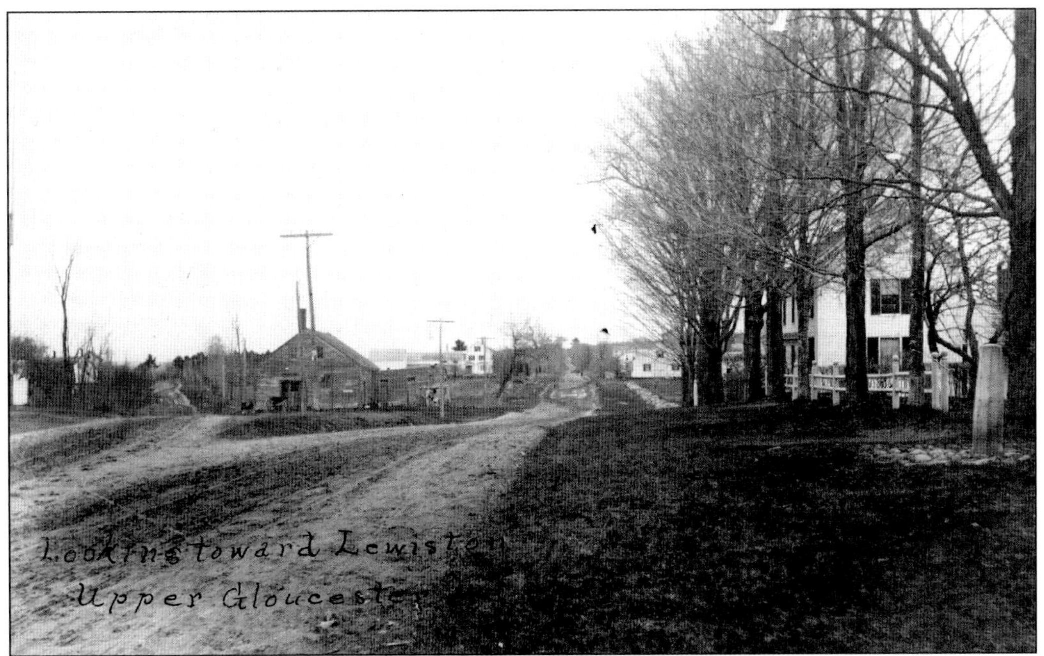

Another postcard view of the intersection, this one offers a view of the old homes along Peacock Hill Road. Capt. Moses Greenleaf, charter member of the Masons, resided on top of Peacock Hill, where he raised peacocks. His son Moses (1777–1834) became "Maine's first mapmaker" and author of the 1829 A *Survey of the State of Maine*.

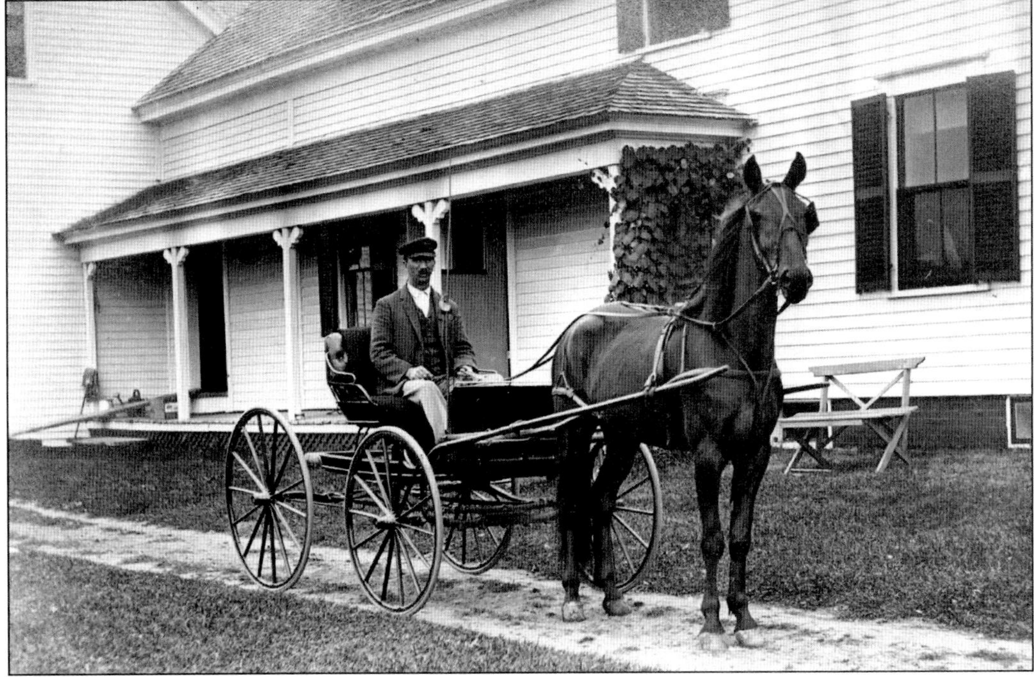

Fred M. Nevins is shown here at home at 30 Peacock Hill Road with his colt, the standard mode of transportation at that time. Lester L. Whitman resided on top of Peacock Hill and was well known for manufacturing the Whitman Horse Sled (Pung) in the 1890s.

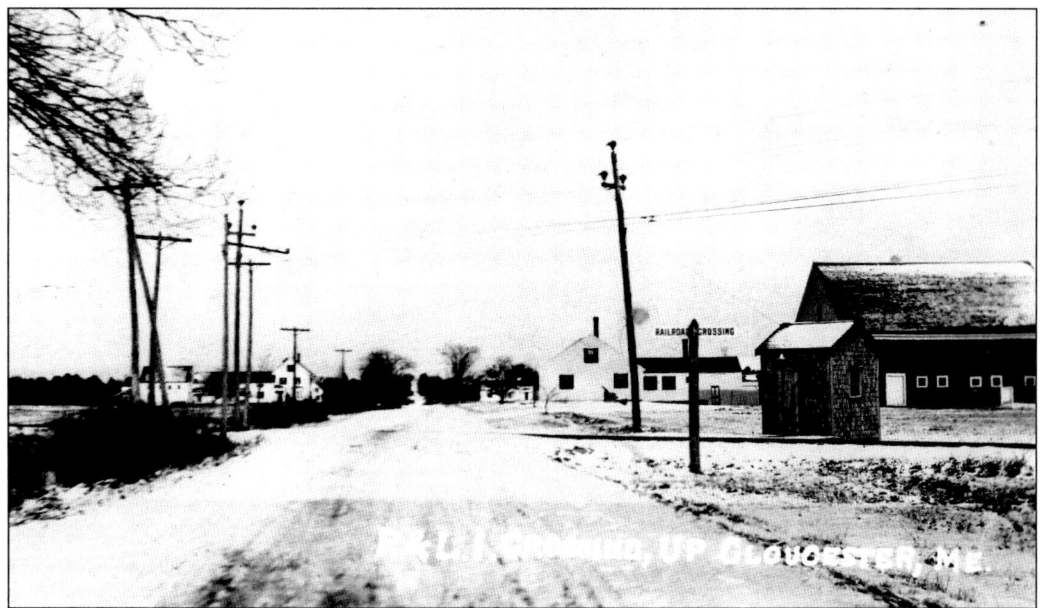

Here is a view of the Portland-Lewiston Interurban crossing on Peacock Hill Road. Notice the waiting station to the right of the Railroad Crossing sign. The cars would travel up to 70 miles per hour, and without crossing signals early on, road travelers were forced to be careful. Reportedly, three of the five interurban fatalities occurred in New Gloucester.

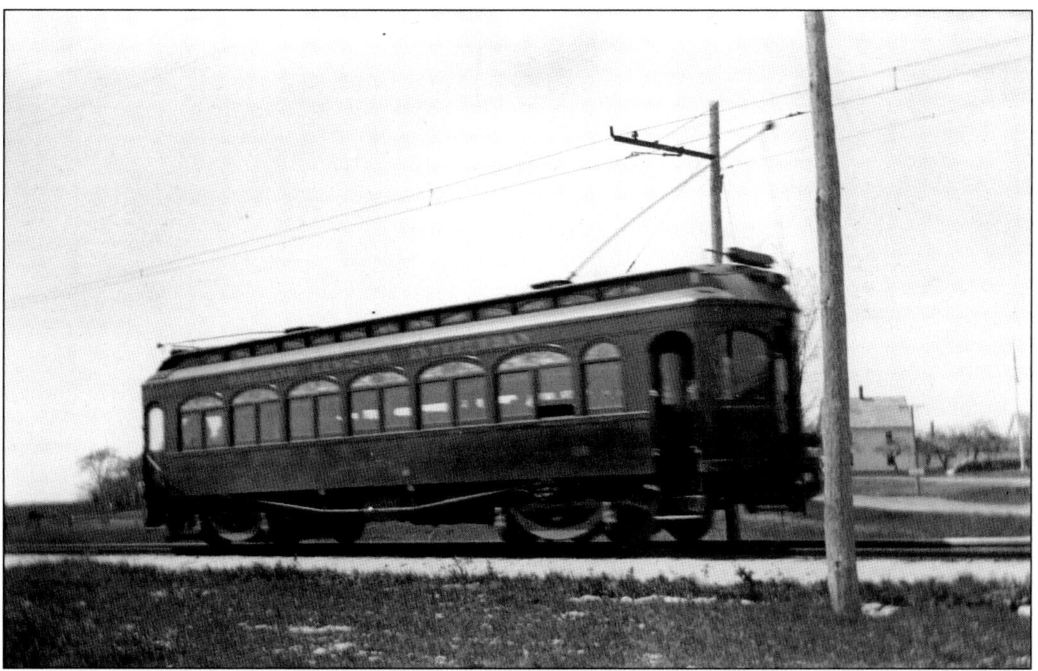

Car No. 16, *Clematis*, is shown traveling by Peacock Hill Road. Former president Theodore Roosevelt was a guest of the interurban on August 18, 1914, on a round-trip run from Portland to Lewiston. He made a brief speech from the back of car No. 14, *Narcissus*, in Gray, declaring the line to be "bully."

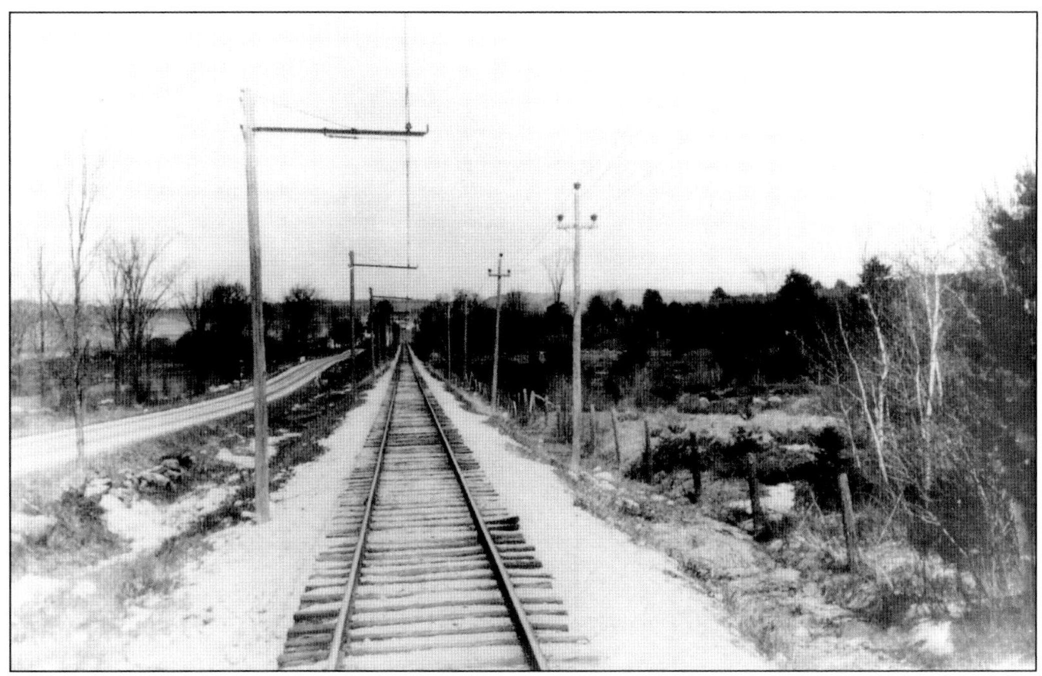

The interurban ran alongside Lewiston Road for one of its fastest stretches, as can be seen looking toward the Danville town line. The poles on the left held arms for the overhead trolley wire, while the poles on the right carried high-tension wires.

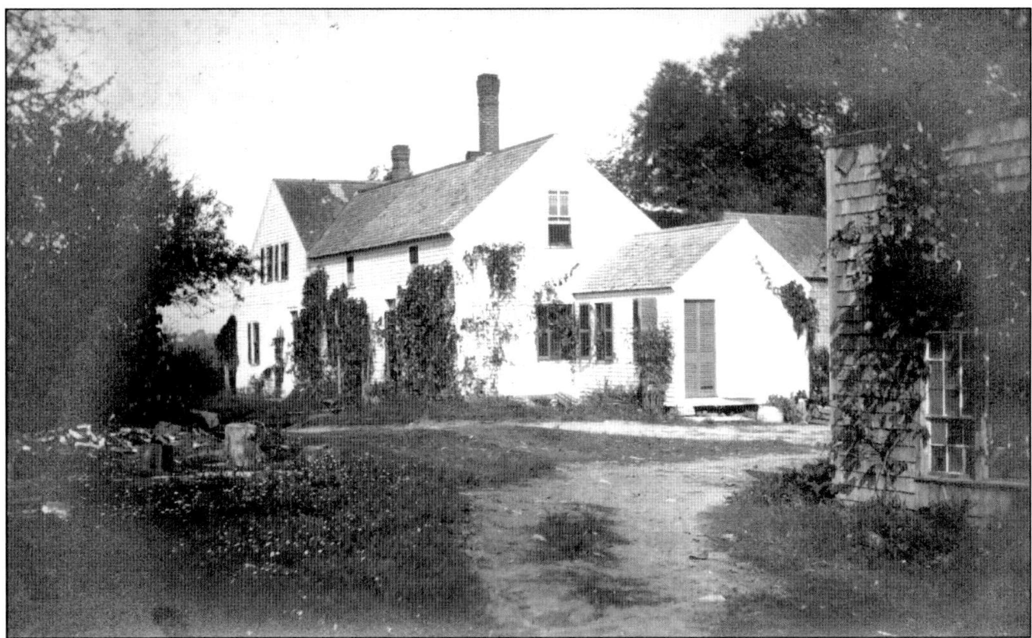

The orchard and former Woodbury residence at 181 Peacock Hill Road is shown on this early postcard. The Clarks purchased the Woodbury farm in 1963 and developed the area into Royal River Orchards. The house was apparently moved from its original location near the road around the time of the Civil War. (Courtesy of the True family.)

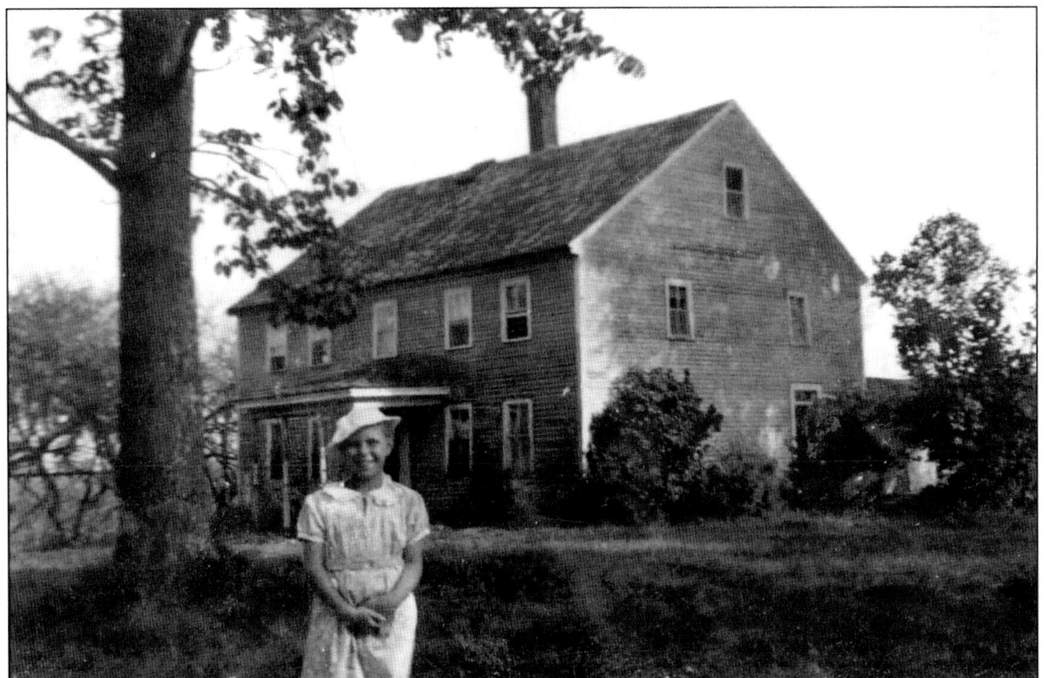

Dorothy Ford Bowie stands before the Capt. Moses Greenleaf house (built around 1790) that stood at 198 Peacock Hill Road. Greenleaf served alongside Gen. George Washington and was a charter member of Cumberland Lodge. His son Moses became Maine's premier mapmaker. The house was dismantled in 1969 by Thomas Moser, who used some of the material in his 1762 Col. Isaac Parsons home.

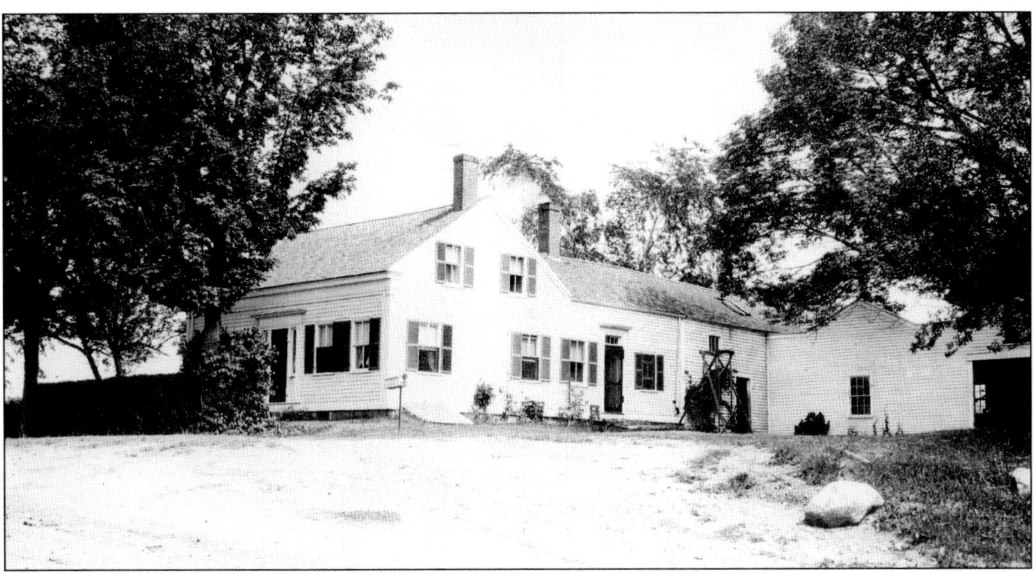

The house at 46 Hatch Road formerly sat at 862 Intervale Road, as depicted on this postcard. It was built in 1844 by Reuel Fogg and was later occupied by his son Reuel, who was known for his humor and was always sought after to take the comedy part of any play. The building burned and was moved in 1982.

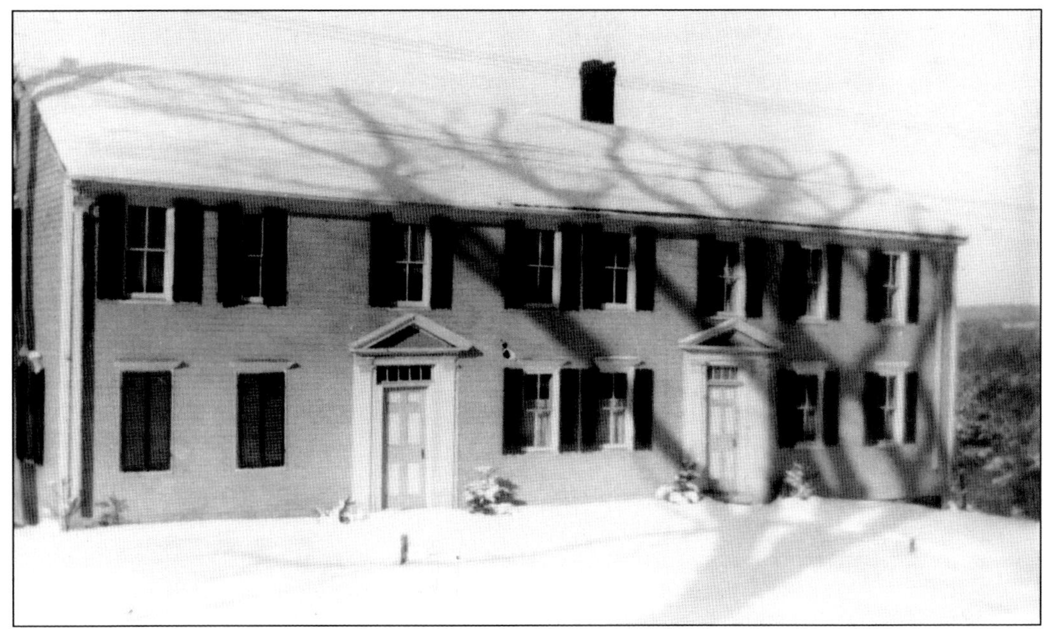

The Capt. Seth Hathaway house at 26–34 Bald Hill Road was built in 1783, the same year as the Moses Merrill house across the road. There was a store on the first level and a private ballroom on the second floor. Hathaway acquired a slave named Peter in 1790 who later lived with his daughter's family. Peter was well thought of and buried in the family lot at the Upper Cemetery in 1871 with his own headstone.

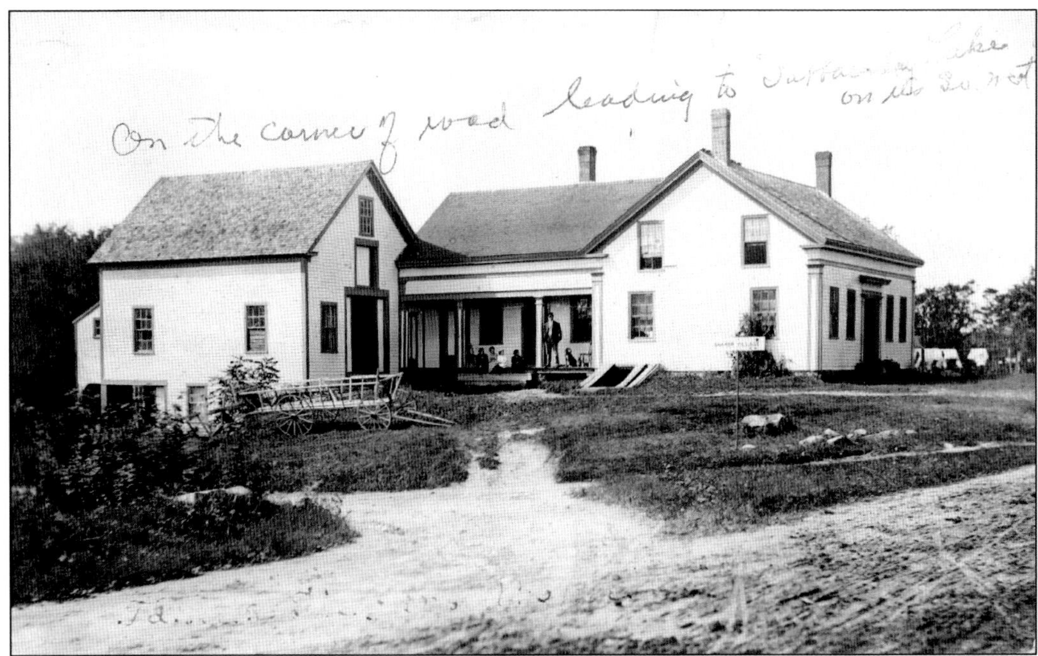

The Segars house at 72 Bald Hill Road is shown on this early picture postcard, complete with the family on the porch. The guidepost at the junction of Bald Hill Road and Snow Hill Road shows four miles to Shaker Village.

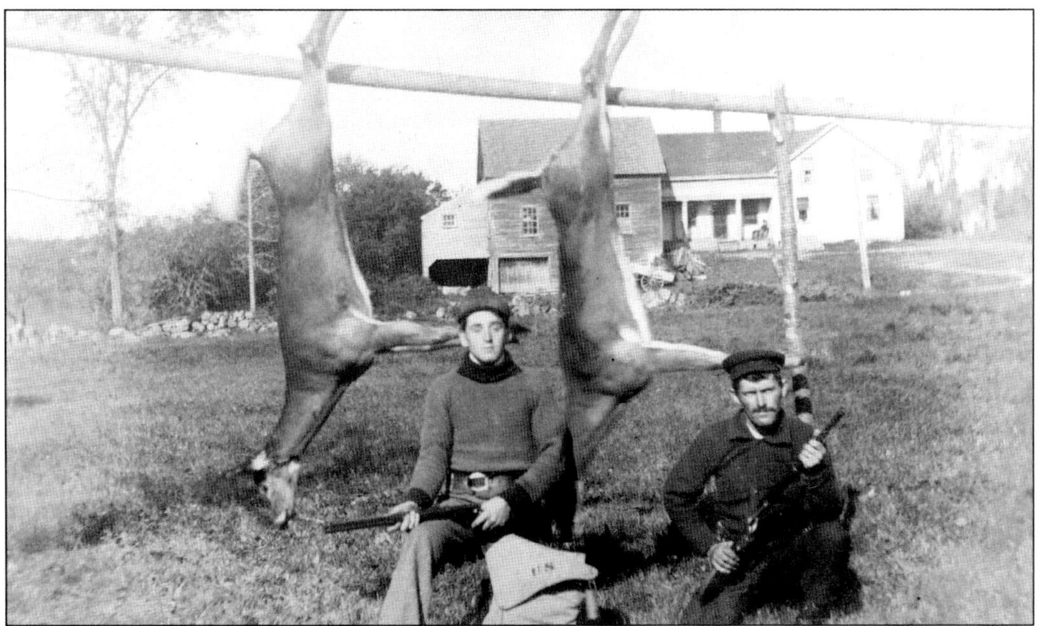

Bernald Segars (left) and James Tukey pose with their trophies in front of the Segars home and Snow Hill Road. Segars, who spent 20 years working for the Portland-Lewiston Interurban, died while hunting in 1960 at the age of 74.

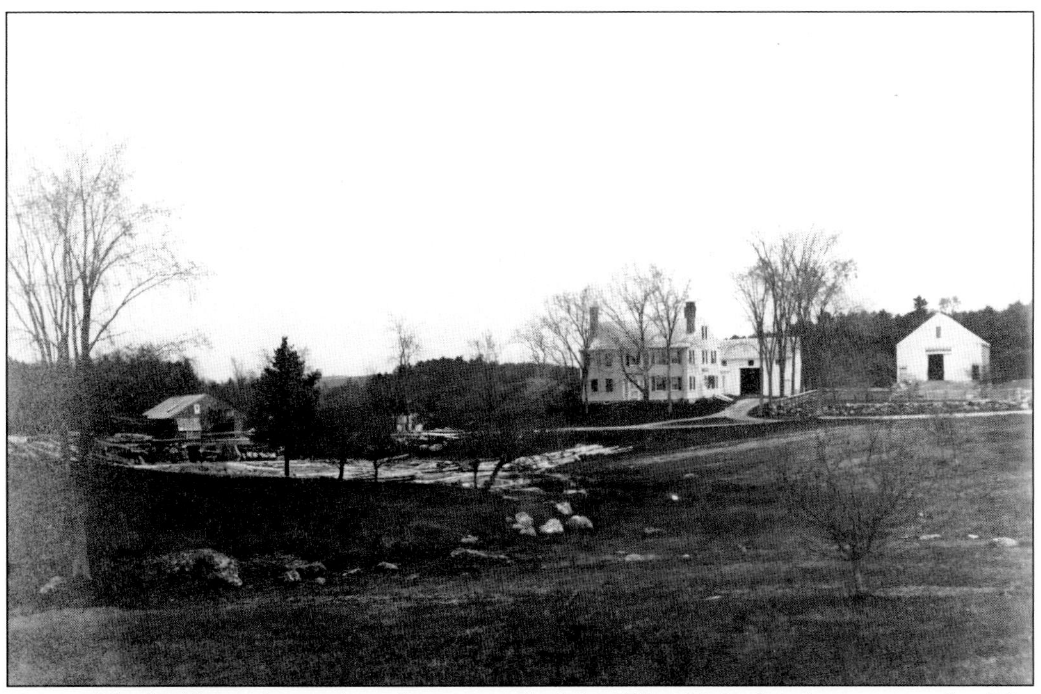

None of the buildings depicted on this postcard of the Allen H. Jordan farm exist today. The house was built by Andrew Campbell around 1800 and was probably financed by his wife, Lydia Hewett. Jordan's Mill is seen on the left on the Royal River. The farm, formerly at 83 Bald Hill Road, burned in 1928.

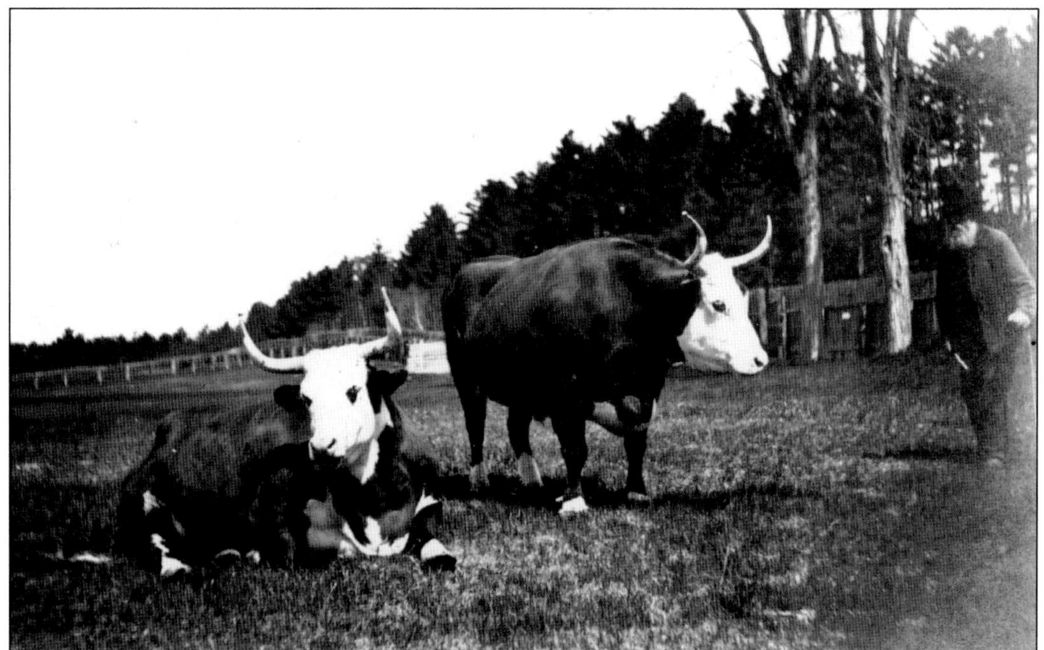

Allen H. Jordan is shown here with the mammoth pair of oxen that he always showed at the New Gloucester and Danville Fair without a yoke because he did not want to hurt their necks. When someone at the fair remarked about a steak from one of them, "he answered heatedly that he would just as soon eat a piece of his grandmother."

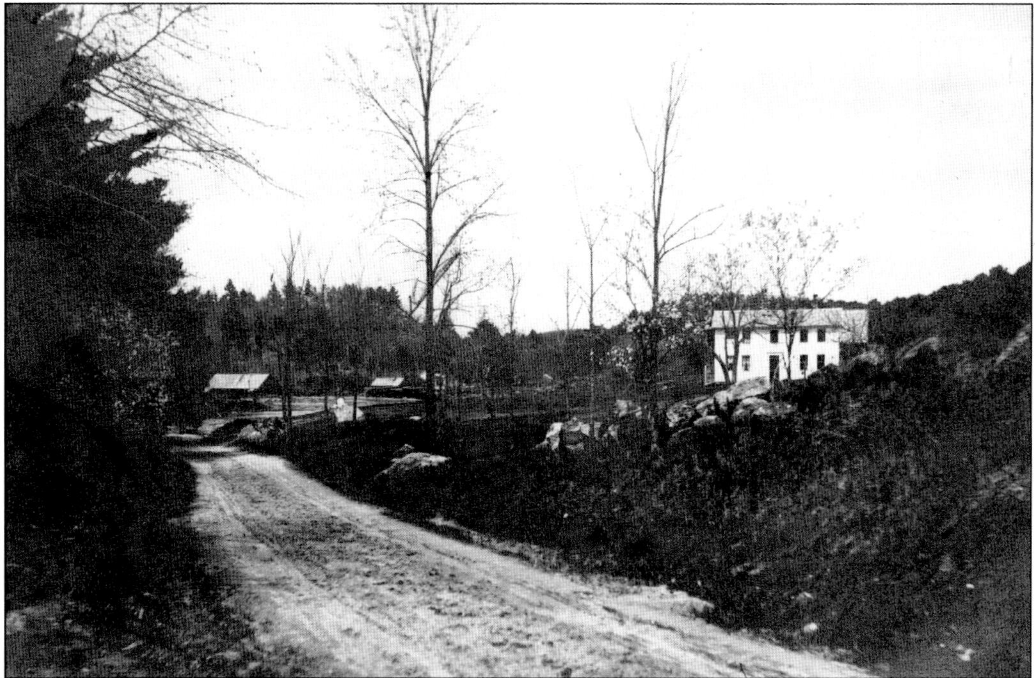

The S. A. Foss residence (right) on Sawyer Road is shown on this postcard. Frank W. Winter's mill (constructed about 1835), formerly Elias C. Lane's, is seen in the background. The mill burned about 1865 but was rebuilt the following year.

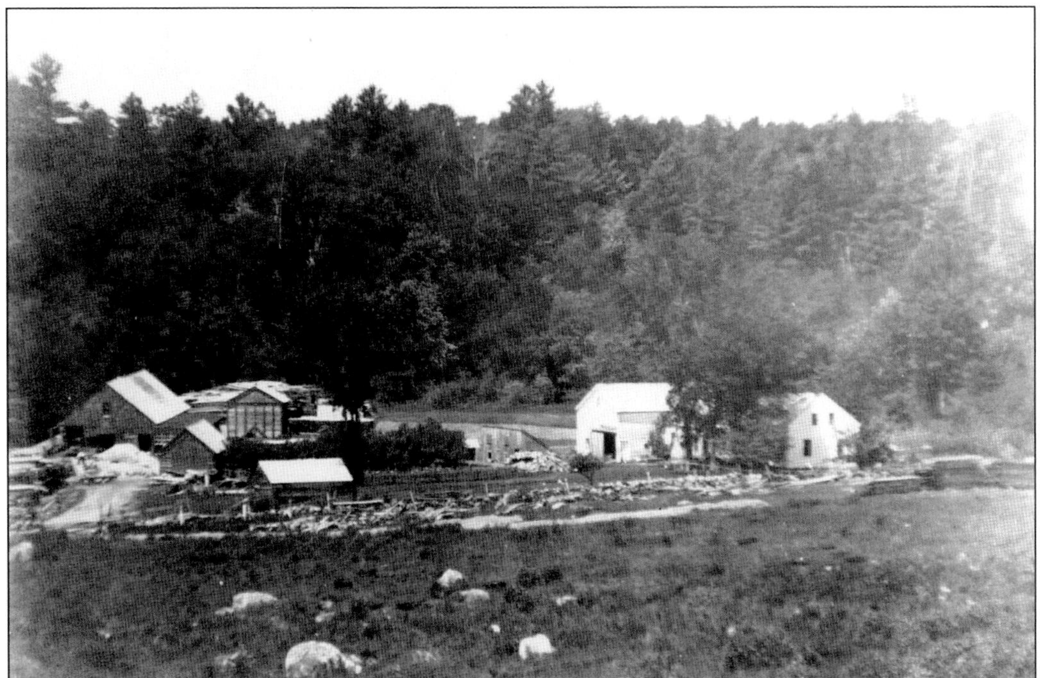

This postcard shows Lane's mill and home. He operated the long lumber and boxboard mill until his death in 1878. The mill, later owned by Frank W. Winter, is gone, but the house (built about 1835) was a longtime residence of Ethel Estes Sawyer and remains at 60 Sawyer Road.

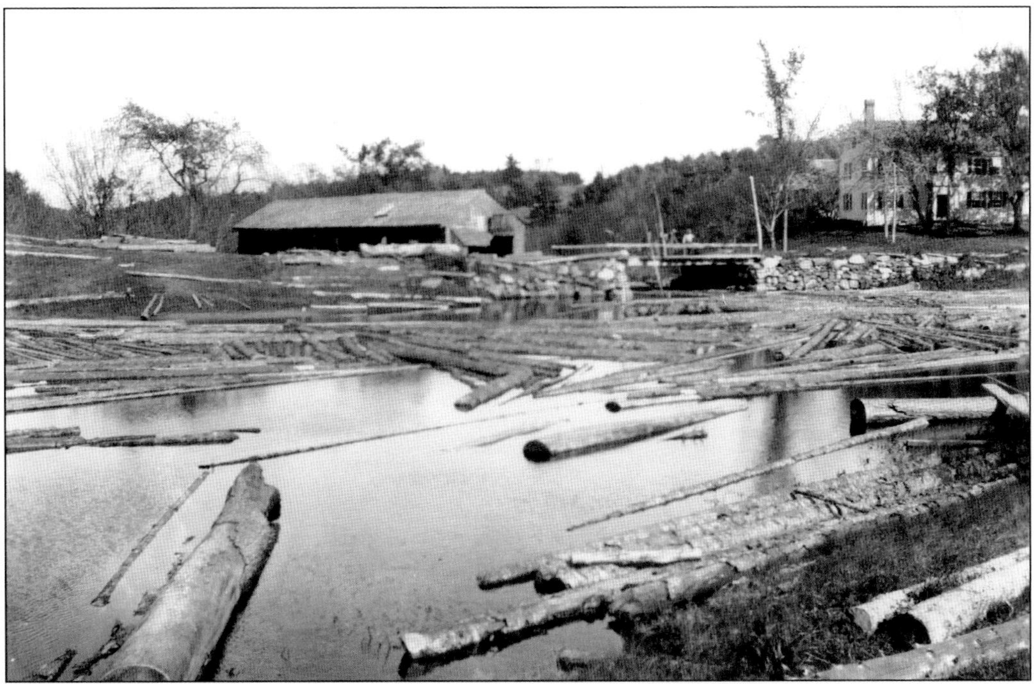

This photograph depicts the millpond on the Royal River filled with logs for Jordan's Mill. The Allen H. Jordan home can be seen on the right. Jordan was described as a "farmer, philosopher, and friend." It was said he could raise 38 big pumpkins on a single vine.

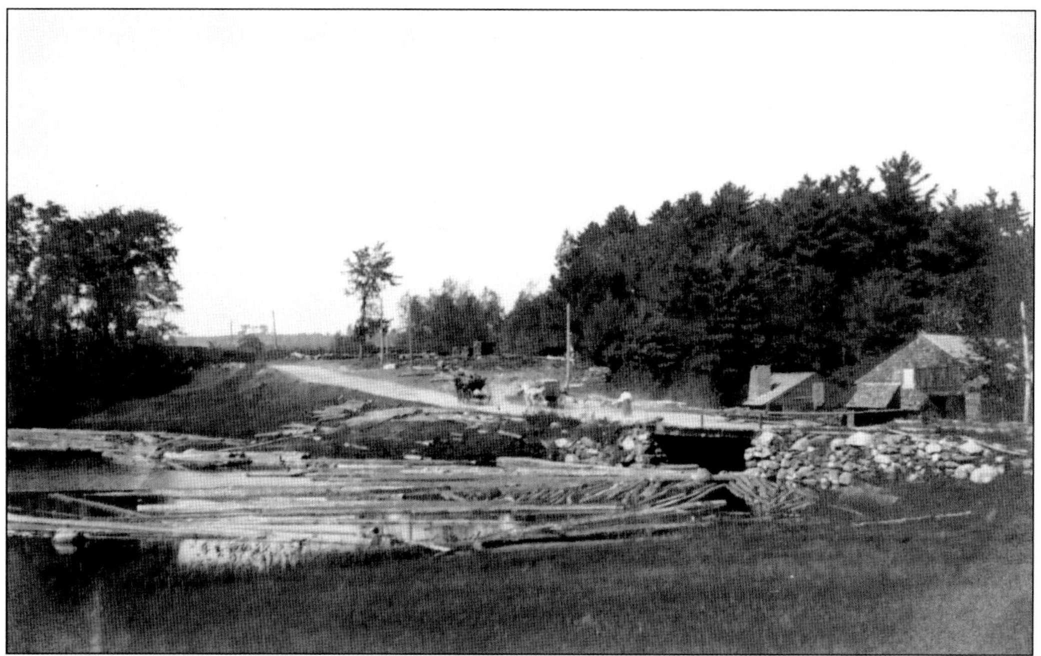

This postcard shows travelers on Bald Hill Road passing by Jordan's Mill and the Royal River, with the fairgrounds seen in the distance. The mill was owned and operated by just five families beginning in 1761. Before it burned down in July 1948, it was believed to be the oldest working mill of its kind in the state.

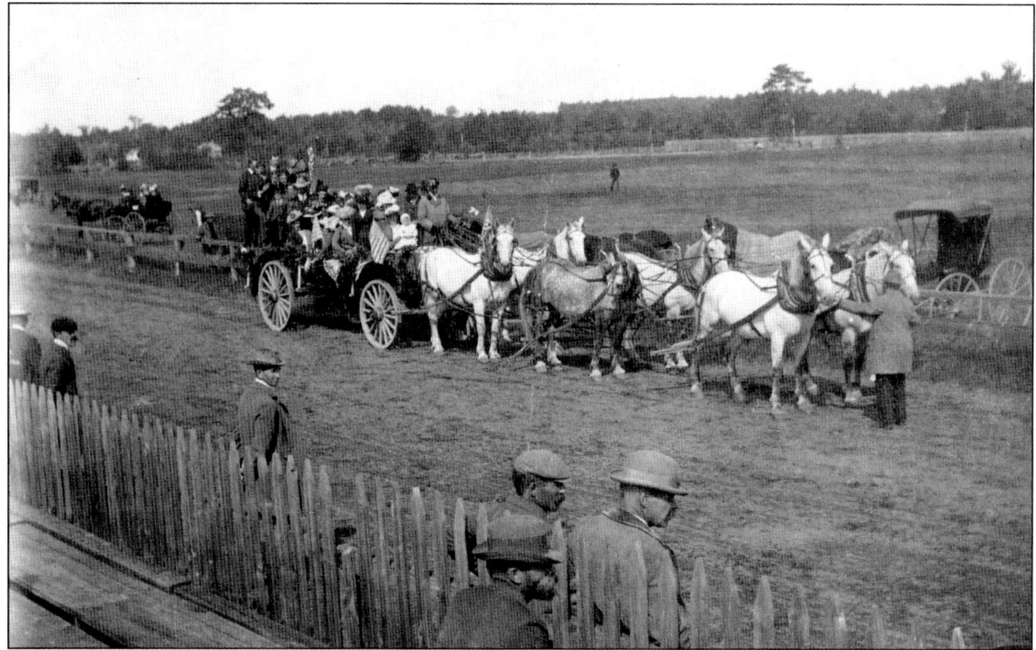

An early photograph depicts the Shakers with a cart at the New Gloucester fairgrounds. The farm of Jacob Osgood Haskell on the banks of Royall's River (now Royal River) was purchased in 1887 and a half-mile racetrack was built, followed later by an exhibition hall and cattle and horse sheds.

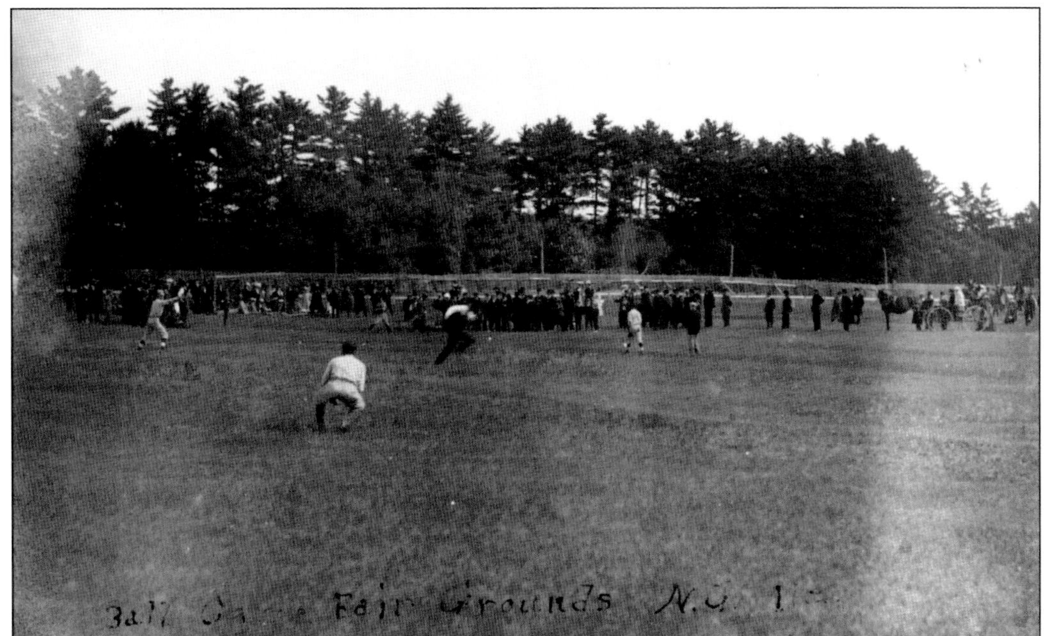

A good old-fashioned baseball game played by the town team is enjoyed at the fairgrounds in this scene. Charles A. (Charlie) Small of New Gloucester was signed by the Boston Red Sox after graduating from Bates College in 1927. After winning the Eastern League's Most Valuable Player award, he was called up to Boston and was an outfielder in 1930 and 1931.

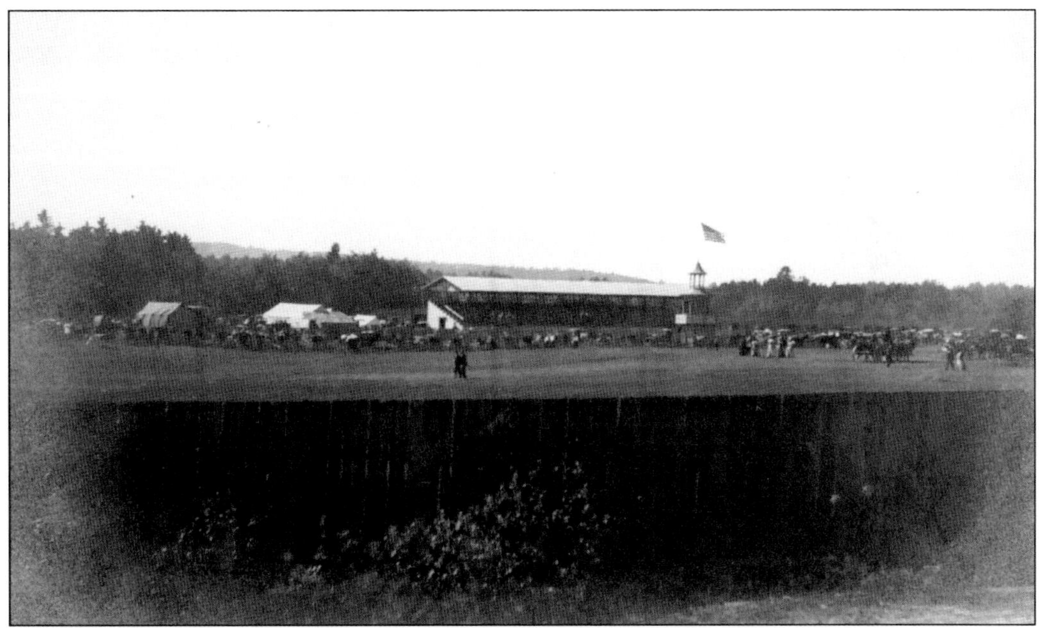

In November 1904, at the dissolution of the Gray Fair Association, the grandstand (top, center) and judges' stand were purchased and moved to New Gloucester. Beginning in the fall of 1891, the New Gloucester and Danville Agricultural Association held a fair on these grounds annually into the 1930s.

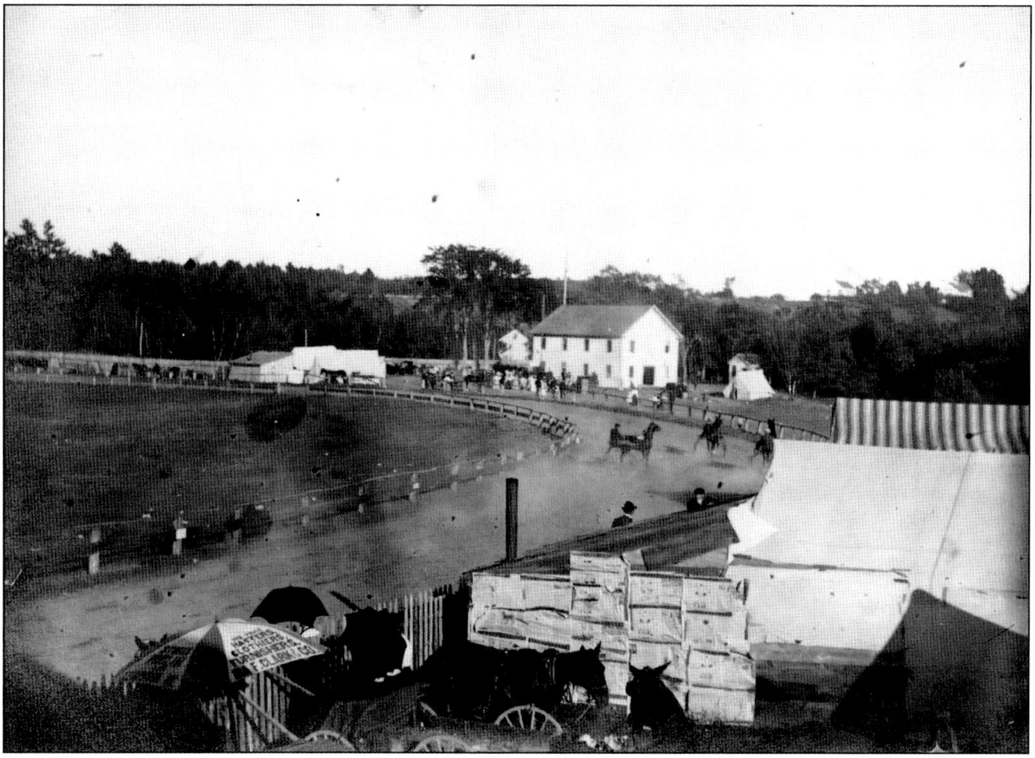

The race is on at the New Gloucester and Danville Fair. The exhibition hall is shown on this postcard and is the only building that remains on the site. It served as a horse stable in later years but had housed many prize jams, art, and knitted items in its early years.

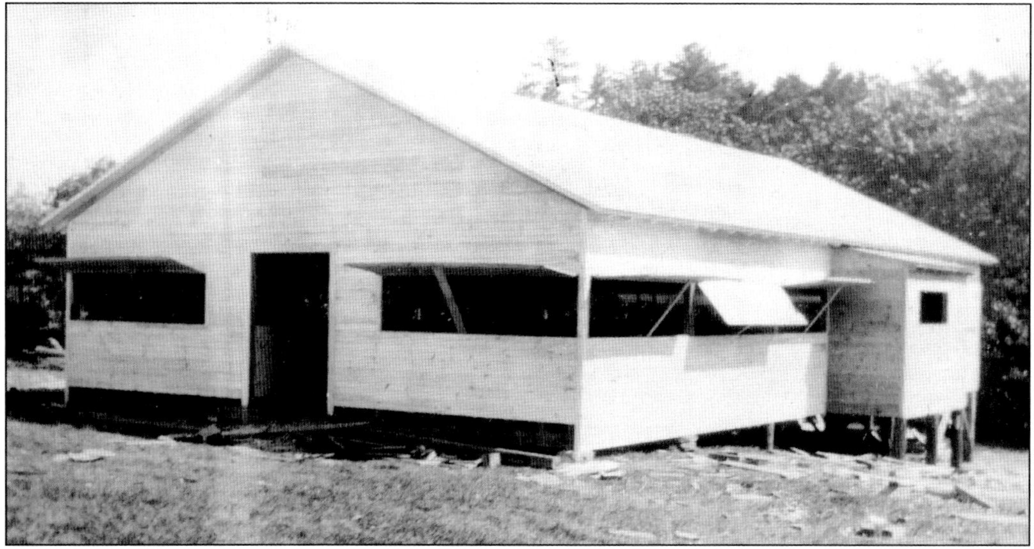

The New Riverside Pavilion is shown here shortly after construction in 1924. Built for manager Ernest Mingo, it was home to hundreds of dances—old-fashioned dances on Thursday nights and modern ones on Saturday nights. After being used as a stable, it was burned by the fire department in 1970.

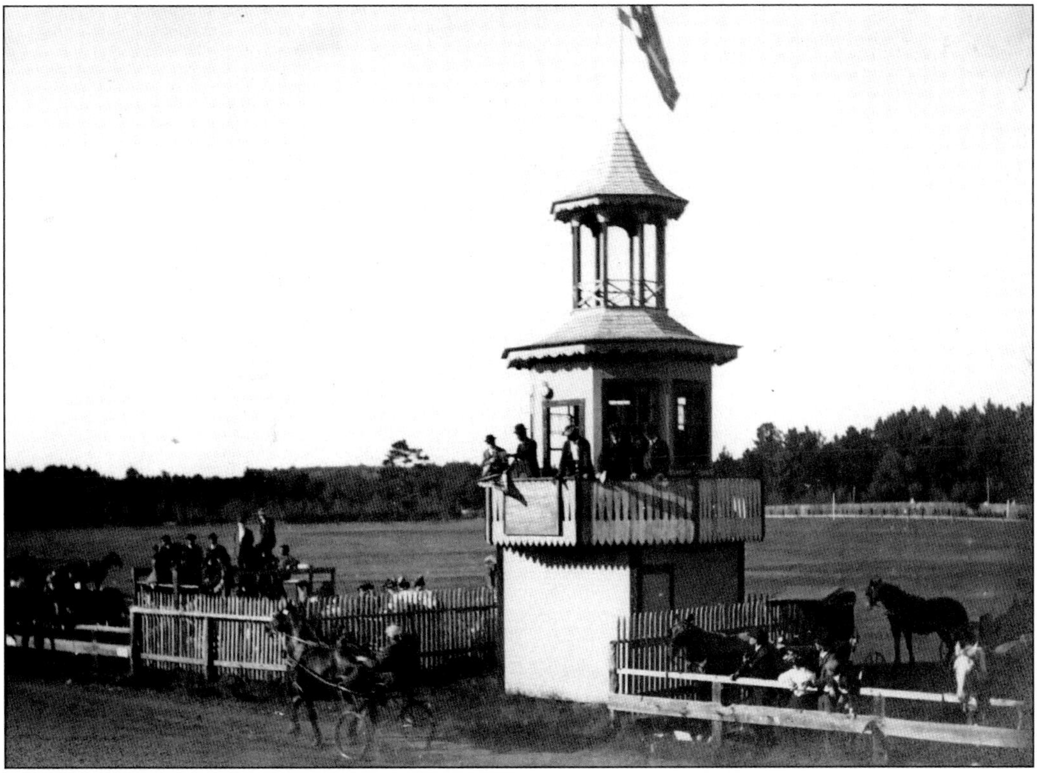

The 1904 judges' stand overlooked the track, allowing evaluation of the passing teams of oxen or determining the fastest horse. Formerly there was a track located across the road about 1870 beside the Upper Cemetery. The fairgrounds served as a training facility for racehorses in later years but became town owned in 2002 and home to the annual New Gloucester Community Fair.

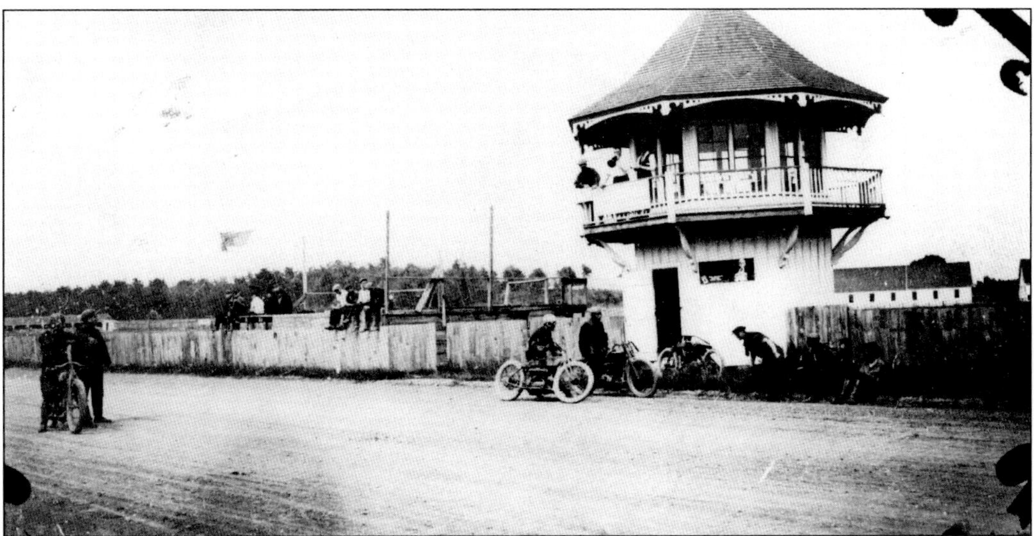

Howard I. Small bought the old fairgrounds property and dedicated it on May 30, 1946, as Royal River Park. He also opened an amusement center and held outdoor movies, a rodeo, and baseball games with the New Gloucester Townies. Motorcycle races were held that summer for $1.20 per ticket, with music by the Royal River Circus Band.

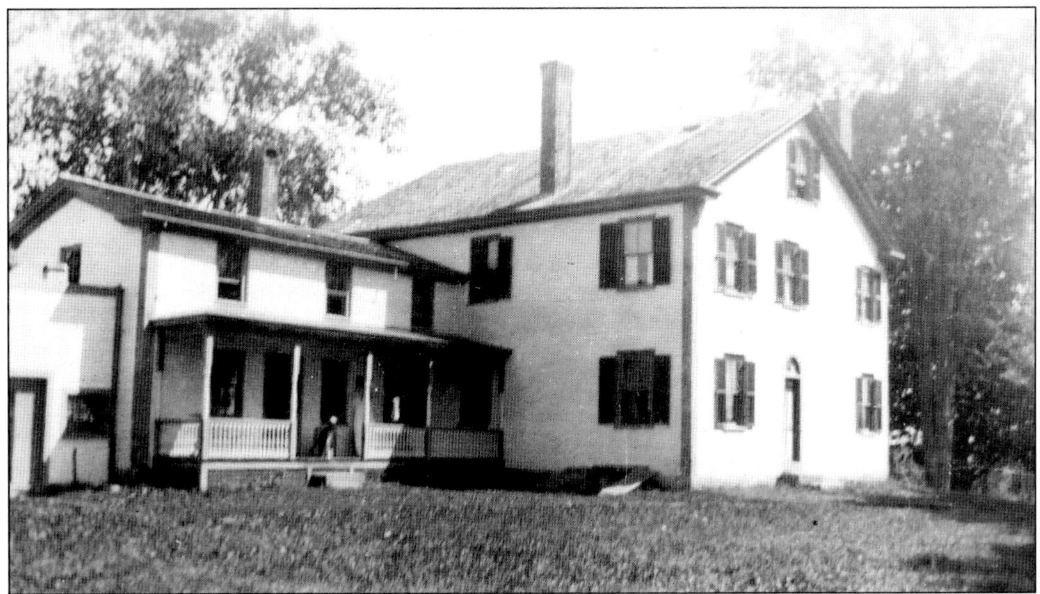

The 1803 Dea. David Nelson brick tavern is pictured here in 1924. The original tavern was built on this site in 1787 but was moved across the road and used as a well-known cider mill. The brick house, considered to be the second in town, still sits at 313 Bald Hill Road.

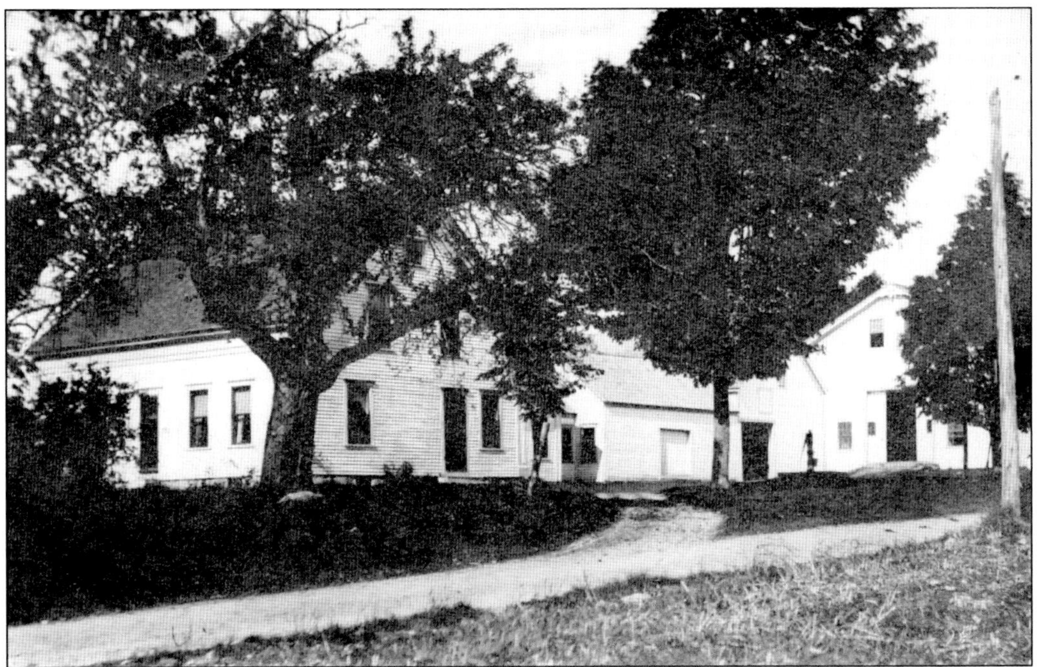

The Jordan farm is shown here in the early 1900s. Embodied in the house is a portion of the first schoolhouse on Bald Hill. The ell is all that remains of the home at 500 Bald Hill Road. The Jordan family also had a shoe shop across the road from 1845 to about 1865.

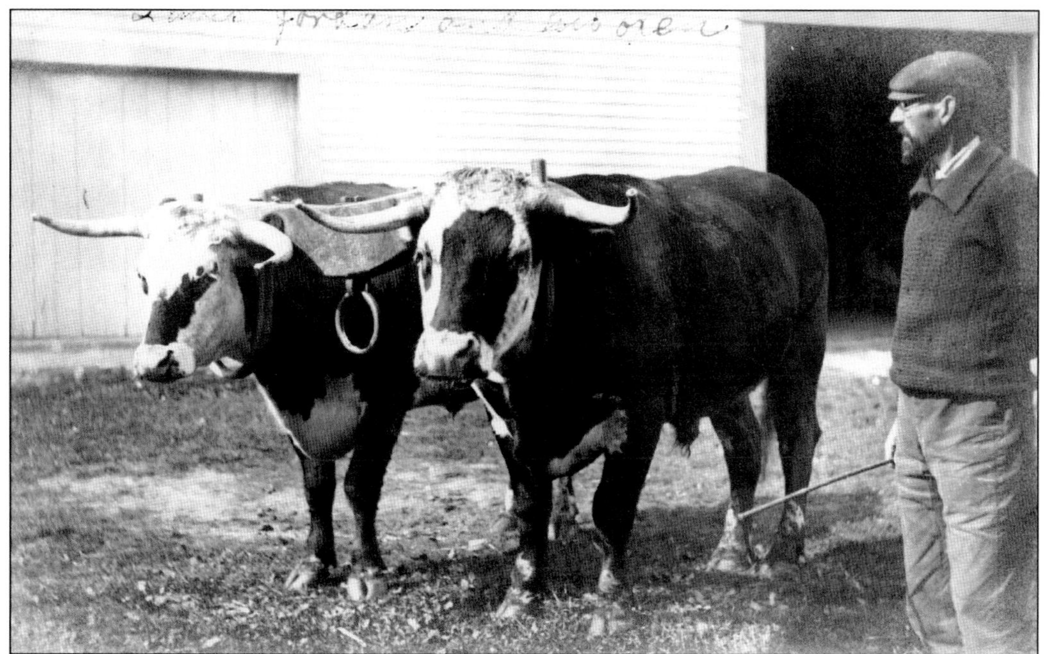

Lewis Jordan is shown here with his team of oxen at his farm at 500 Bald Hill Road. As late as 1824, not less than 100 oxen teams might be seen each day delivering huge pine logs to the Royal River so they could float to the coast or continuing along the road to Yarmouth.

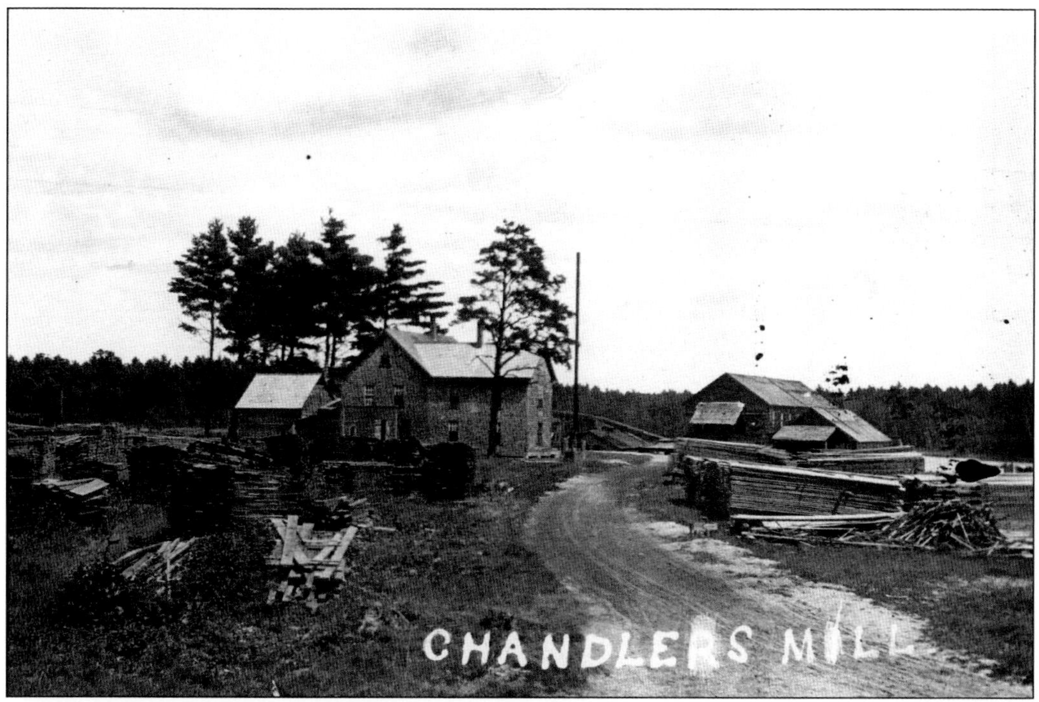

In about 1890, Solomon Hewett built the first mill at Lily Pond and then sold it to his four nephews the Chandler Brothers around 1898. Charles Peleg Chandler served as the general manager until his death in 1926. They eventually switched from wholesale to retail, even building boats.

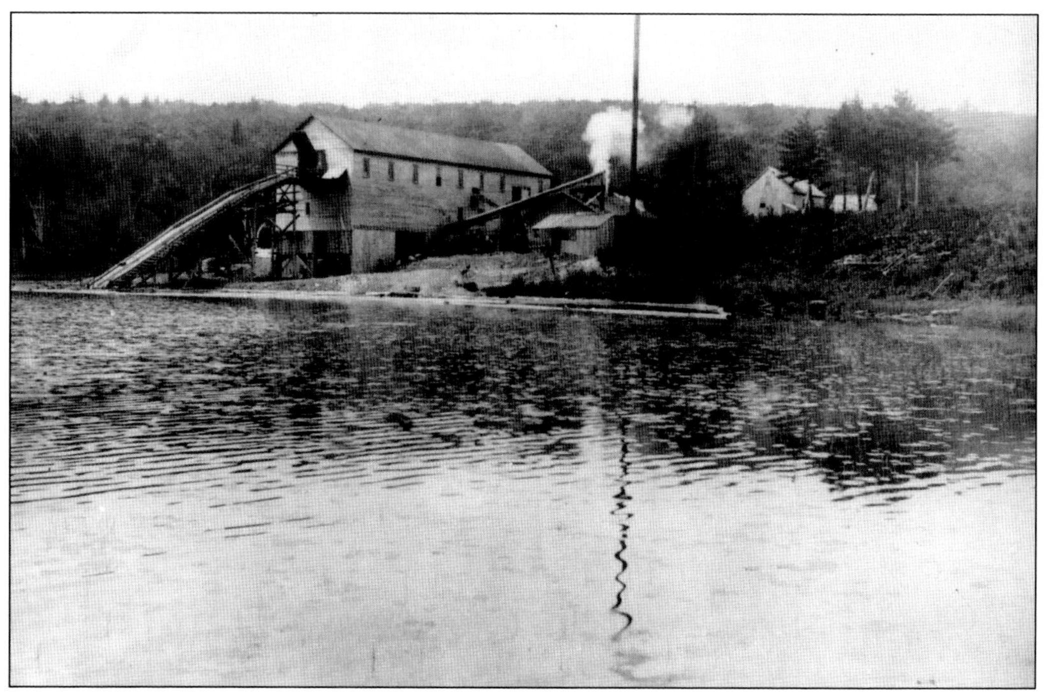

Here is Chandler Mill in operation. The mill was run by steam, as there was no stream to power it. Timber was cut in the winter, and logs were skidded to the frozen pond and stored on the ice until spring. On April 7, 1927, the two mills burned flat.

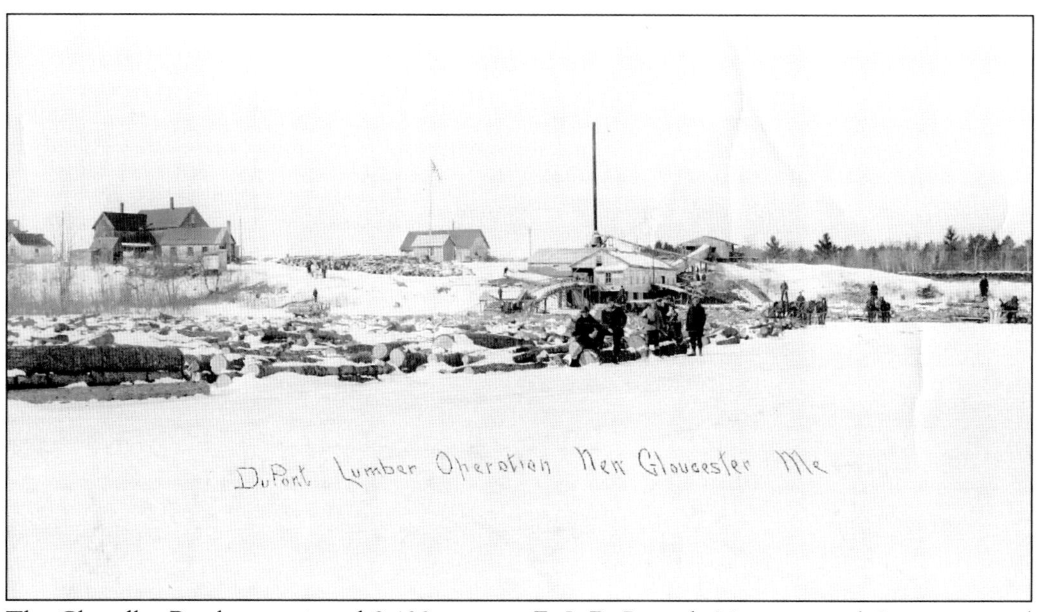

The Chandler Brothers optioned 2,400 acres to E. I. DuPont de Nemours and Company, and the mill was rebuilt, as shown here in 1929. Following the worst fire in town history when over 1,000 acres burned near the mill in 1934, it was torn down and rebuilt into a warehouse for Oliver Stores at 411 Intervale Road.

Six

The Intervale

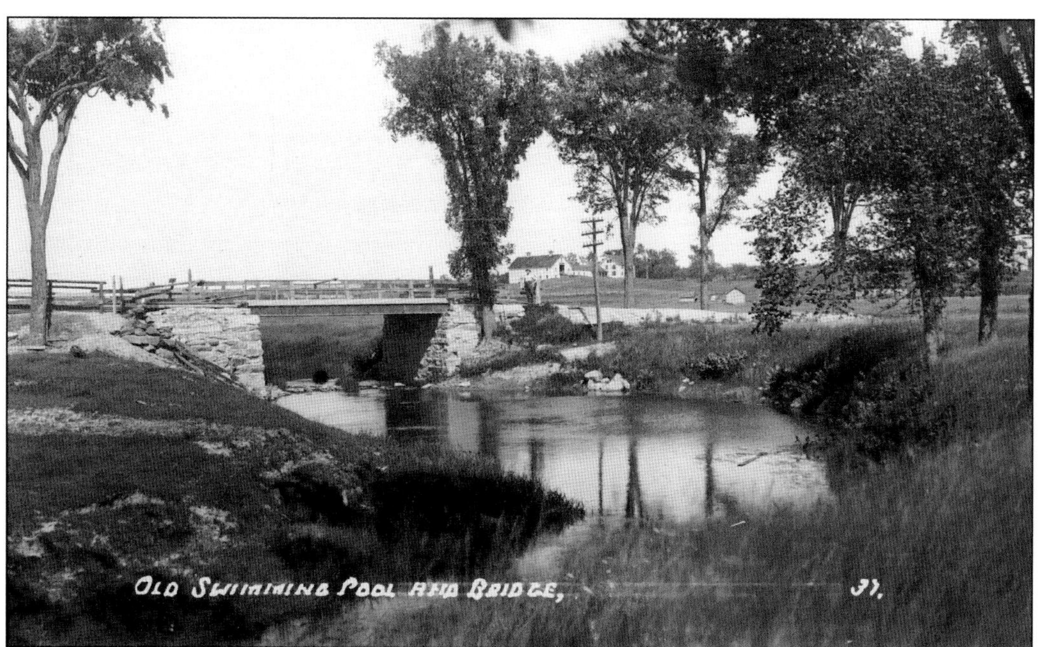

Seen here is the old bridge where Intervale Road (Route 231) crosses the Royal River, with the Rideout farm seen in the background. In 1646, William Royall purchased a farm along the river near its mouth in Yarmouth, giving it the name Royall's River. The Royal River begins at Sabbathday Lake in New Gloucester and meanders through the meadows of the Intervale.

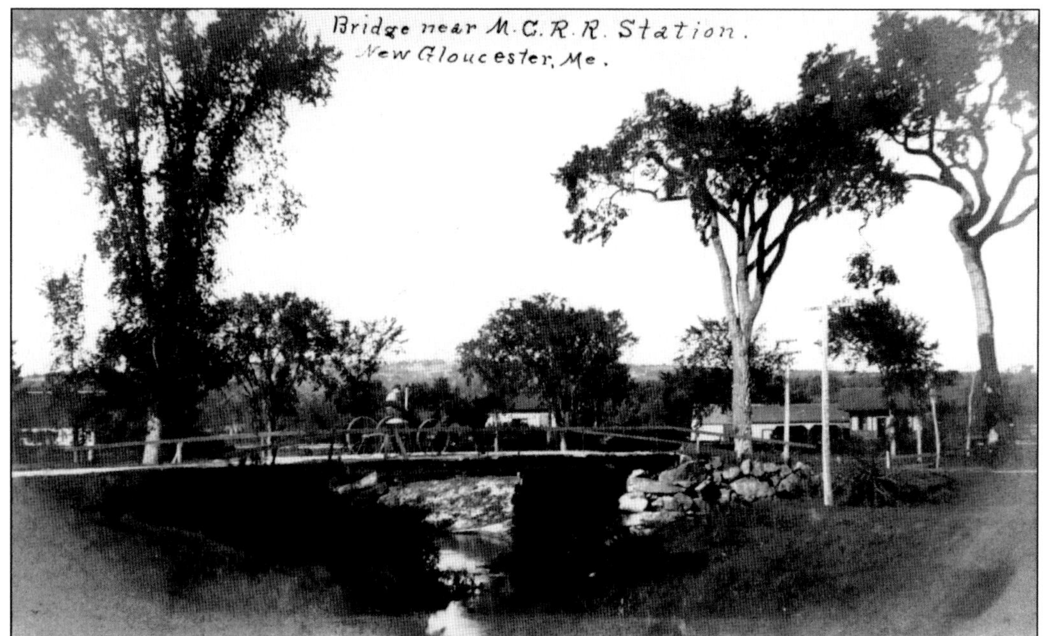

A horse and carriage cross Royall's River in this view of the bridge taken in the opposite direction of the previous image, with Gloucester Hill seen above the head of the man in the carriage. The river was lined with majestic elm trees.

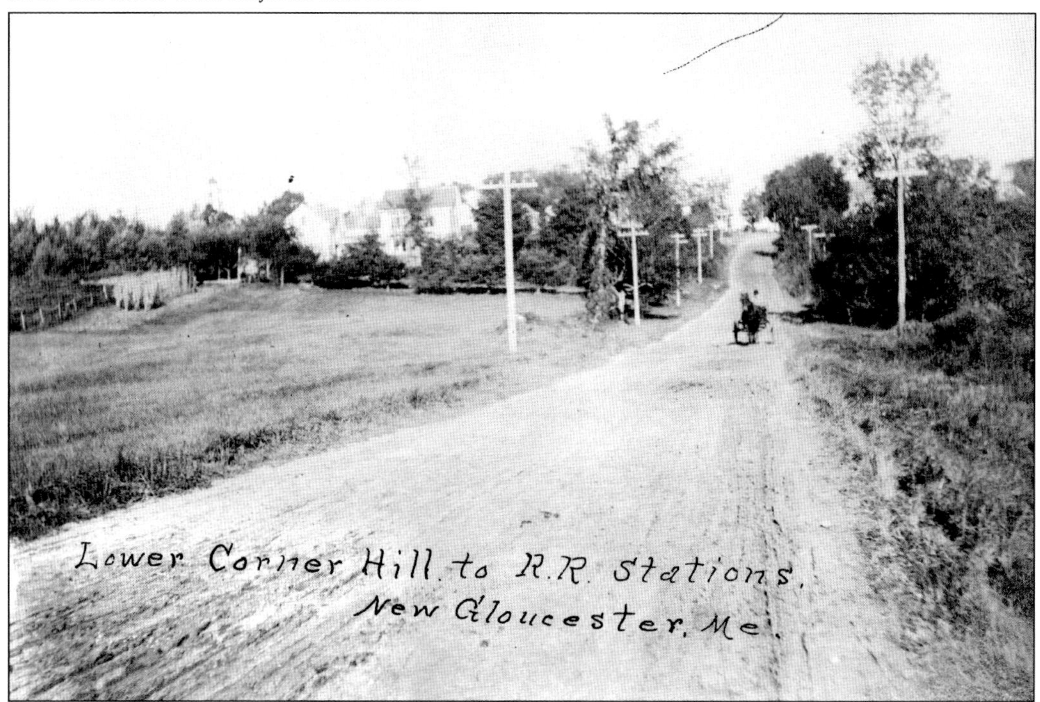

A horse and buggy are shown racing down the hill from Lower Corner toward the railroad tracks. The New Gloucester Creamery (butter factory) was built in this area (right) in 1883 and burned in 1902. Melville Berry was the manager and had a pipe that would feed buttermilk to a piggery owned by Andrew Chandler down the hill.

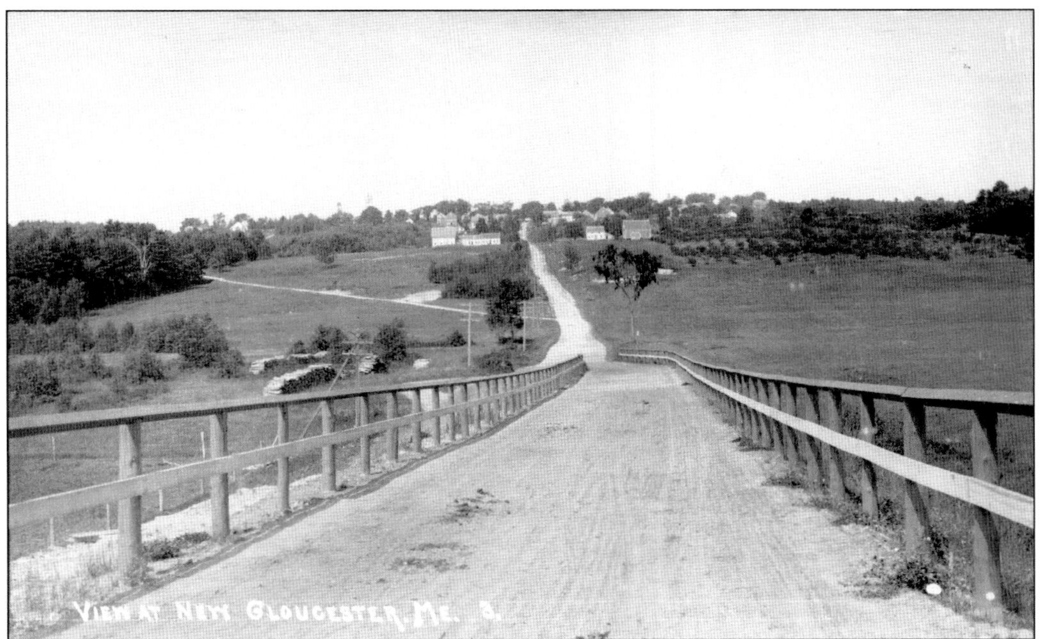

This picture postcard depicts the view from the newly built bridge (1911) over the Maine Central Railroad looking back toward the village. Foxcroft Road can be seen heading left across the field to come out opposite Church Road beside the parsonage. The bridge was removed in 1975 and reverted to a grade crossing.

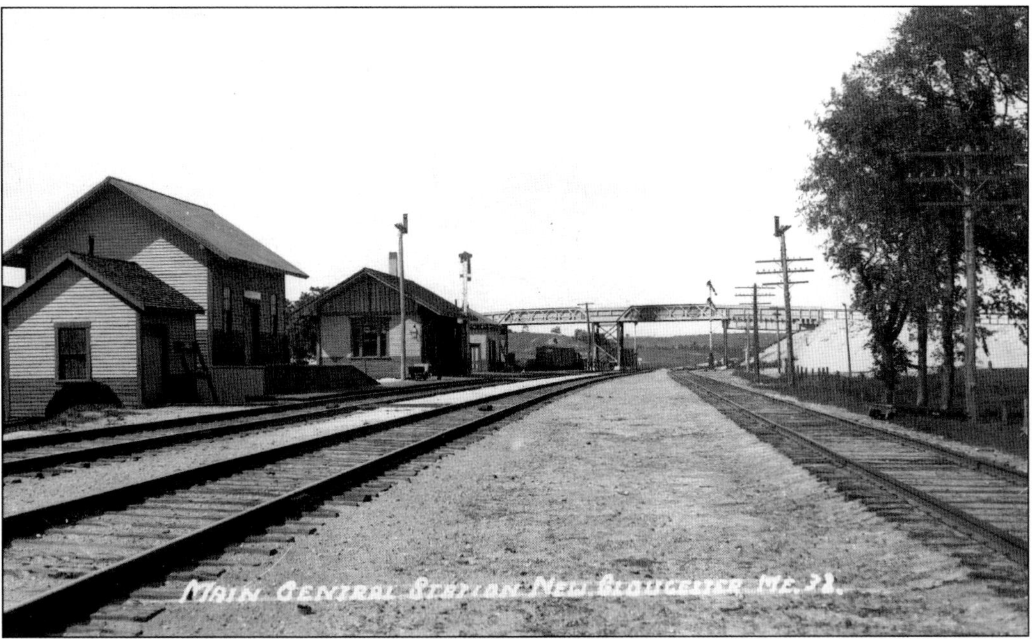

Looking north, the bridge can be seen here crossing three sets of tracks at the Maine Central Railroad station. Located here were freight sheds, a passenger station with a telegraph office, and toolsheds. The Maine Central Railroad came to town in 1870, connecting Danville Junction to Cumberland Junction. Barker Holt served as its first station agent.

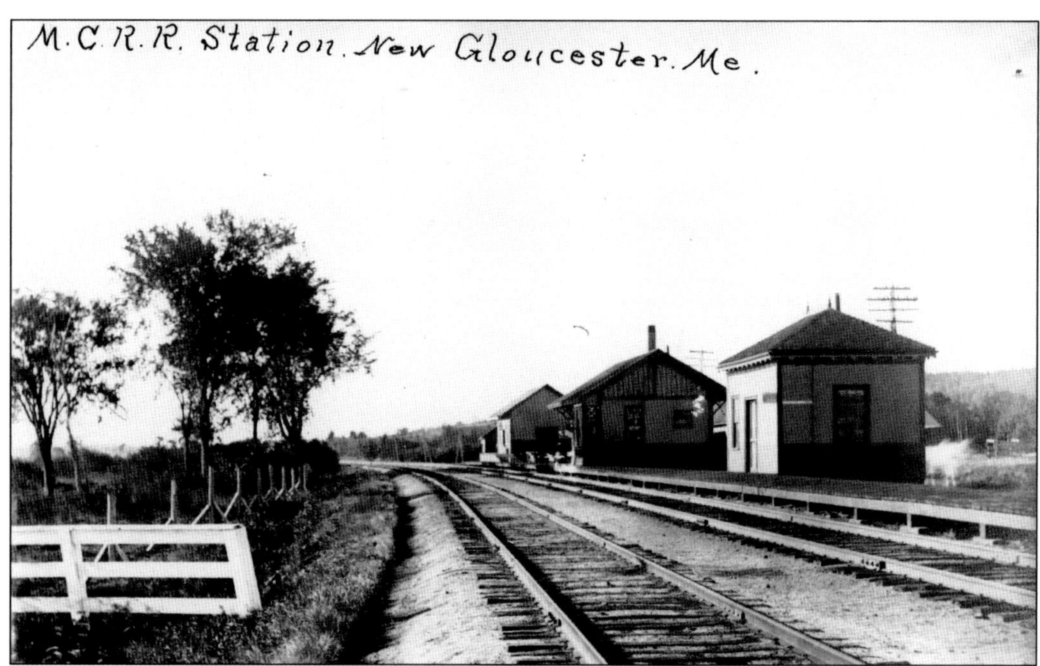

This view of the Maine Central Railroad station looks south. The 38-by-20-foot passenger station shown here, along with the 34-by-29-foot freight shed, was purchased by Donald Chandler in 1956. Complete with an office and waiting room and washroom, the station was moved to 417 Intervale Road, where it was burned in 1967 to make way for a new post office.

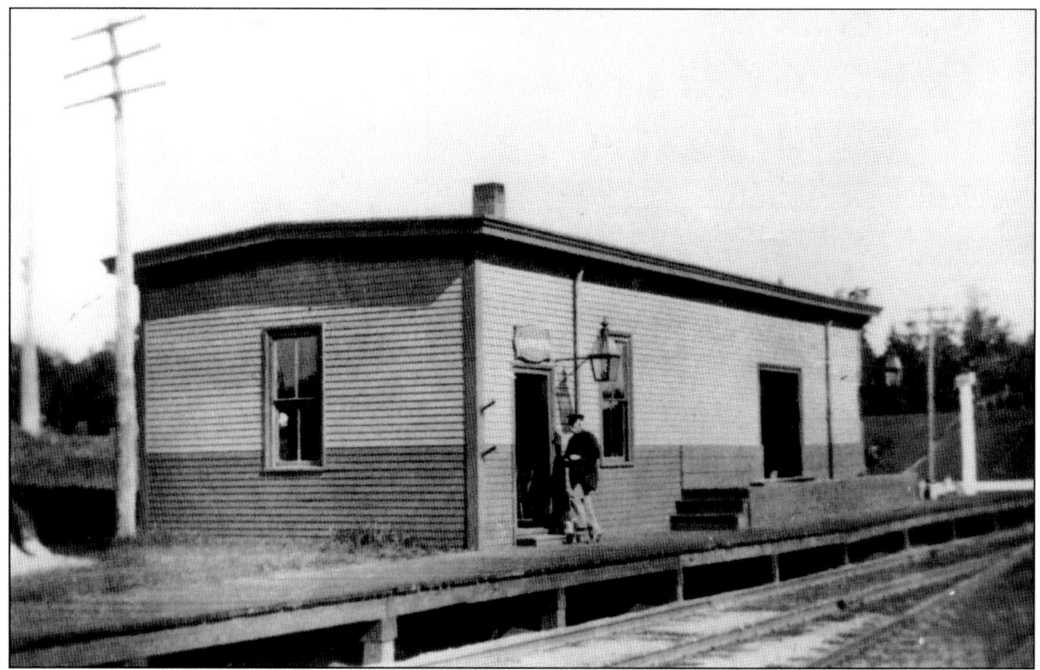

Rowe's Station sat off Cobb's Bridge Road along the Maine Central Railroad near the present overpass. Ed Rowe, shown above, served as the station agent for several years. Farmers brought their milk here to ship to Portland or Lewiston.

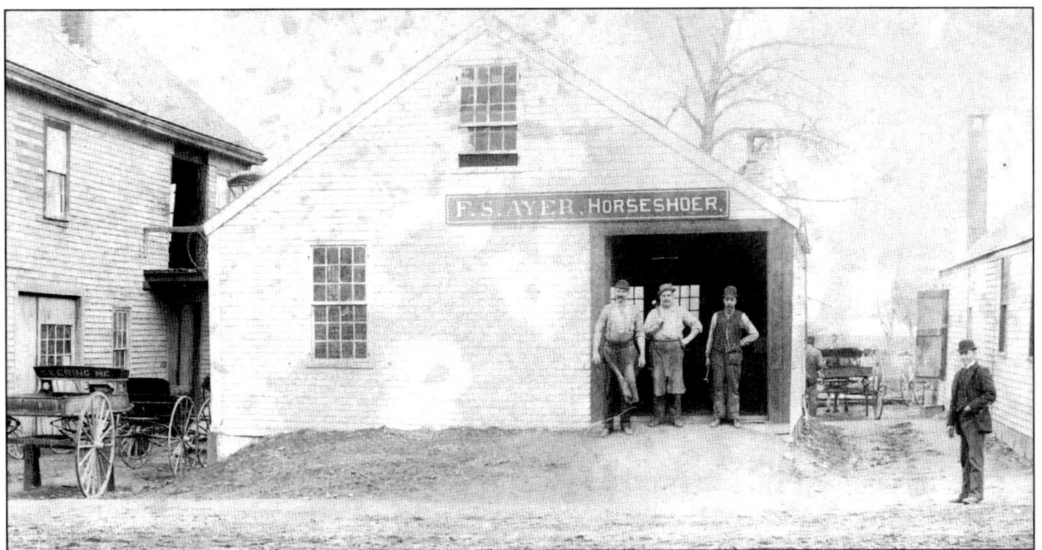

Here is a view of F. S. Ayer's blacksmith shop, which was believed to be near the two railroads on Cobb's Bridge Road. Winthrop Cobb ran a store nearby for several years, while many Cobb family members resided in this area in the early days of the town.

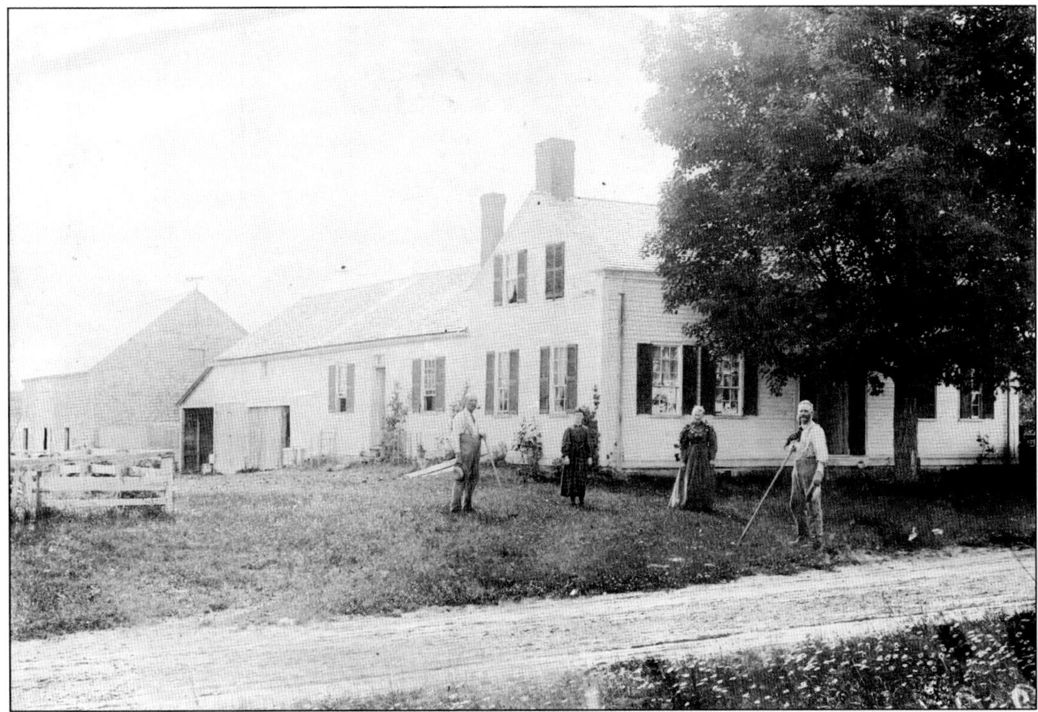

The Hunnewell farm is shown in this early photograph. The barn burned in 1969, while the stable was moved to 457 Intervale Road. The house remains at 346 Cobb's Bridge Road near Meadow Lane.

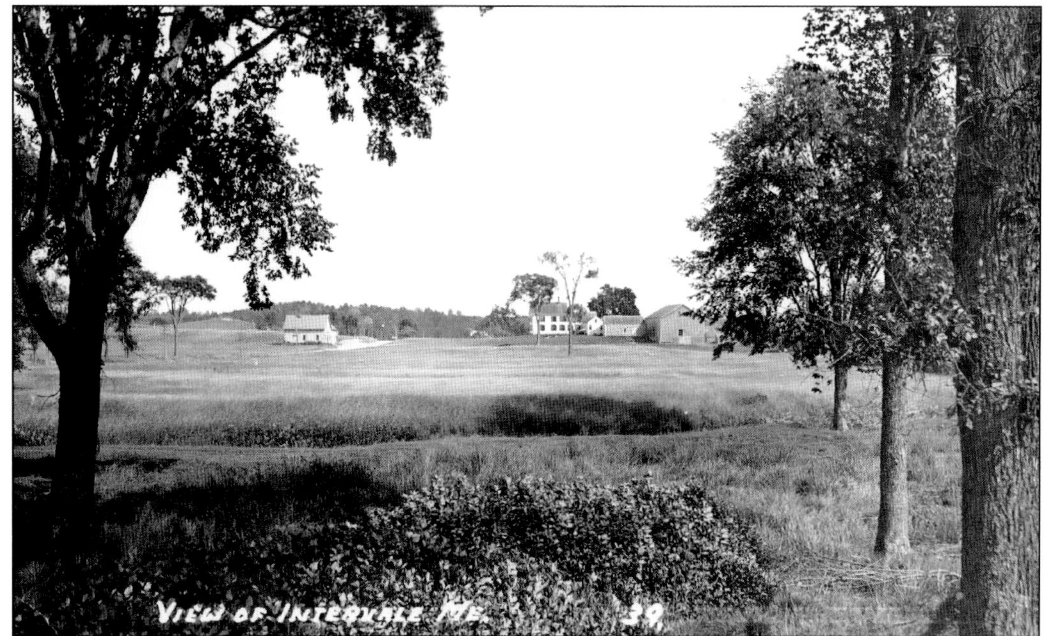

Across the meadow is the John Woodman Rideout store (left, formerly owned by Frank M. Hawkes) and the John Woodman farm (right). Woodman, purchaser of the blockhouse, built a log house near this site in 1761. Jabez Woodman built the ell section of the main house in 1770 where it still sits at 633 Intervale Road, home of Conifer Industries.

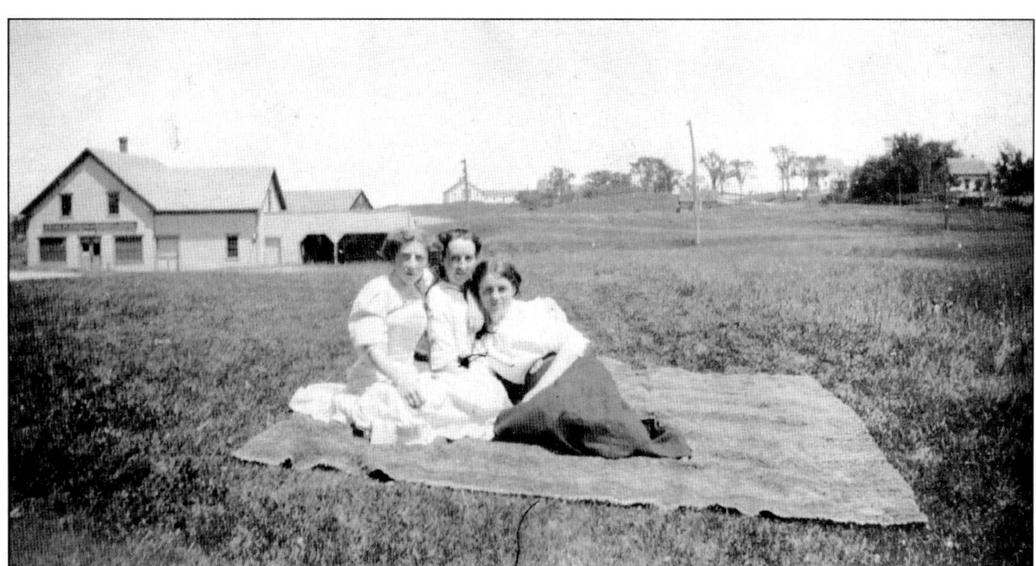

Isabelle Wharff Hawkes (left), Angie Hawkes True (center), and Georgie Hawkes Ayer relax in front of the new Frank M. Hawkes store. The store, which also housed the Intervale Post Office, replaced Joseph True's store/post office/gristmill beside the tracks of the Grand Trunk Railway.

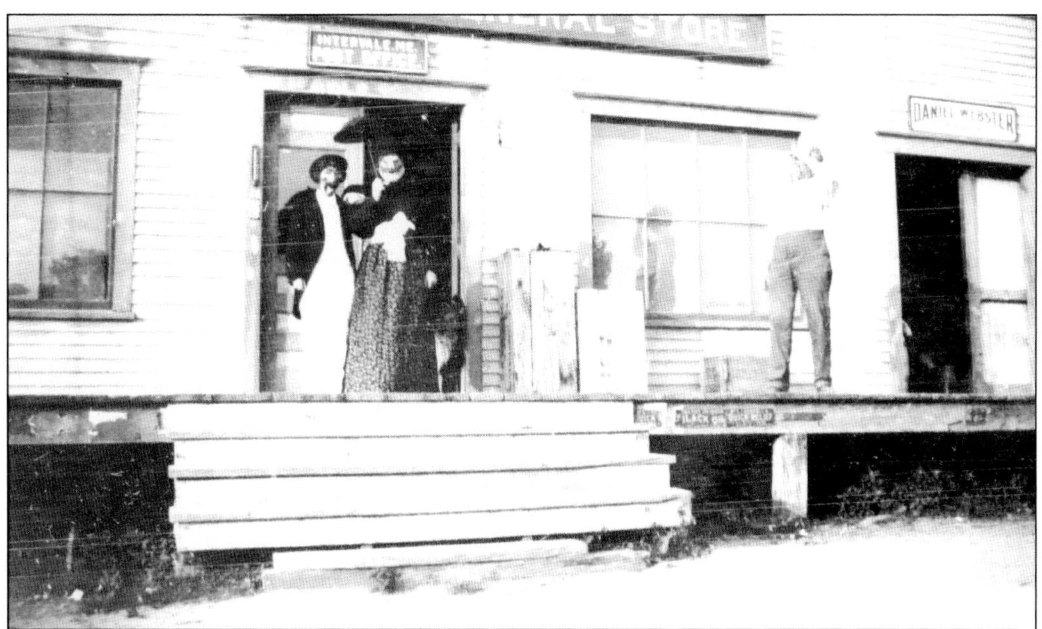

Some folks are gathered at the general store/post office in this postcard view. Postmasters were Joseph S. True, Frank M. Hawkes, John Woodman Rideout, and Carroll and Georgie Hawkes Ayer. The building burned down on September 29, 1945, and the post office was relocated across the road to the Woodman farm until closing in 1954. (Courtesy of the True family.)

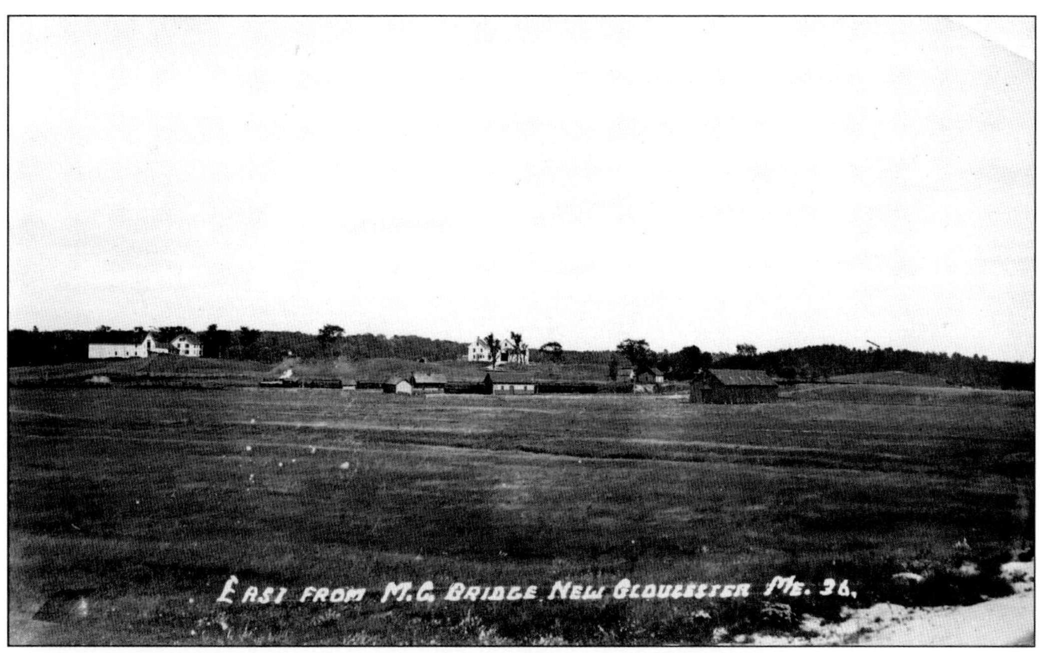

The Grand Trunk Railway (Canadian National Railway) buildings can be seen in the distance. The 1851 Nicholas Rideout farm (left) still stands at 58 Woodman Road, while the John C. Hammond farm (center) burned in the 1930s.

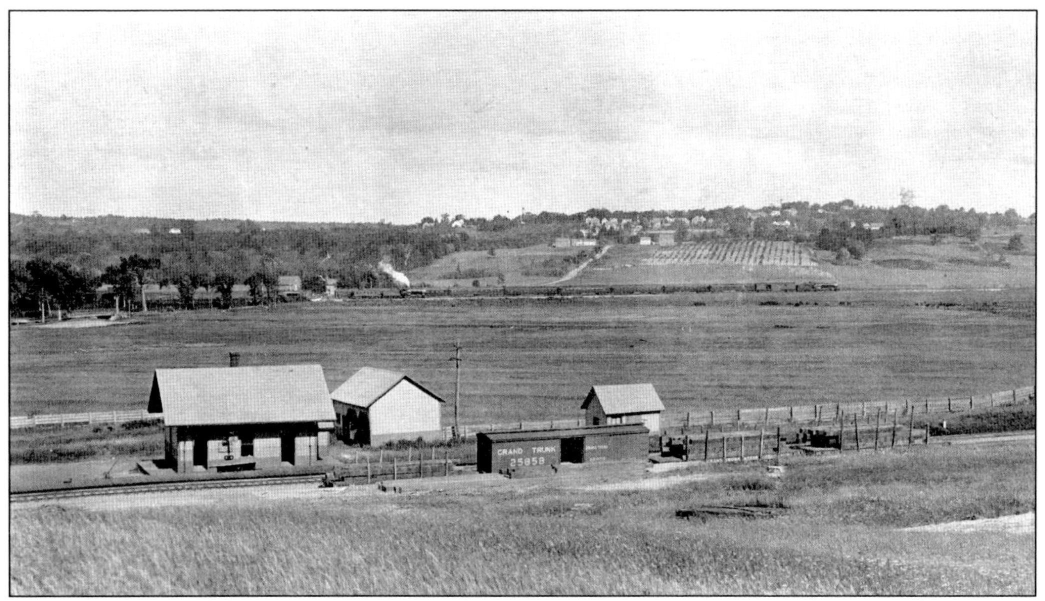

This postcard view depicts the Grand Trunk Railway station in the foreground and a steam locomotive on the Maine Central Railroad in the background. Mail arrived from Portland on the Maine Central Railroad until 1957 when truck service began.

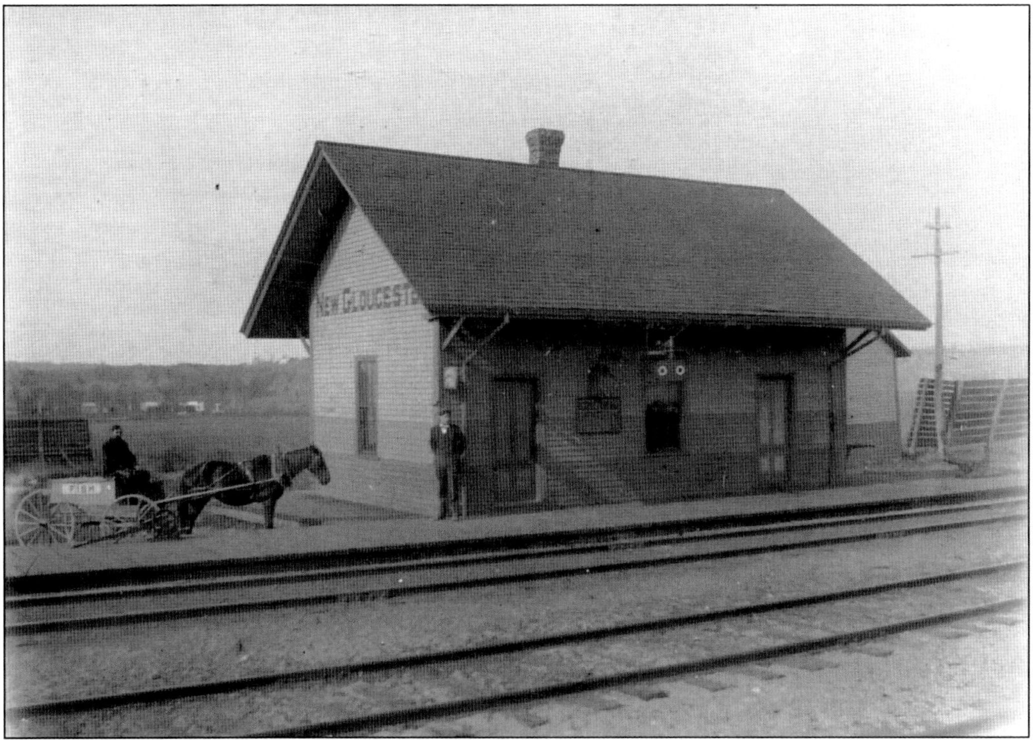

The Grand Trunk Railway station, which also had a grain mill and store, is shown in this postcard view. The Atlantic and St. Lawrence Railroad Company laid tracks through town in 1848 and leased them to the Grand Trunk Railway Company. Nicholas Rideout was the first station agent, accepting wages of $1 per day.

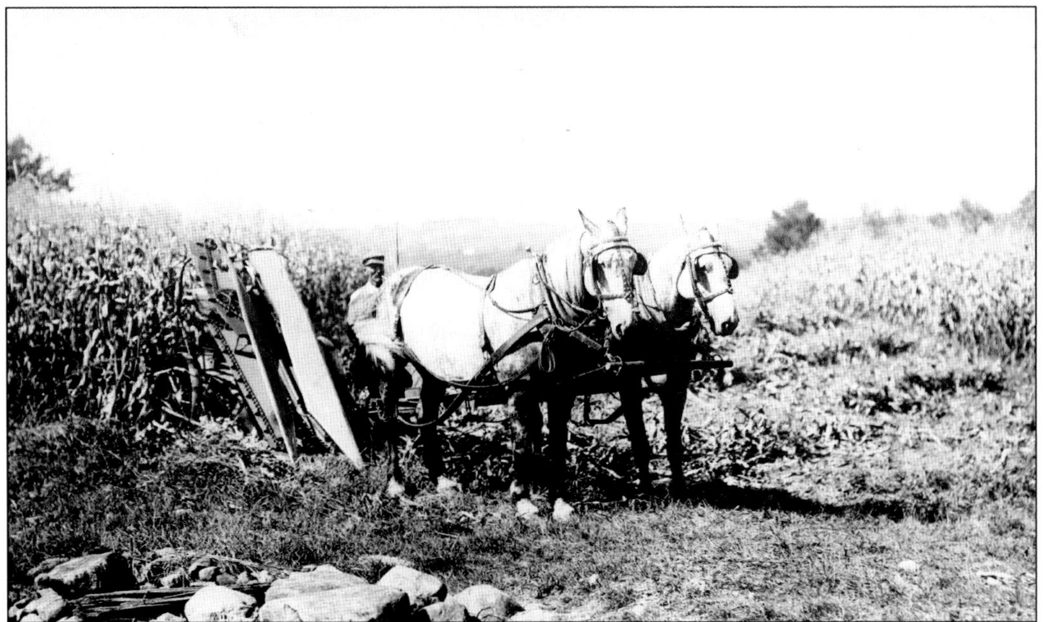

This picture postcard depicts an Intervale farmer and his team of horses hard at work. The Intervale provided natural farmland for the early settlers while they also worked at clearing the forests near the blockhouse.

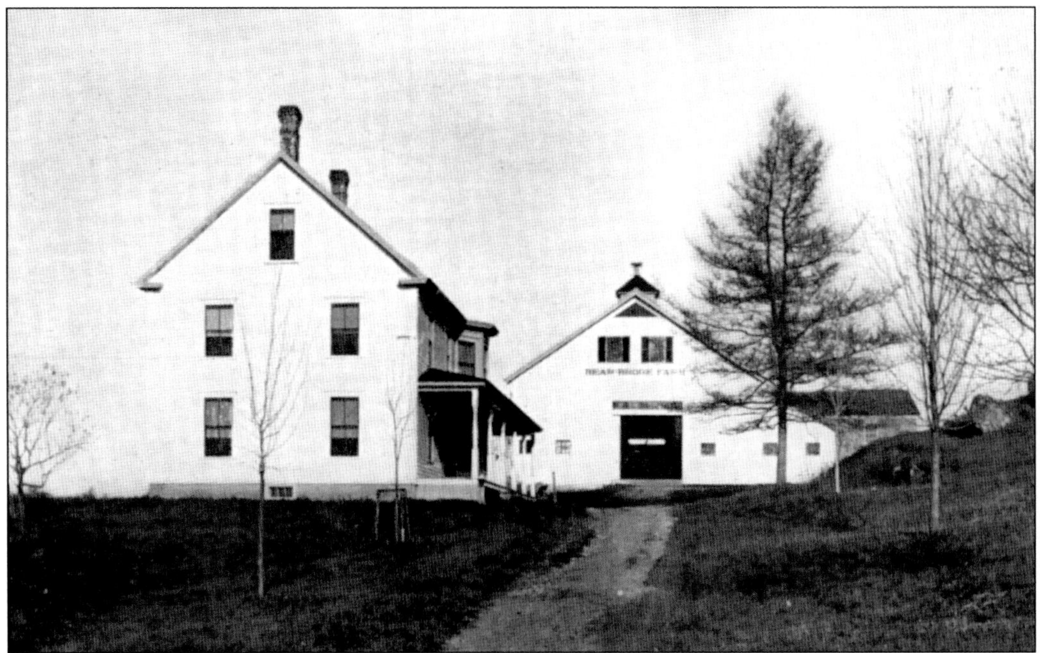

Bear Brook Farm is shown in this postcard. The longtime home of Elliott Fogg can still be found on Fogg's Corner at the intersection of Intervale Road and North Pownal Road. (Courtesy of the Blake family.)

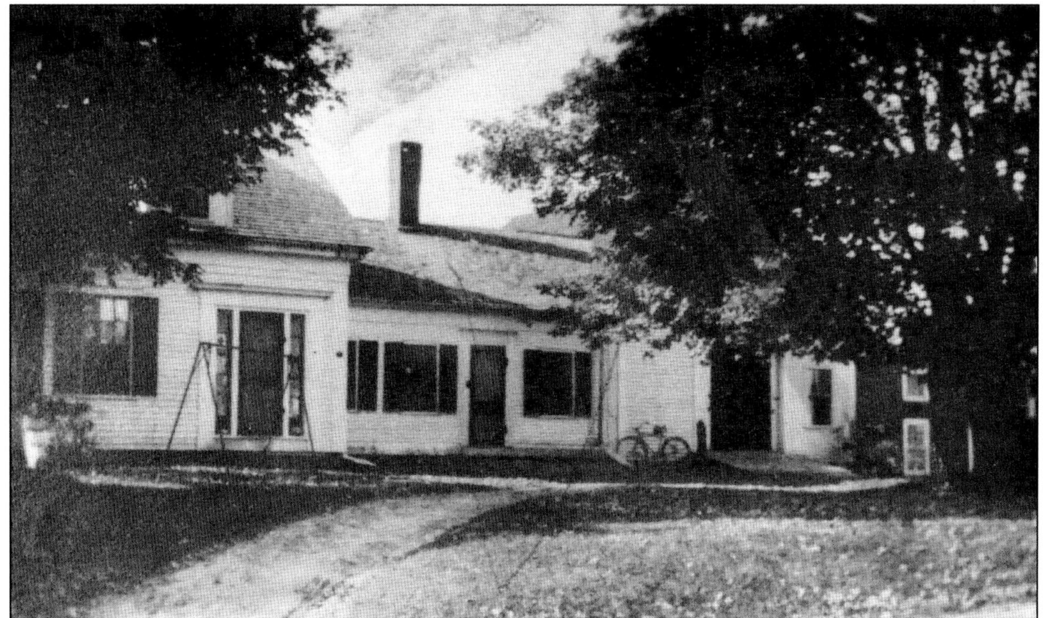

The Albert Rideout farm at 210 North Pownal Road is seen in this photograph. In 1963, the barn and shed burned, and the house was so badly damaged that it had to be taken down. Another building very similar in size, shape, and appearance was moved from North Pownal onto the old foundation.

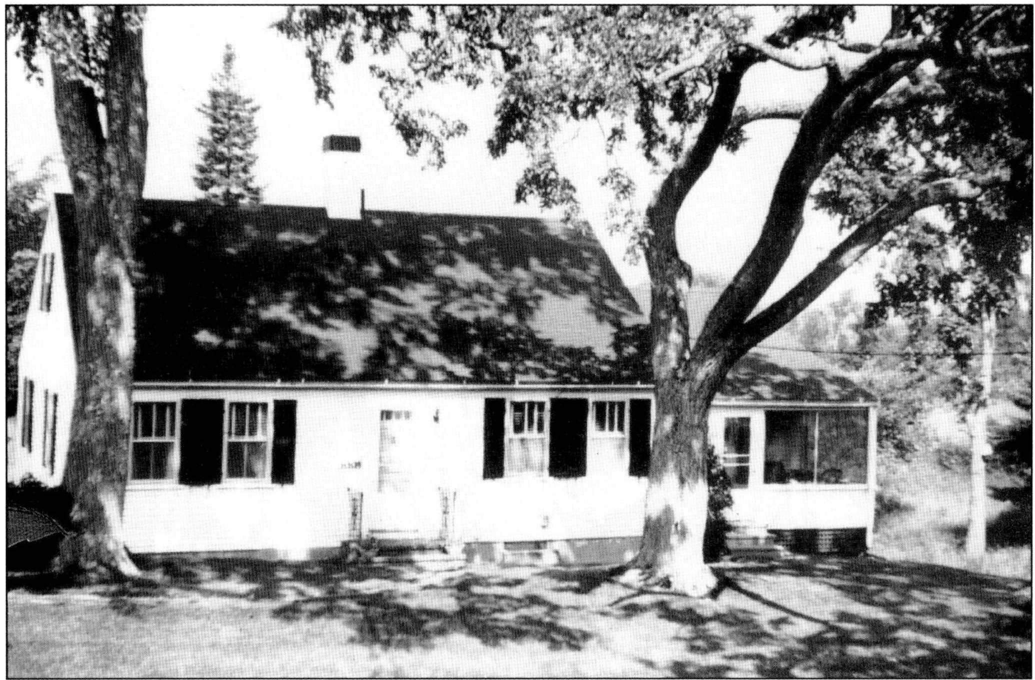

The Moses Parsons Haskell house (built about 1794) is shown here at 971 Intervale Road. Originally the ell and the barn connected to the house on the north until 1892 when the barn was dismantled. It was later the longtime home of local historian Elizabeth Sedgley.

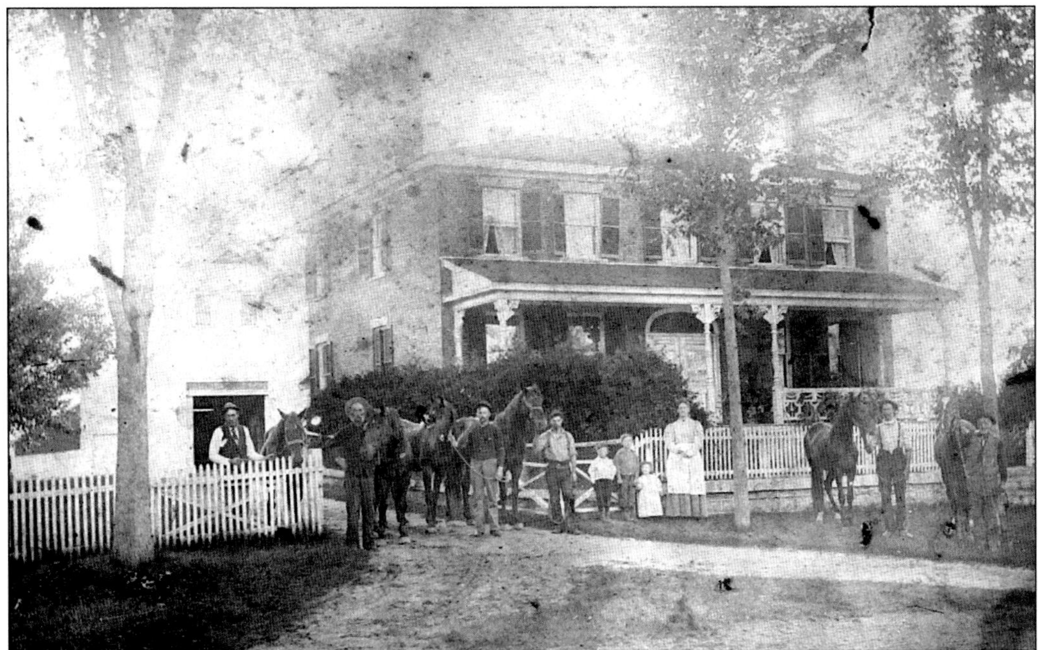

This early photograph is of Intervale Farm, located at 1047 Intervale Road. Thomas Clark is believed to have built the Colonial brick house in 1811. Land for the 1838 Universalist church came from this farm. The farm is now on the National Register of Historic Places. (Courtesy of the Wilcox family.)

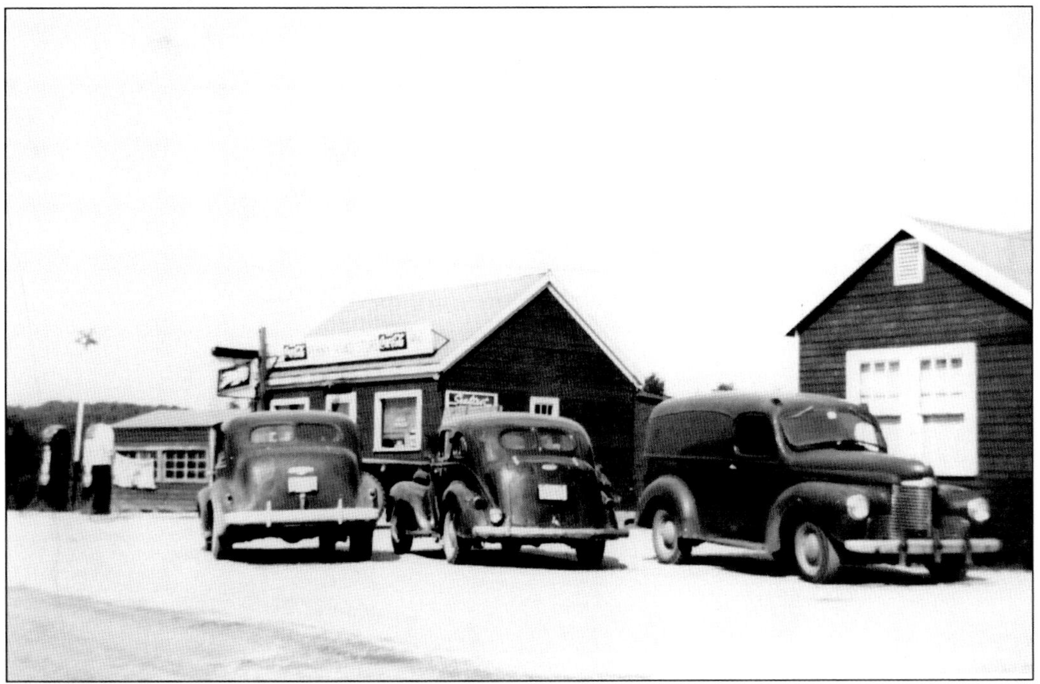

Penny Road Store is seen here in its early years at 1224 Intervale Road. Virgil Best built the store in the 1940s, and it was run by different owners through the mid-1960s. Delbert and Mary Ray reopened the store in 1986 with a new building on the same site.

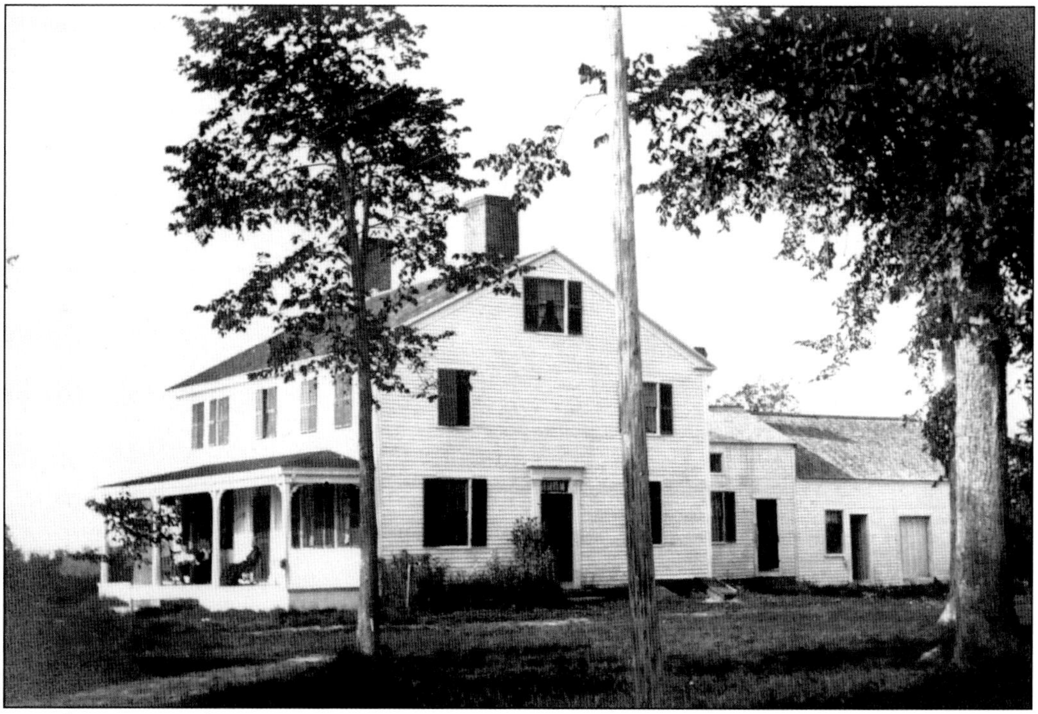

Seen here is an early postcard view of the Webber family on the porch of the old Micah Webber homestead at 1296 Intervale Road. Built in the 1820s, it was later known as Echo Farm and was home of Pownal Springs, renowned for its medicinal properties. Water was bottled in five-gallon glass demijohns that sold for $2.50 with $1.50 allowed for returns.

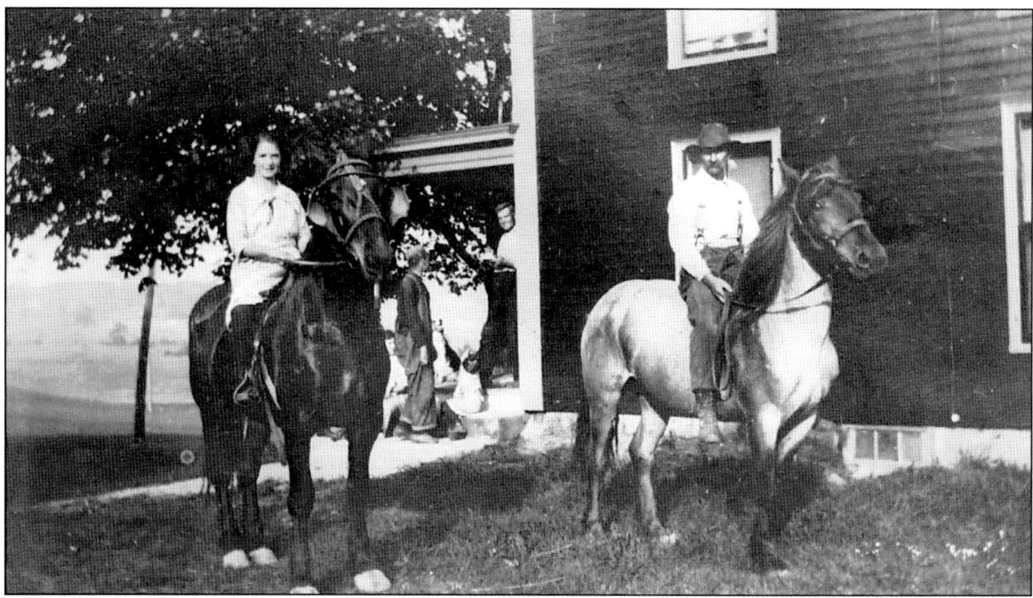

Mae Blake (left) sits on her horse at the Blake farm at 421 Penney Road. Hired hand Nat Bubier is on the other horse, with Fred Blake speaking to Herbert Blake (on the porch) in the background. The farm had been part of the Penney estate and was in the Blake family from 1860 to 1974. (Courtesy of the Blake family.)

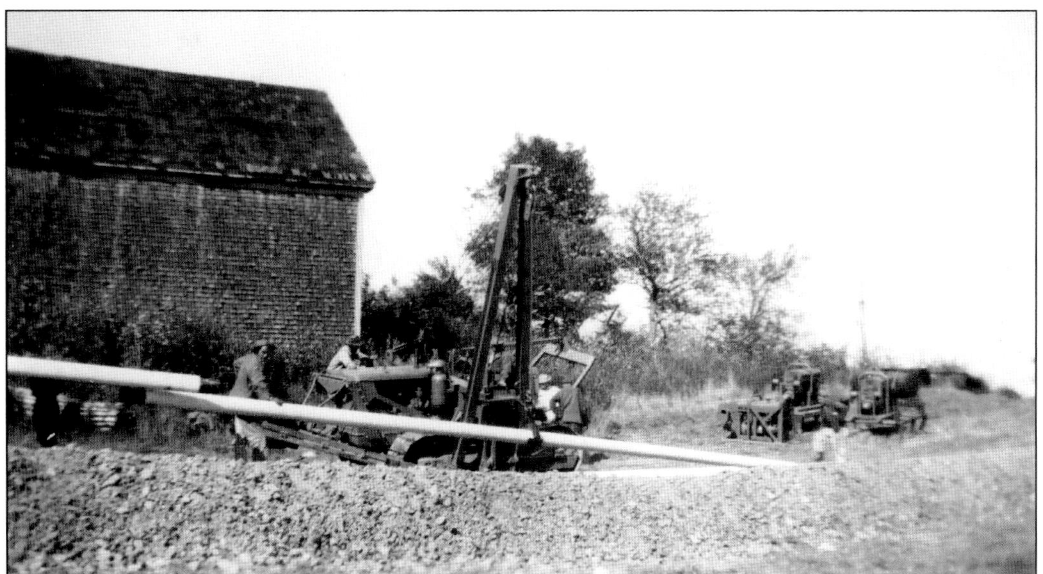

The Socony Vacuum Oil Company pipeline is being placed in ditches two feet wide by three feet deep in this 1949 photograph. The ditching machine came here from Texas. The hay barn seen standing opposite the Blake farm at 421 Penney Road came down in the early 1950s. Central Maine Power installed the nearby overhead power line in 1933. (Courtesy of the Blake family.)

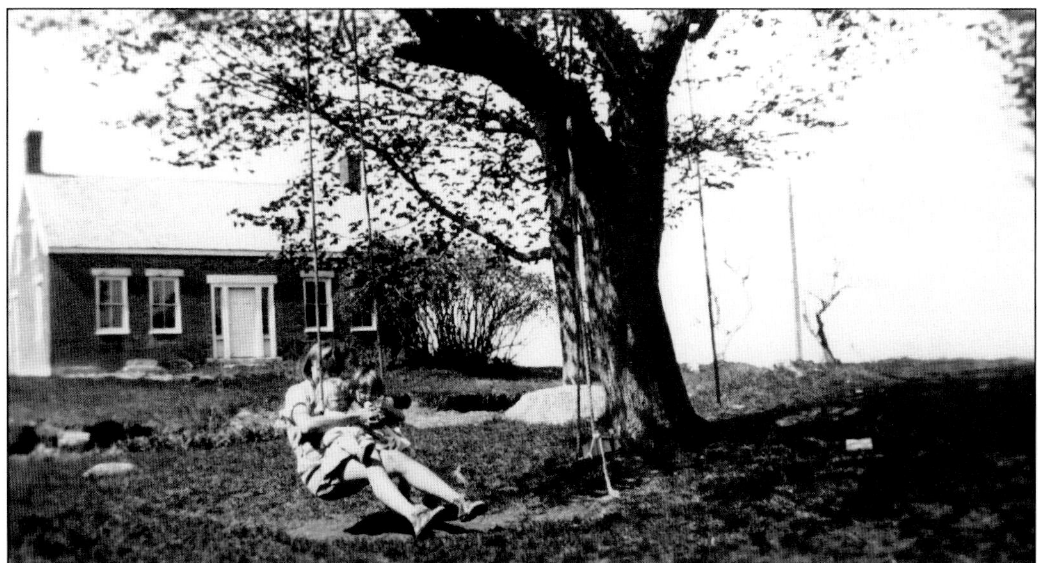

The 1838 Mark Penney brick house is seen at 399 Penney Road. It was built at the site of the original Penney homestead where his father, Thomas, built a house in 1793 to replace the log home he built when settling here in 1778. On the swing are, from left to right, Hazel, Herbert, and Madaline Blake. (Courtesy of the Blake family.)

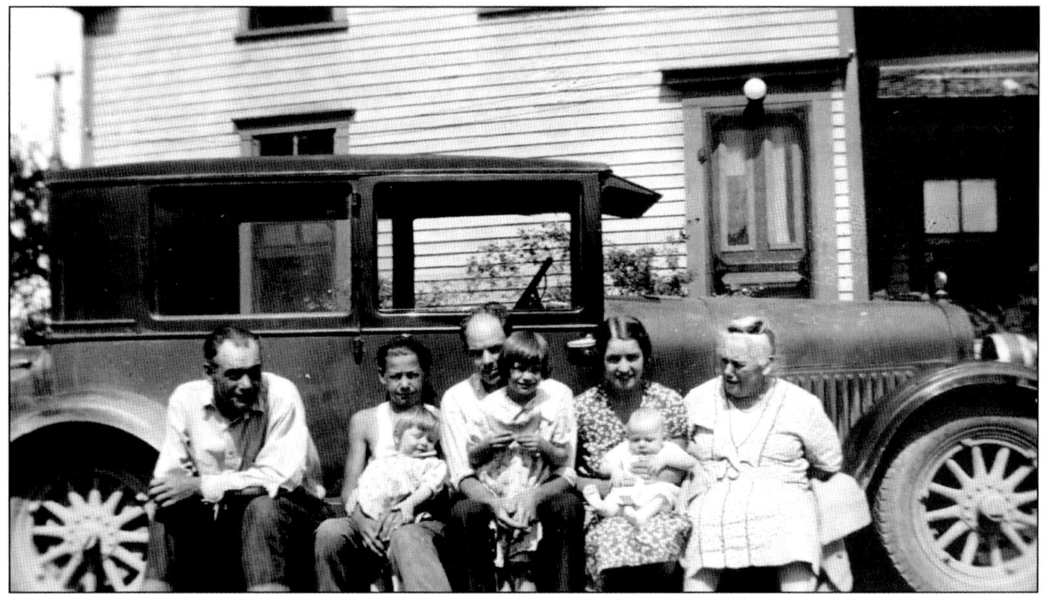

The Blake family is seated on the running board of their 1926 Hudson on Hillcrest Farm at 398 Penney Road. From left to right are Fred Blake, Everett Blake holding Madaline Blake, Albert Gilmore holding Colleen Blake, Mae Blake Gilmore holding Herbert Blake, and Lizzie Blake. This picture was taken on July 4, 1932. (Courtesy of the Blake family.)

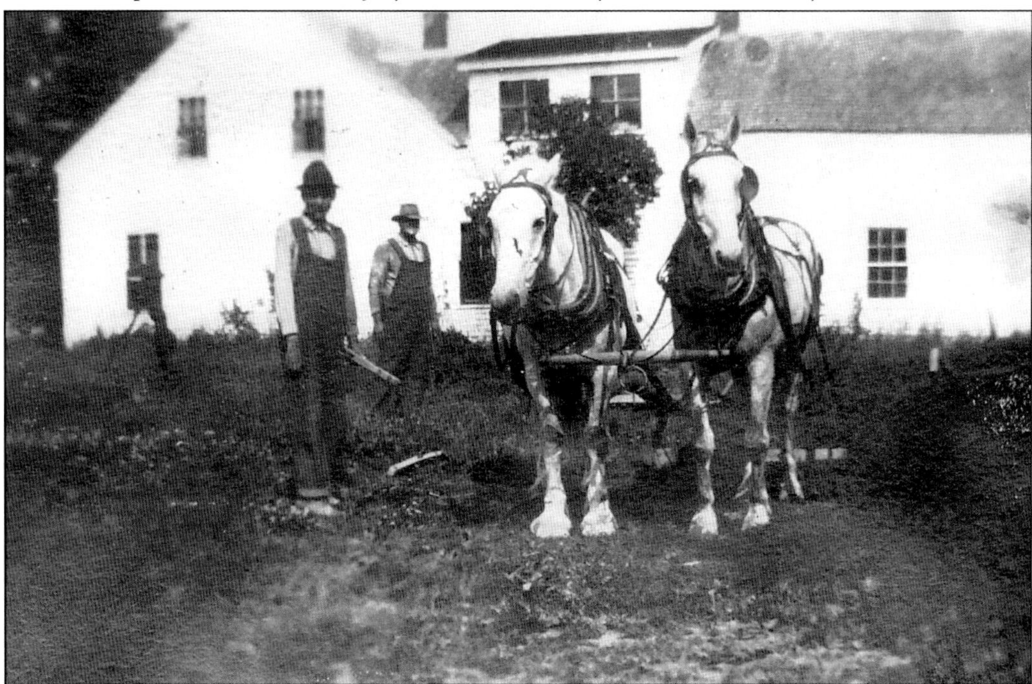

Fred Blake (left) and his father, Herbert Blake, are standing in the yard of Oscar C. and Clara Stinchfield at 376 Penney Road. Fred was married to Muriel Stinchfield, daughter of Oscar and Clara and last of the Stinchfield family line. Herbert was an imposing local constable, standing six feet five inches tall, and served as a civil and criminal deputy sheriff for Cumberland County. (Courtesy of the Blake family.)

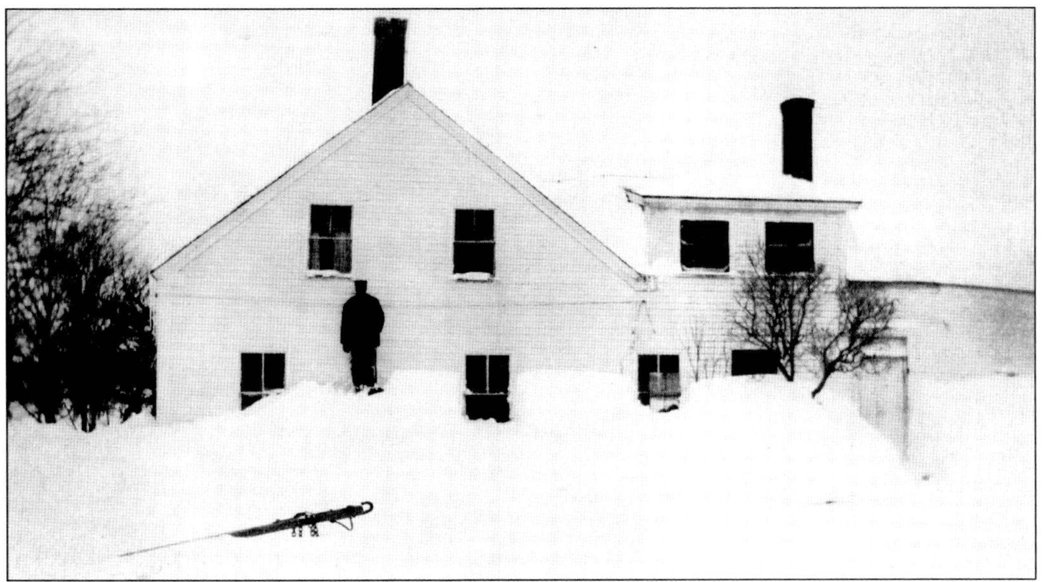

Oscar C. Stinchfield (1868–1940) is seen standing outside his upstairs bedroom window at his home at 376 Penney Road after a blizzard in March 1920. With no snowblowers or snowplows, the men worked hard for days to clear out the snow around the farm buildings. Horses hauled a roller to pack the roads or pulled a harrow if there was crust to break up. (Courtesy of the Blake family.)

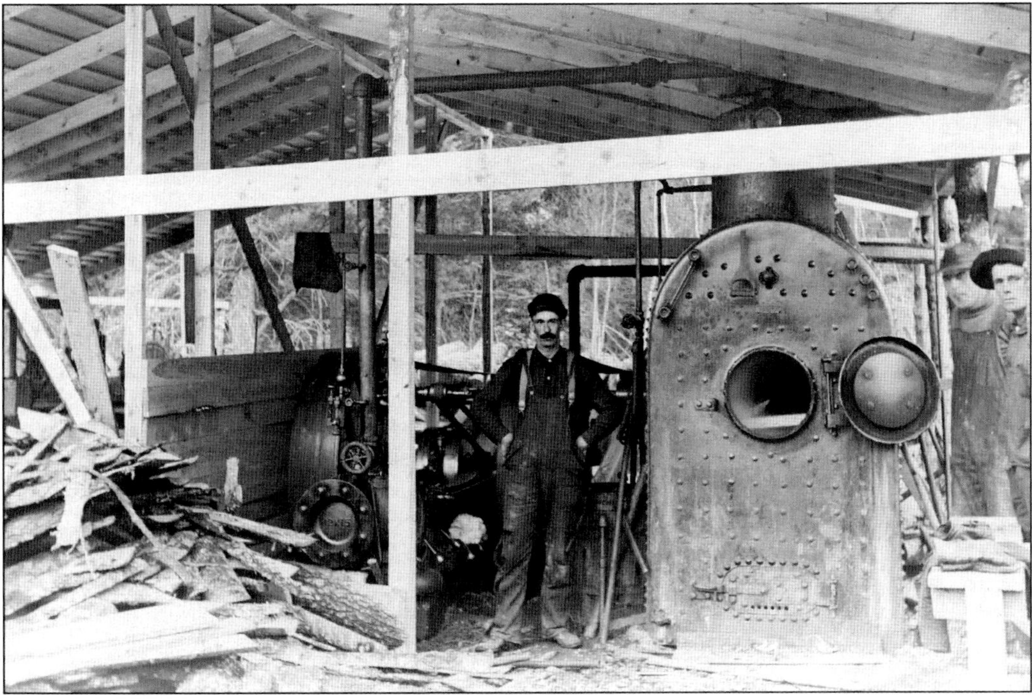

Oscar C. Stinchfield poses with his boiler and sawmill while his workers look on. He grew up on Dougherty Road but later purchased the Ebenezer Bennett farm at 376 Penney Road. His portable mill visited a large part of Maine and New Hampshire. Oscar was descended from John Stinchfield Sr., "father of the blockhouse." (Courtesy of the Blake family.)

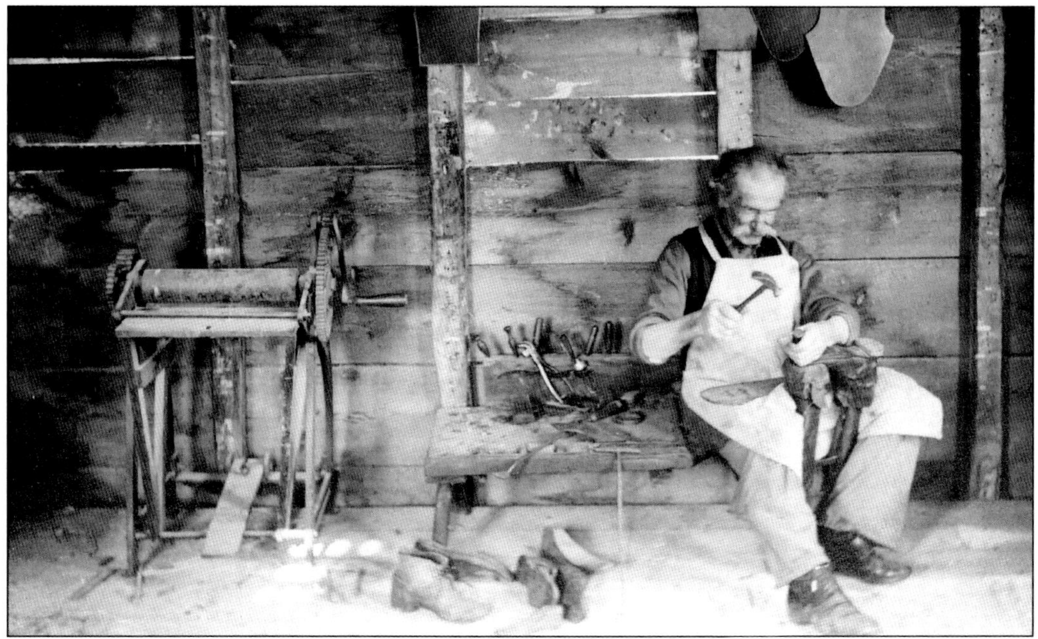

Cyrus Latham Stinchfield (1839–1914) is at work in his cobbler shop. Cyrus left his family's farm (the Rev. Ephraim Stinchfield homestead at 320 Penney Road) as a young man to work in a shoe factory in Lowell, Massachusetts. He returned with his new trade and took over the family estate. (Courtesy of the Blake family.)

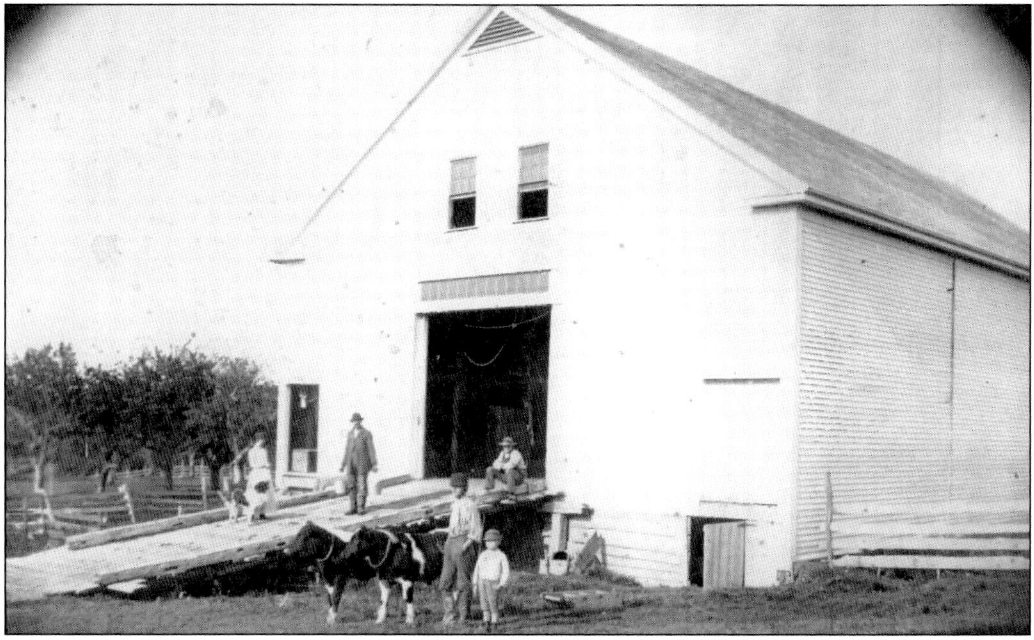

According to the 1880 book *Cumberland County*, "The practice of selling the poor was abandoned in 1834, and a town farm purchased." The town farm was closed in 1928, and the buildings burned in 1947. Individual pauper stones can be seen at the Hill Cemetery at the entrance of Town Farm Road. The 42-by-72-foot barn seen here was built it 1883 on the site of the previous barn in fields at the end of Town Farm Road.

Seven

The Shakers and Sabbathday Lake

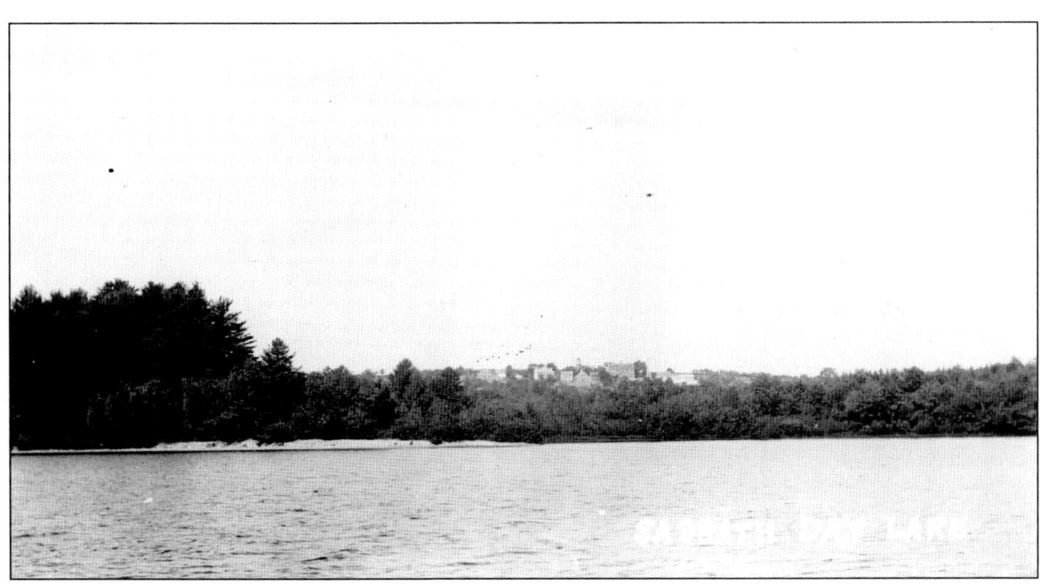

The Shakers settled near Sabbathday Lake in 1782 in what was then called Thompson Pond Plantation. Shaker societies were set up in nine states, but this is the only active Shaker community remaining in the country. This society in West Gloucester was organized in 1794, and it now has 18 buildings on 1,800 acres of land.

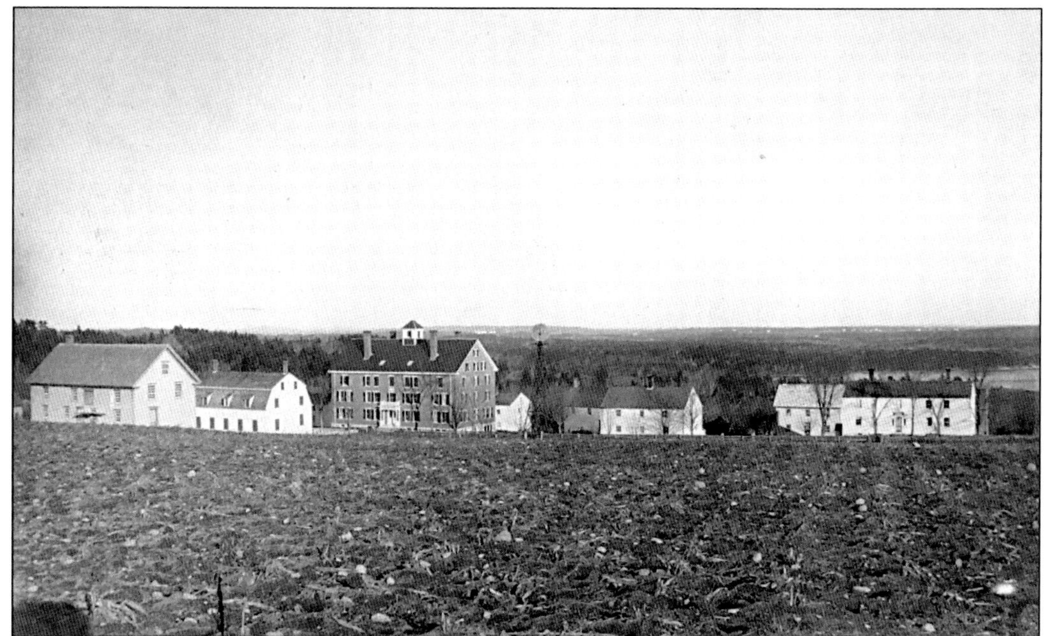

This view of the church family was taken around 1890 looking east. From left to right are the garden seed house (1796), meetinghouse (1794), dwelling house (1884), infirmary (1770s), herb house (1824), brethren's shop (around 1800), boys' shop (1850), and trustees' office (1816), with Sabbathday Lake in the background. (Courtesy of the Shaker Library Collection.)

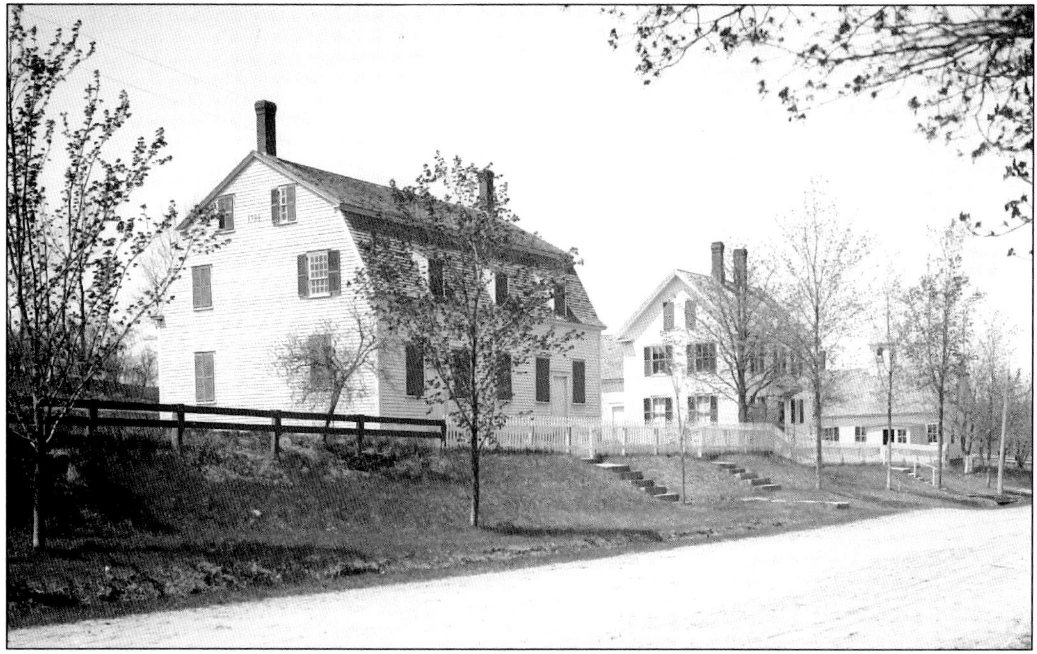

Brother Delmer Wilson took this photograph, which shows the maple trees that still stand along Shaker Road (formerly Route 26), around 1910. From left to right are the meetinghouse, ministry's shop (1839), and schoolhouse (1880). The meetinghouse is still used for public worship. The schoolhouse is now used as a research library. (Courtesy of the Shaker Library Collection.)

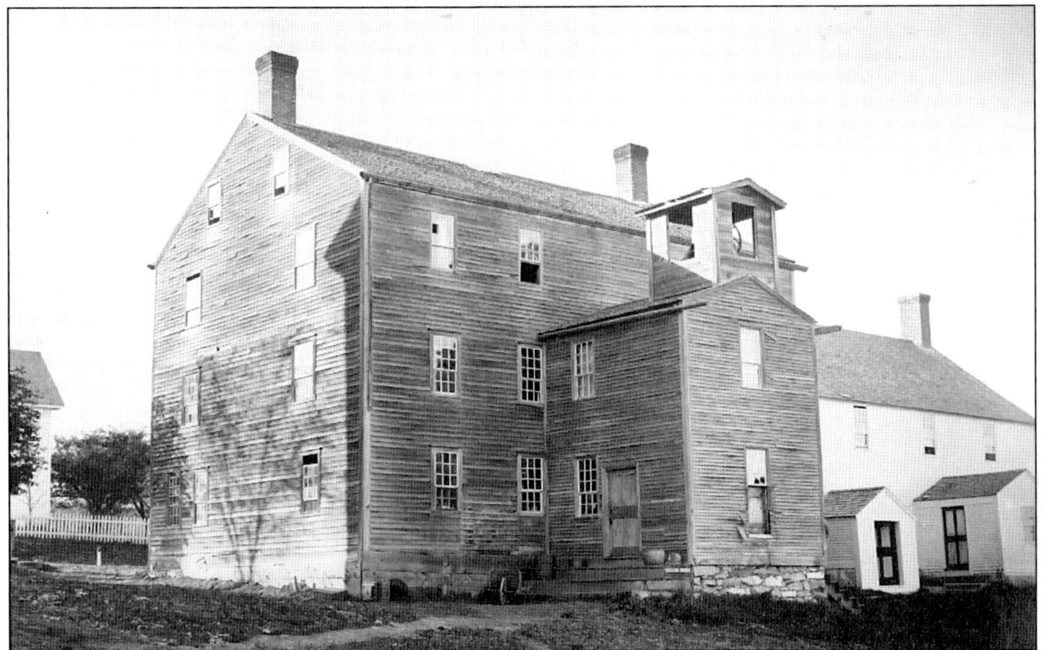

The original dwelling house (1795) is seen in this 1884 photograph. The house had been moved into the driveway, requiring close to 20 yoke of oxen to make room for a new dwelling house on the same foundation. To the left is the 1796 girls' shop, which now serves in part as offices for the Shaker museum and herb department. (Courtesy of the Shaker Library Collection.)

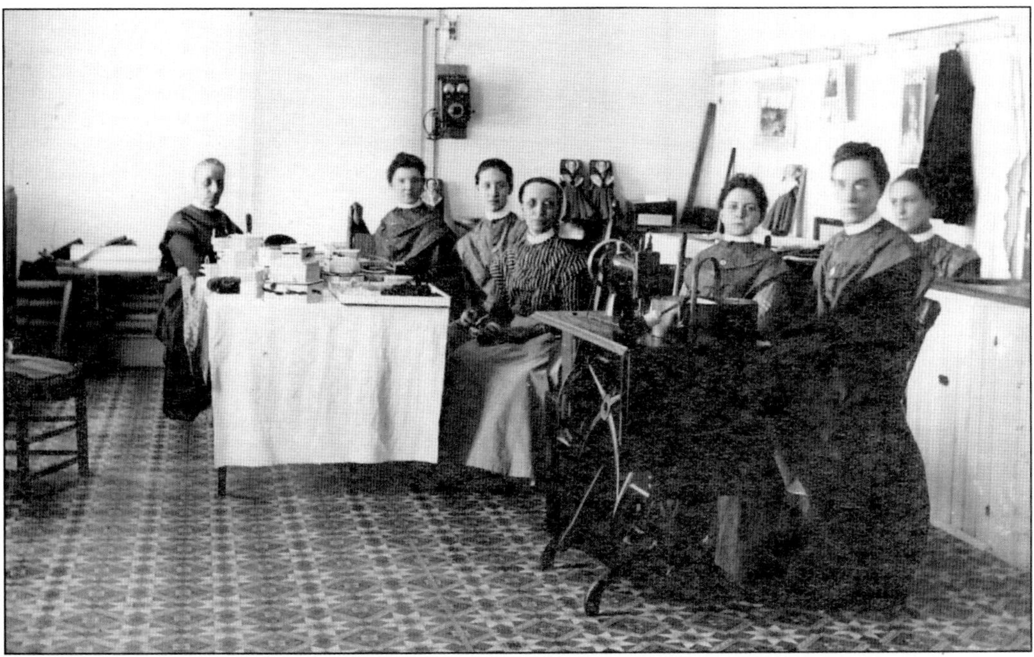

This 1920 photograph by Brother Delmer Wilson depicts the "Bee Hive" workroom in the 1821 sisters' shop. Seated from left to right are Sisters Sarah Fletcher, Laura Bailey, Lizzie Bailey, Prudence Stickney, Claire Chase, Iona Sedgley, and Viola Daniels. The "Bee Hive" now serves as the packing room for the herb department. (Courtesy of the Shaker Library Collection.)

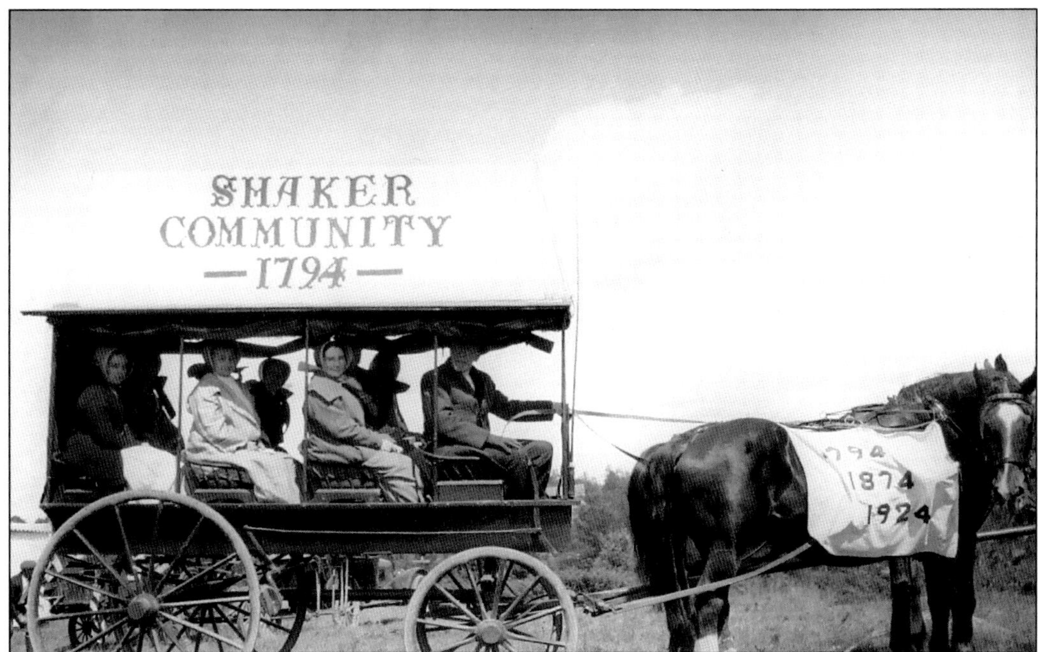

The Shakers have always been active in town affairs and are seen participating in the September 6, 1924, parade. Riding in the fair wagon are, from left to right, Sisters Elsie McCool, Irene Corcoran, Susie Reid, unidentified, Genie Coolbroth, and Viola Daniels. Driving the team is elder William Dumont. (Courtesy of the Shaker Library Collection.)

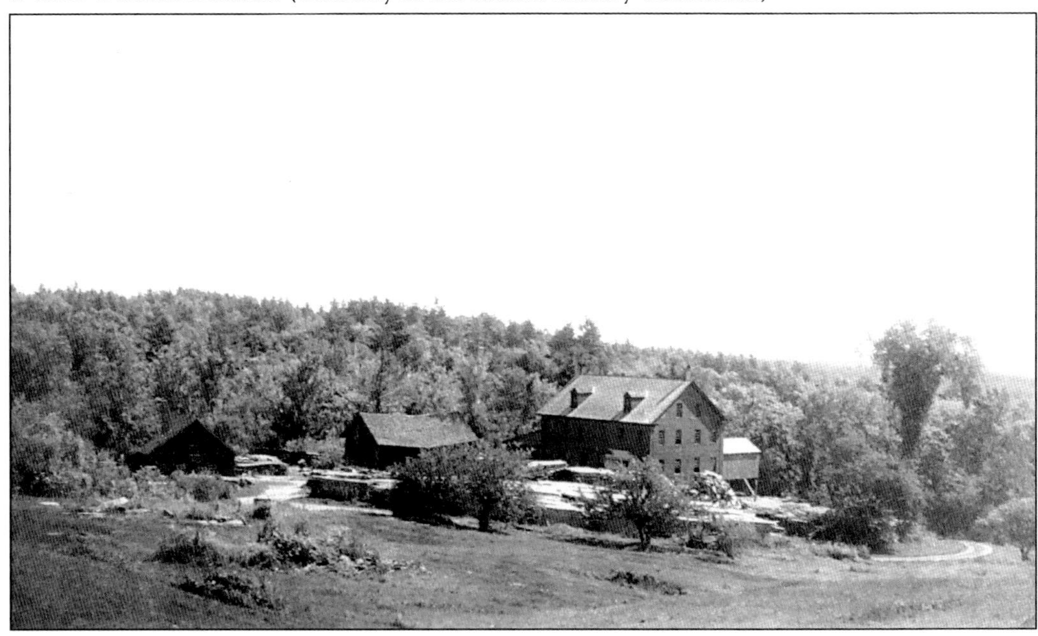

The Great Mill was built in 1853, the last and largest of the community. An overshot wheel 31 feet in diameter, one of the largest in the country, powered the mill. It operated until 1942 and was taken down in 1949. This mid-1920s view shows the blacksmith shop (left), the old Stave Mill (center), the Great Mill, and Outlet Road on the right curving up from the lake. (Courtesy of the Shaker Library Collection.)

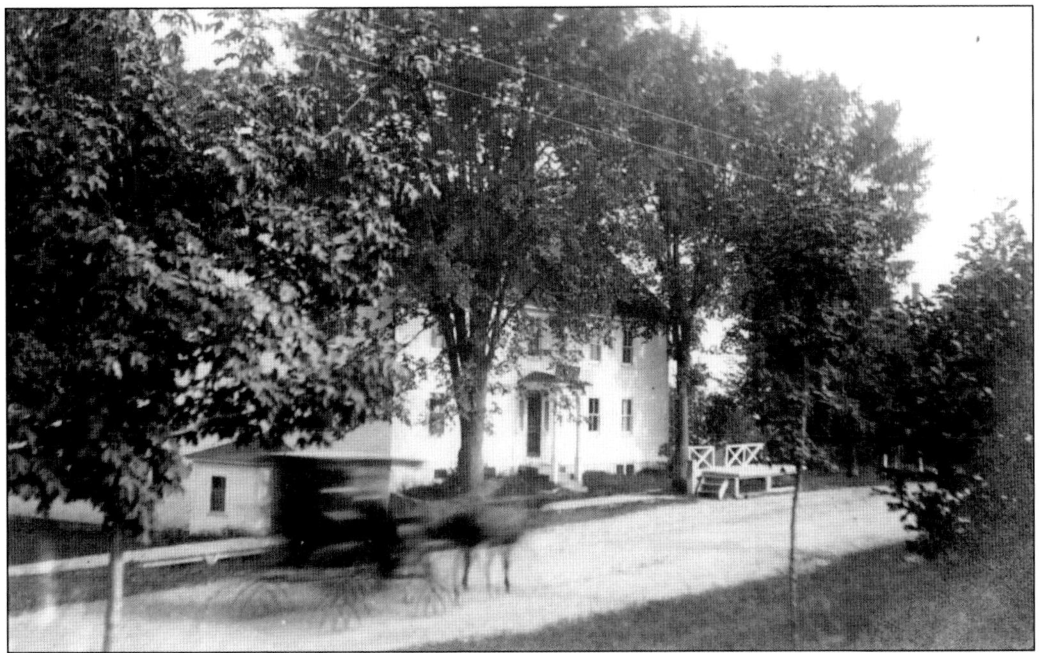

The Sabbathday Lake Post Office and trustees' office is seen on Shaker Road, which officially received its name in 1994 to commemorate the 200th anniversary of the United Society of Shakers in New Gloucester. With the motto Hands to Work and Hearts to God, the Shakers were the first in Maine to package garden seeds.

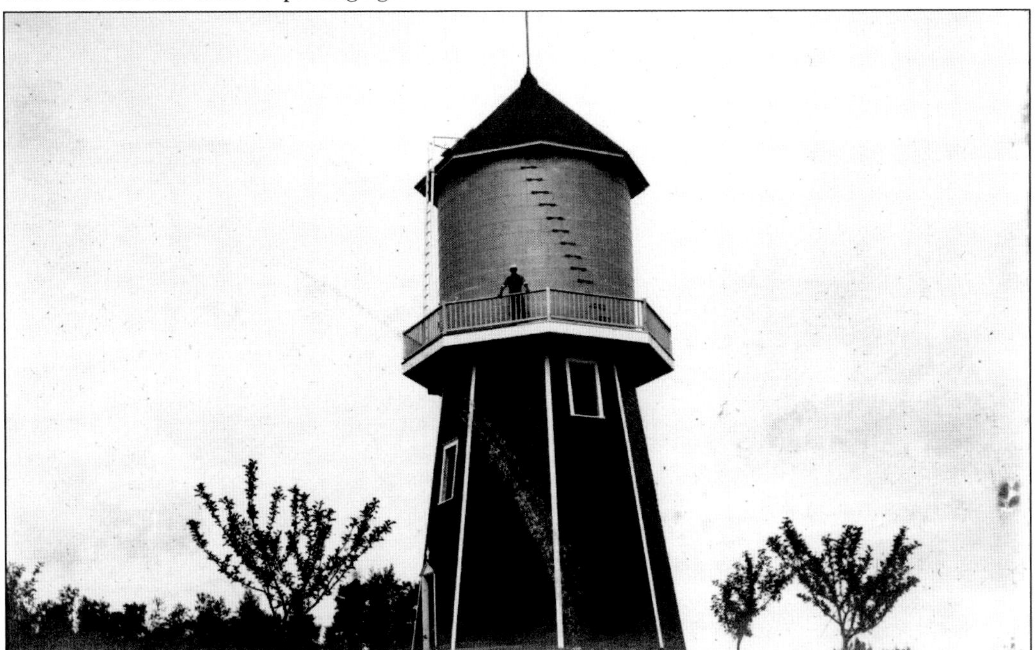

Standing on the Shaker Tower, one could easily see the Shaker community on Poland Hill about one mile north, which merged with the Sabbathday Lake community in 1887. The Shaker society in Alfred consolidated with New Gloucester in 1931, and in 1969, this became the last active community in the country with the closing of the colony in Canterbury, New Hampshire.

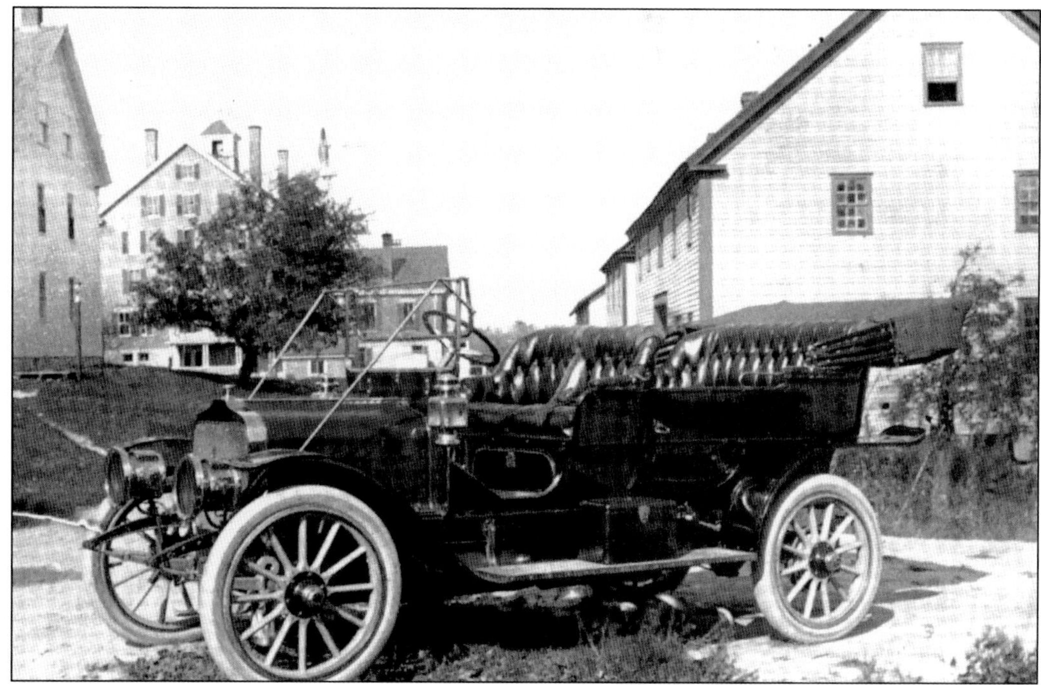

The community's first automobile was a 1908 Selden. The Shakers were often among the first to accept the latest innovations and are responsible for many inventions of their own. They developed water-repellent cloth and an early washing machine and were the first in the country to manufacture metric measurers.

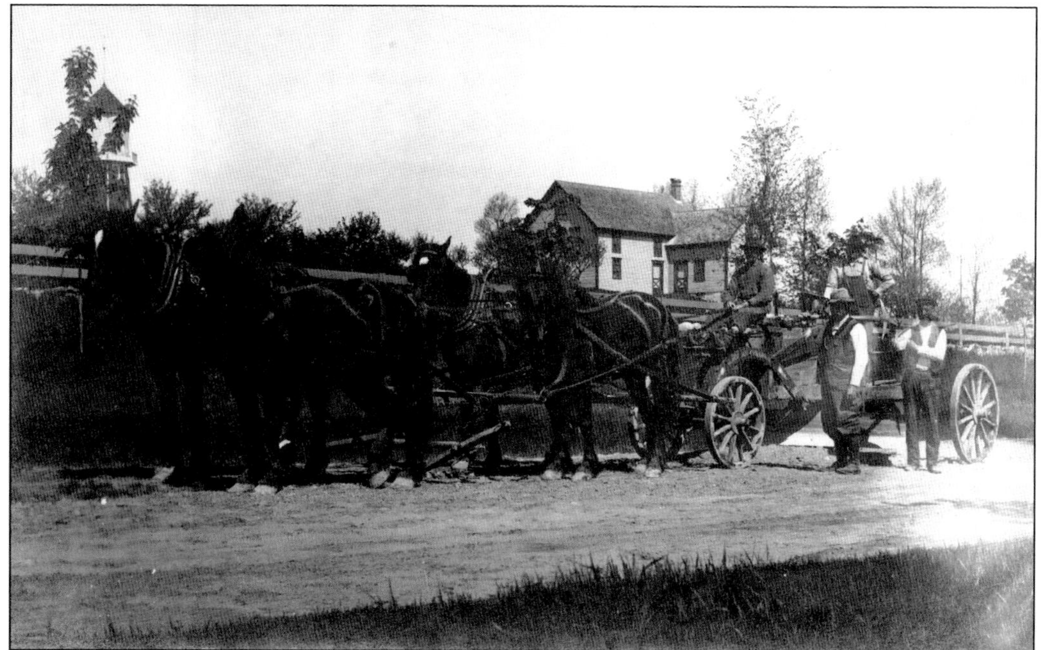

Brother Delmer Wilson took this picture of the town road crew in 1909. Herman Emery was driving in place of the regular driver, Ernest Johnson, who was off that day. The team was kept at Harry Merrill's place nearby. Frank Marston was the road commissioner.

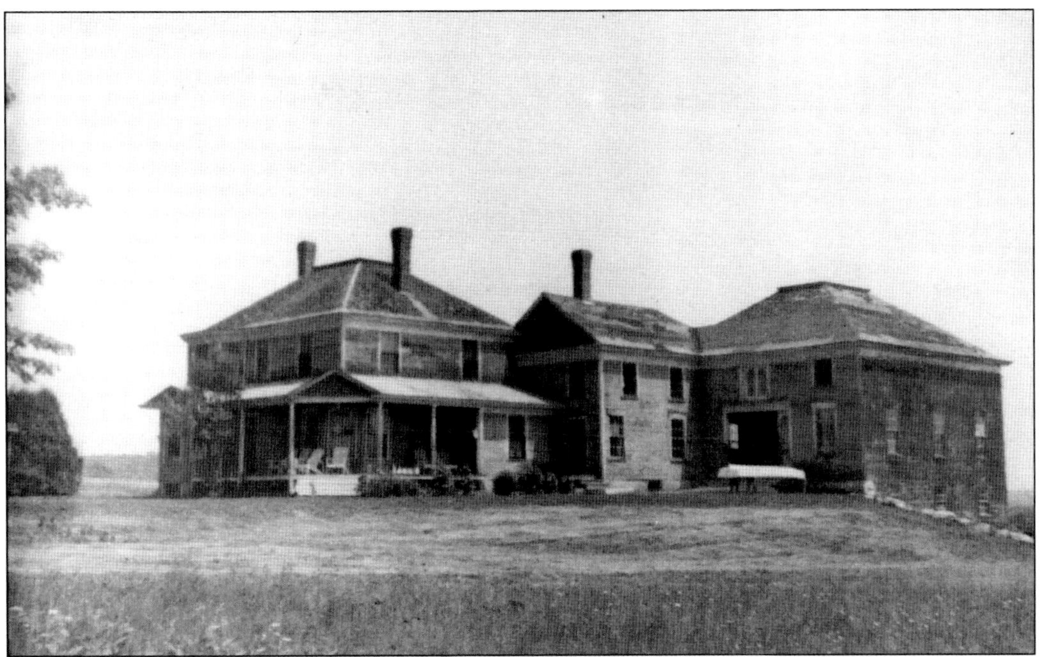

The 1899 Otis Campbell farm stood at 613 Shaker Road on land purchased from the Shakers. The Campbells sold shore frontage to the Catholic Diocese of Portland in 1939 that became part of Lady of the Lake Camp. The farm was destroyed by fire in 1947, and the Pond Schoolhouse was moved to the site and converted to a home.

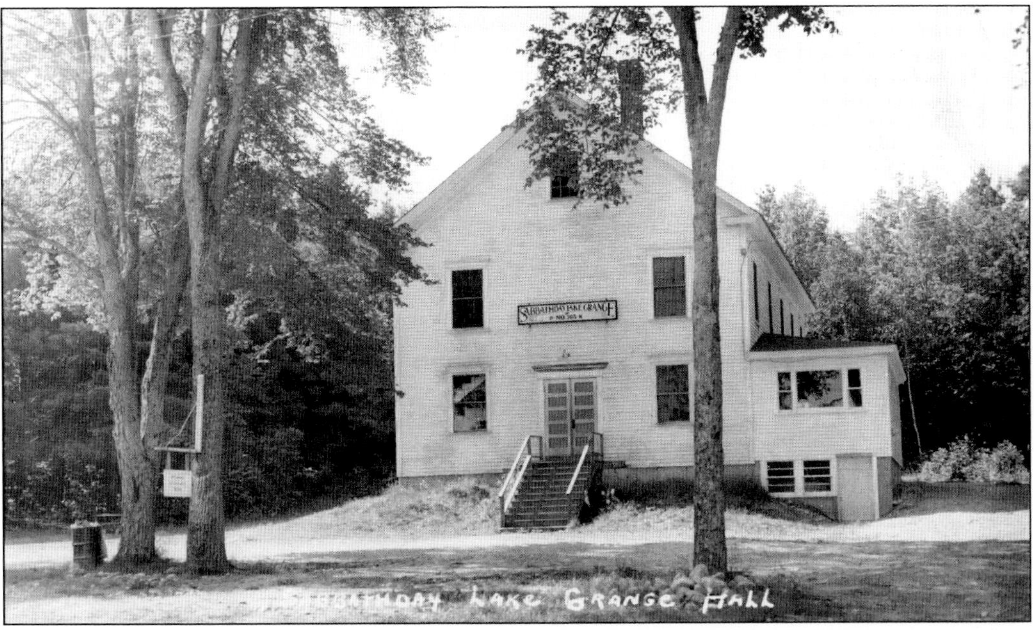

Sabbathday Lake Grange No. 365 was organized on November 15, 1900, with 26 charter members and was incorporated on April 18, 1903, with 107 members. The Sabbathday Lake Grange Hall was dedicated on October 16, 1903, and is the only remaining Grange in town. It faces the southern end of Sabbathday Lake along the old Route 26 on Shaker Road.

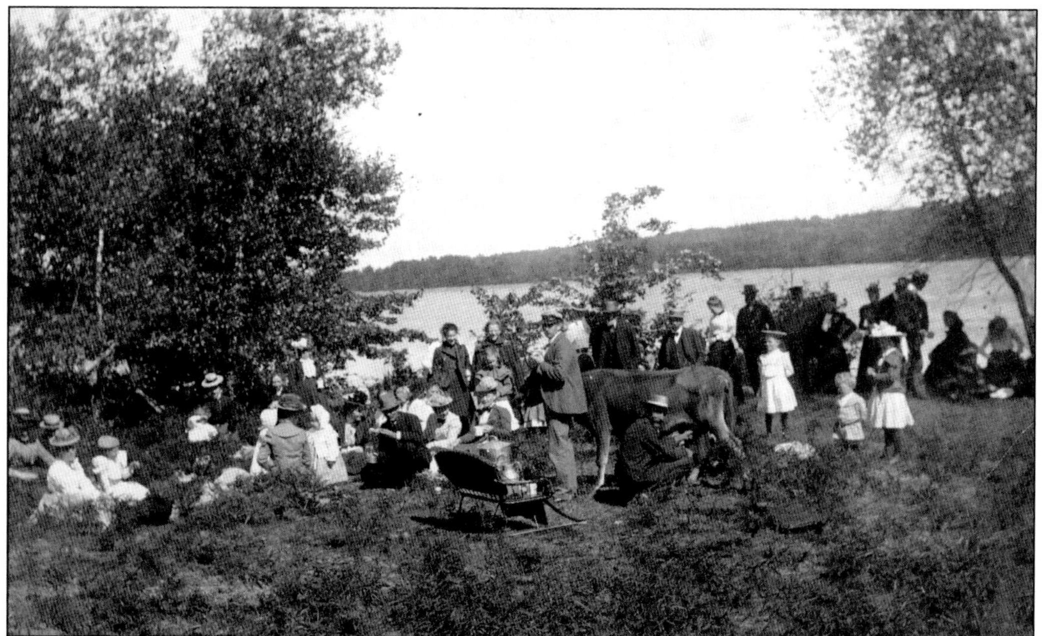

Many picnics have been enjoyed along the shores of Sabbathday Lake, formerly known as Sabbath-Day Pond. Albert Rideout is milking the cow at this Sunday school picnic. Sabbathday Lake is about one and a half miles long and a half mile wide and reportedly derived its name from a number of early hunters who agreed to meet there to keep the Sabbath.

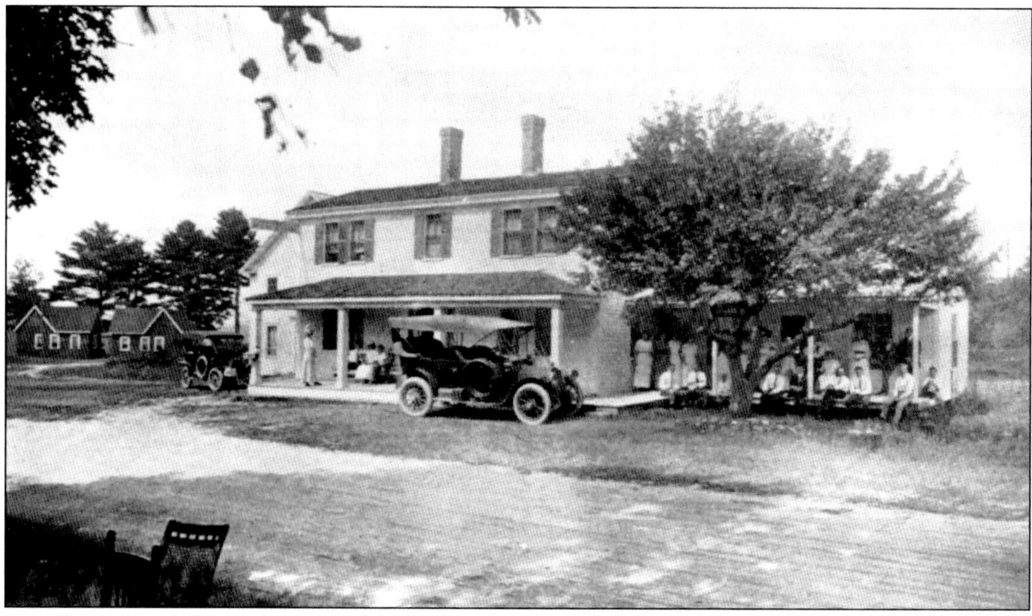

The Centennial Spring house at 341 Shaker Road (now Sabbathday Road) was built in 1842 as a tavern. The Centennial Spring was discovered in 1876. Its bottling company was incorporated in 1881, but the spring dried up in the late 1940s. The main part of the hotel has been torn down, and the dining room was converted to a hall that is now home of the Fraternal Order of Eagles No. 4131.

Eight

PINELAND

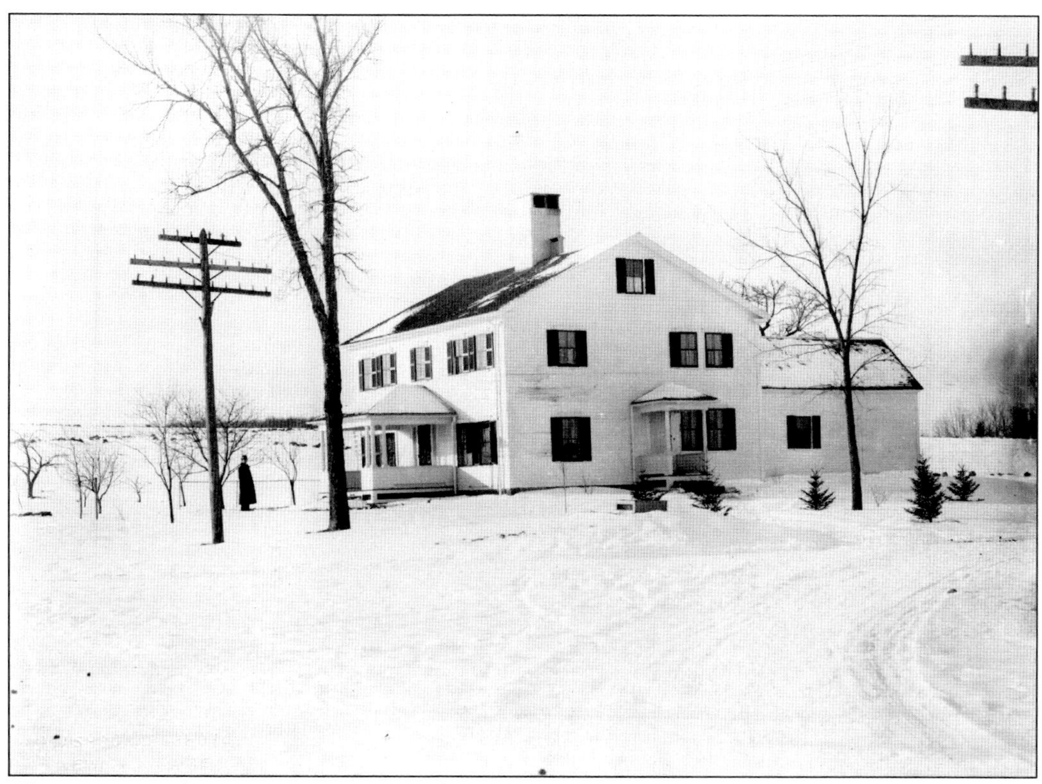

The superintendent's cottage is seen in this 1915 view at the corner of Intervale Road and Depot Road. The old Gould farmhouse was later named Dirigo House. The Maine School for the Feeble-Minded was opened in 1908, with the state purchasing 1,200 acres in New Gloucester, Gray, Pownal, and North Yarmouth. Most of the land and buildings were in New Gloucester but were usually credited to Pownal. It became the Pownal State School in 1925.

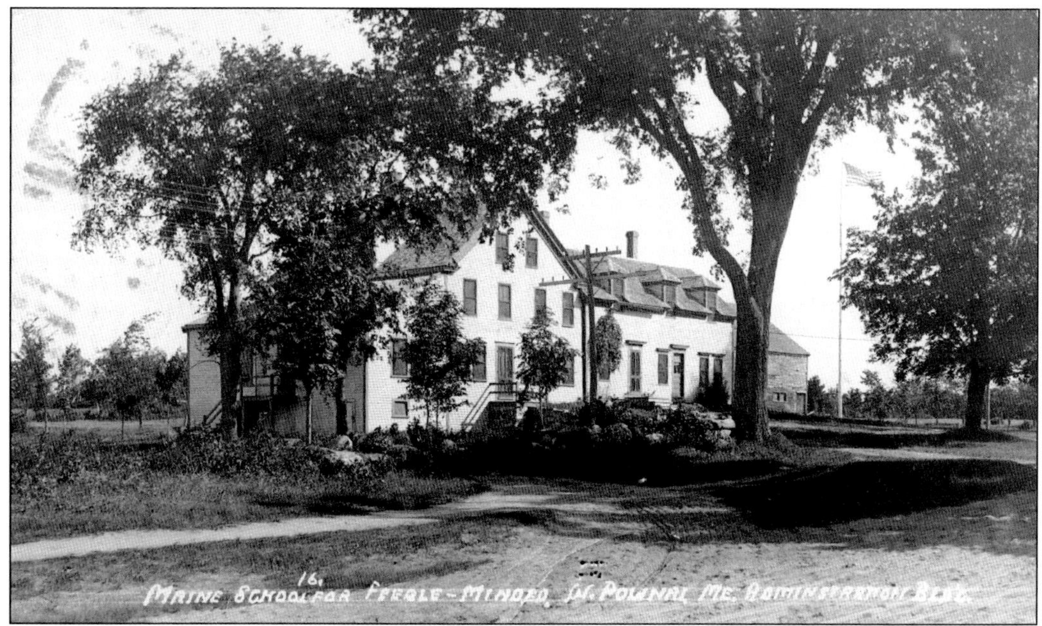

This postcard depicts the old Shailer house used as an administration building that sat at the front of the campus along Intervale Road. In 1957, the school became Pineland Hospital and Training Center, and it closed in 1996. Pineland had over 40 buildings and 1,500 residents at its peak. It was purchased by the Libra Foundation and has been restored as a 19-building campus and a 5,000-acre working farm.

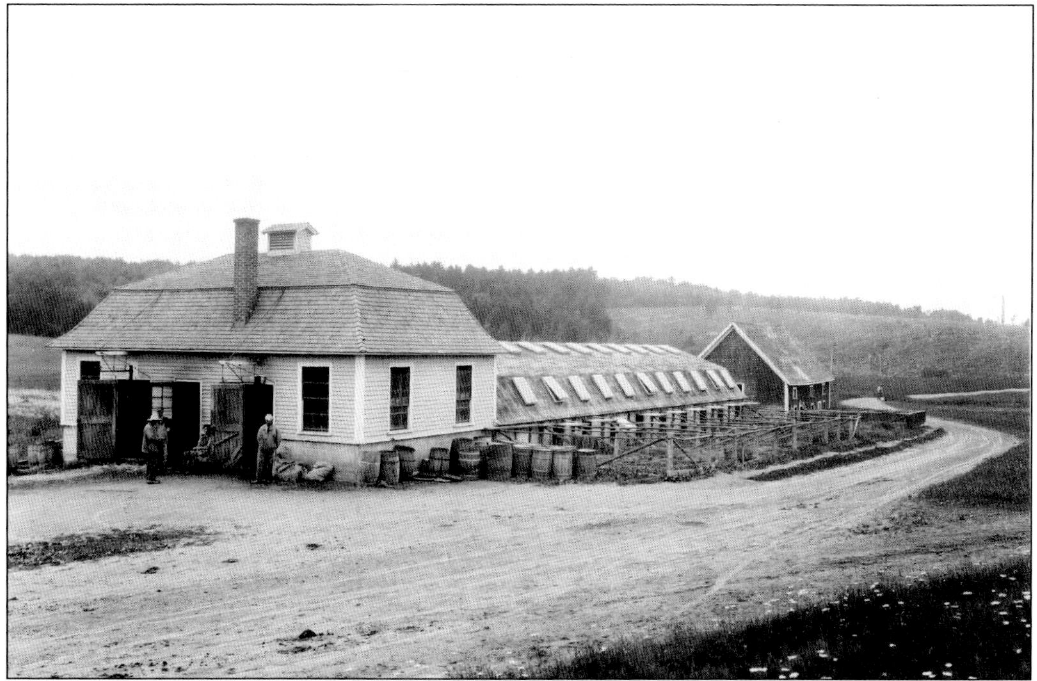

The piggery at Valley Farm is seen here in 1927. Several farms were purchased by the state to create Valley Farm at the north end of the grounds and Hill Farm on the south end. Over half of the food consumed at the institution was grown on-site.

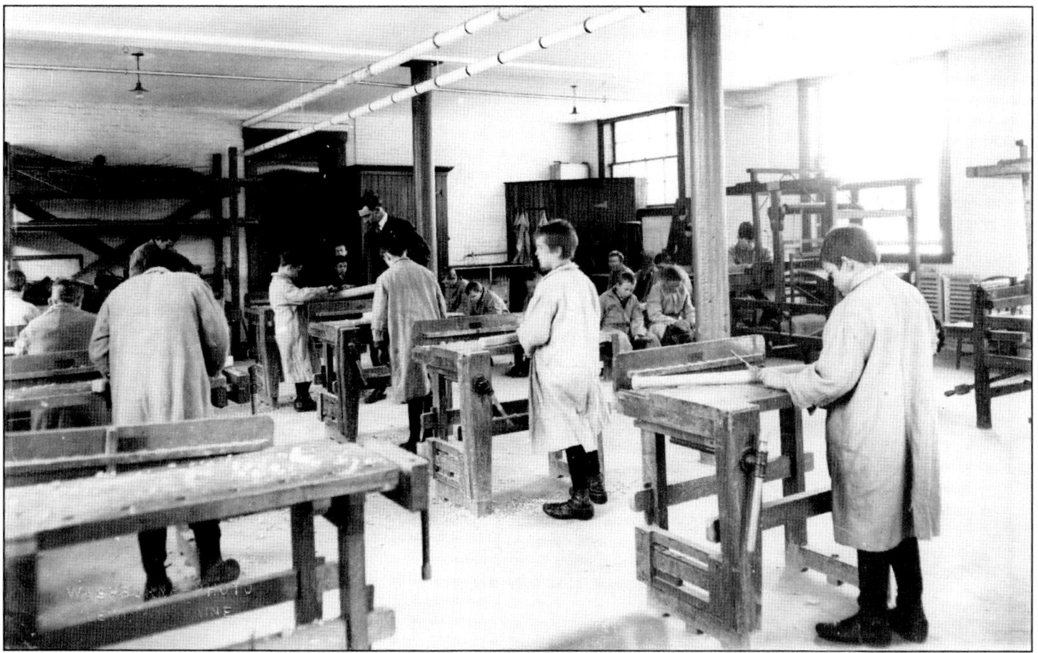

The manual training class is underway in this 1915 photograph. All the furniture used at the institution then was made in this room, including beds, tables, chairs, racks, and wardrobes. The state hoped that the boys of different physical and mental abilities would be able to go out and work and live with the rest of society.

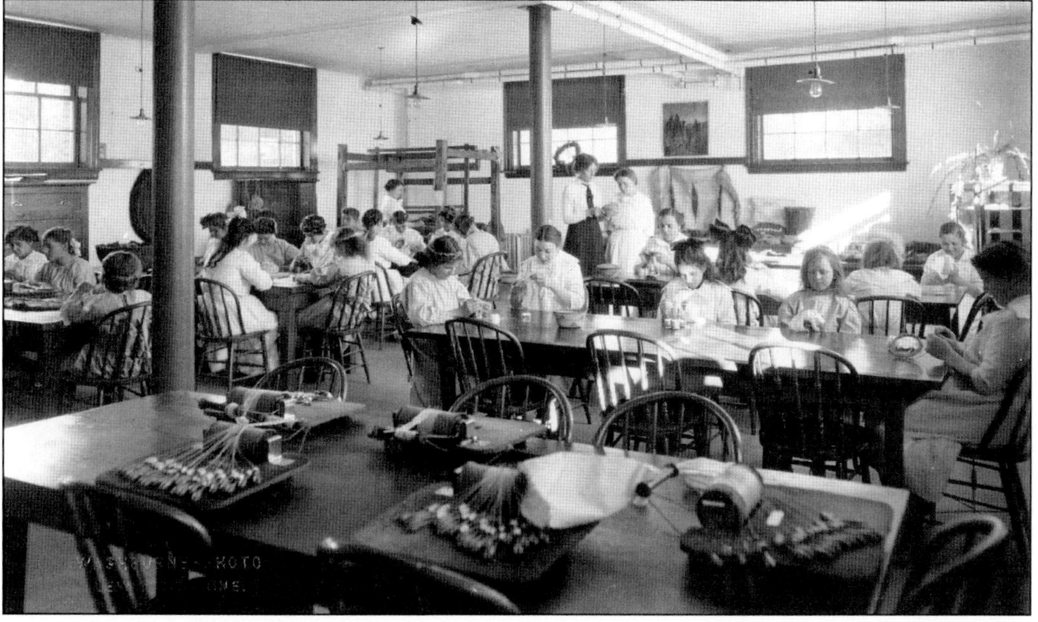

The girls are hard at work in their industrial training class, preparing costumes for their 1915 Christmas cantata. In this sewing room, they made dresses, aprons, bed clothing, curtains, and fancy work. The girls were allowed to sell the articles they produced, giving them money and pride of accomplishment. The table in the foreground is set with equipment for making bobbin lace.

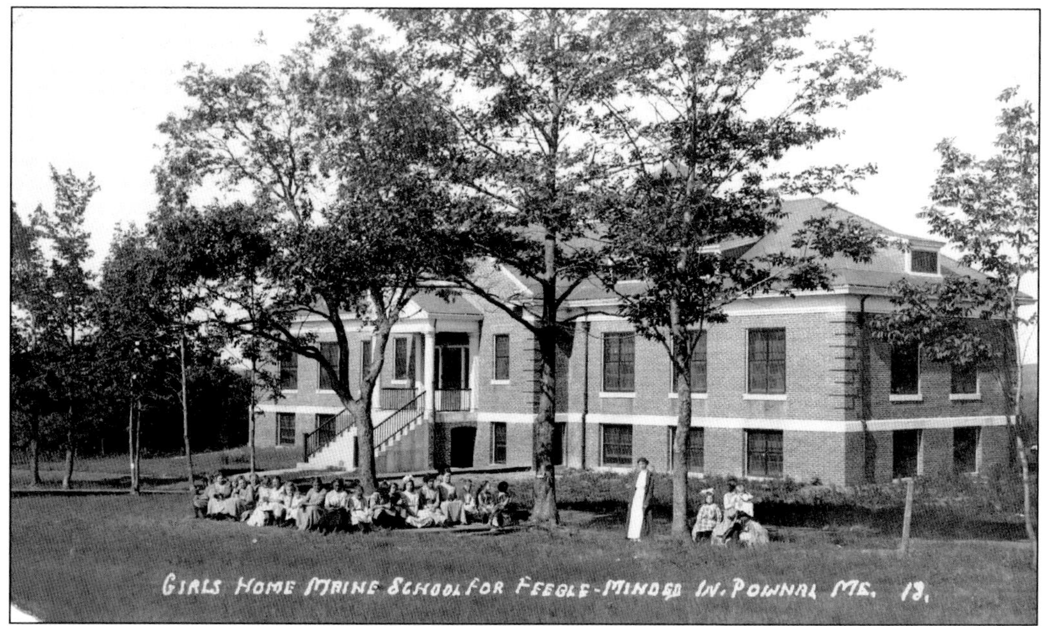

This early postcard depicts the girls' home, later known as Staples Hall. The campus provided its own power, lights, water, and sewage systems. Water was pumped from Collyer Brook a mile away to a reservoir on the property's highest point. The crescent-shaped campus was designed by Olmsted Brothers in 1921, known for Central Park in New York City and hundreds of college campuses.

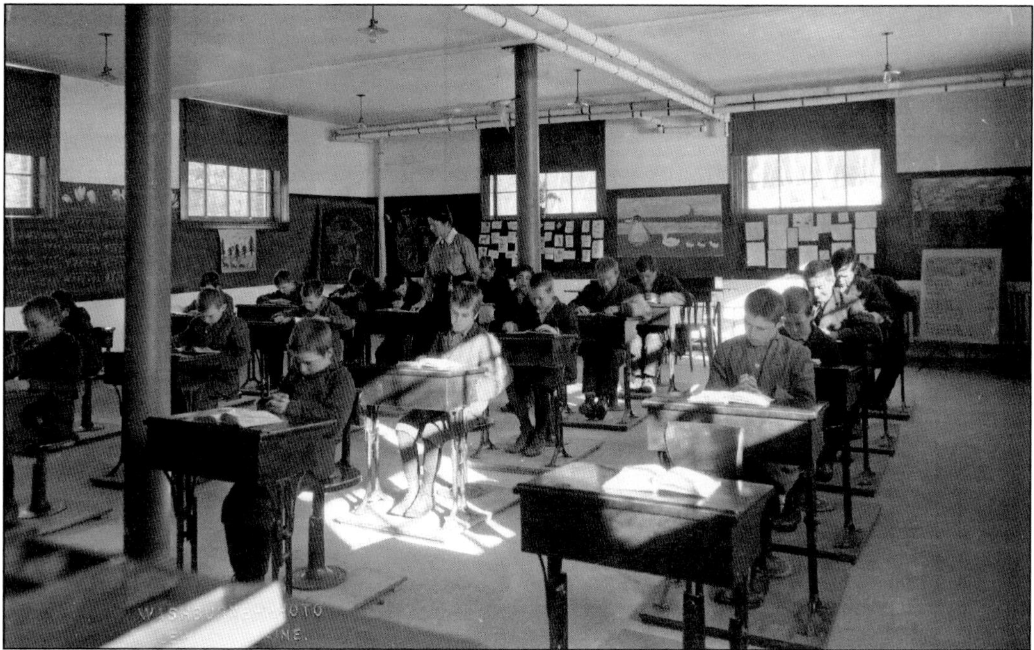

This 1915 photograph shows the boys learning to read. There were regular school classes held, along with music and art. The school had its own baseball team with "two or three really good players," according to Dr. George S. Bliss, who was the first superintendent. A gymnasium was eventually added in 1967.

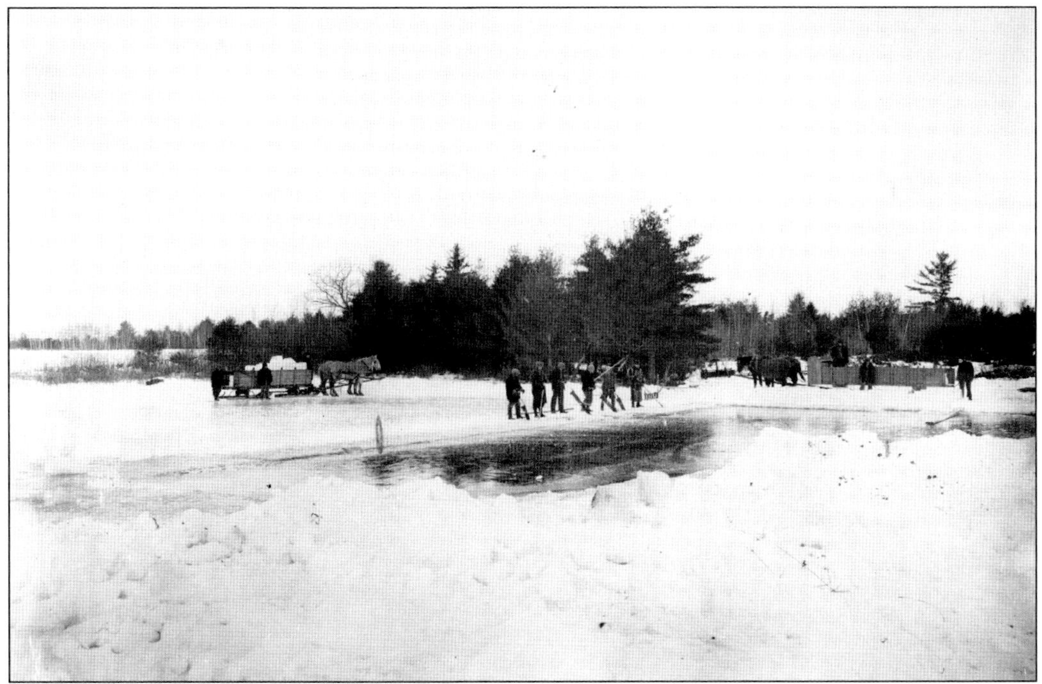

The boys are cutting ice in this 1915 scene. Much of the expansion work in the early days was done by the "inmates" and their supervisors. They picked rocks and made walls, cut brush, planted and cultivated crops, cut and piled the winter's supply of wood, and cared for the livestock.

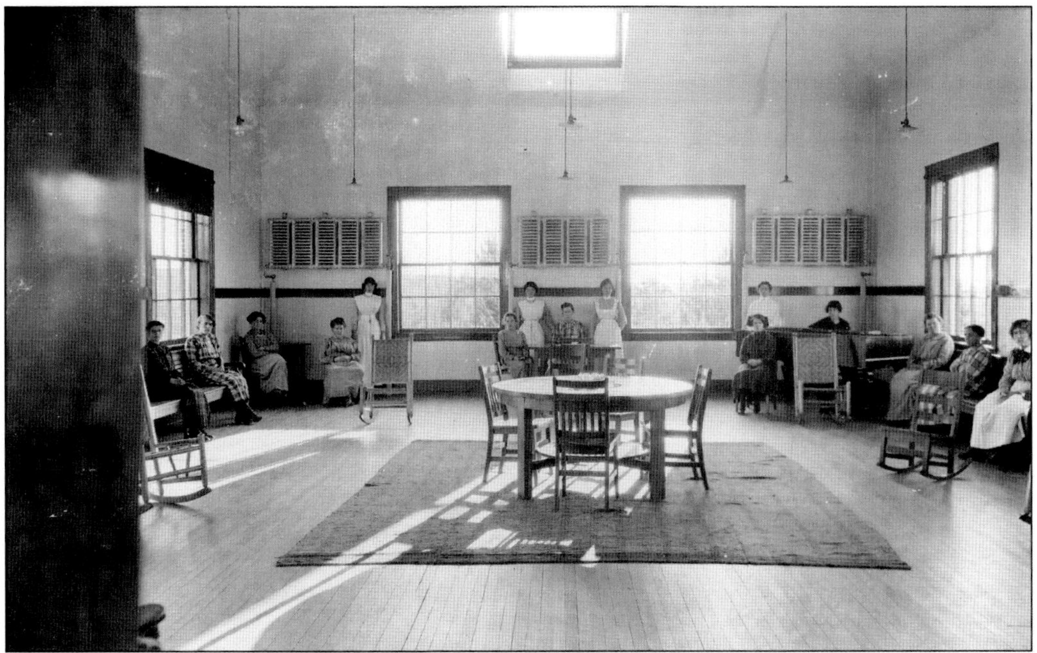

Seen here is an early view of the day room in the girls' home. Visitors could travel here by train, as the site was within a mile of both the West Pownal station on the Grand Trunk Railway and the Gray depot on the Maine Central Railroad. Admission preference was given to women of child-bearing age because the belief was that feeblemindedness was hereditary.

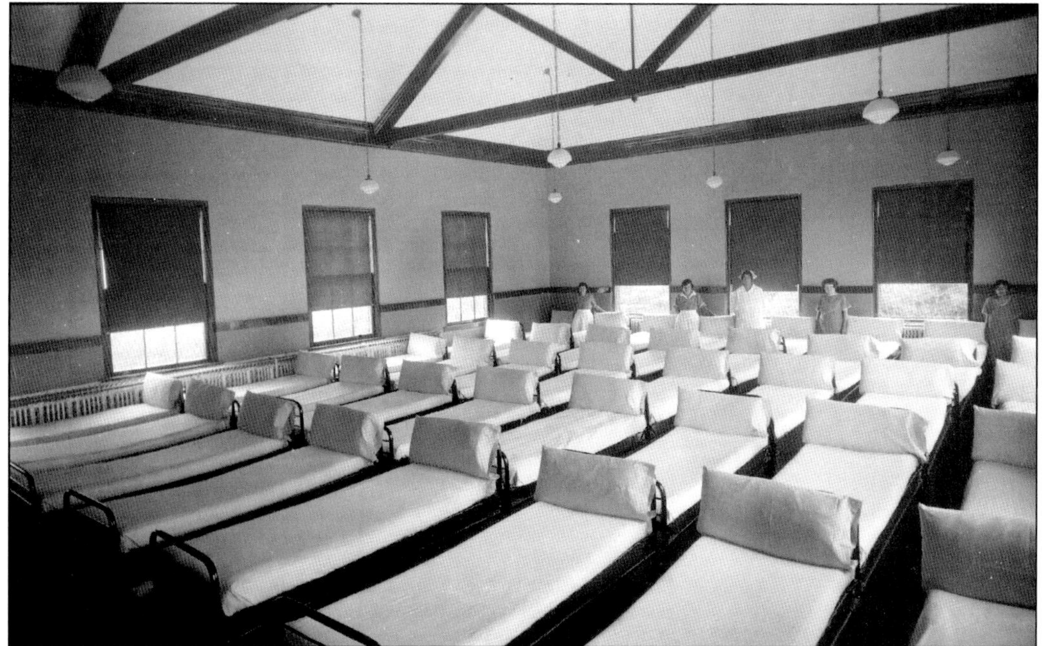

Here is a 1927 interior view of the dormitory in New Gloucester Hall. The institution was expanding at great rates into the 1950s, and overcrowding was always an issue. With a changing society, the "inmates" were later called residents, patients, and, eventually, clients. In 1980, the institution was renamed Pineland: A Comprehensive Center for the Developmentally Disabled.

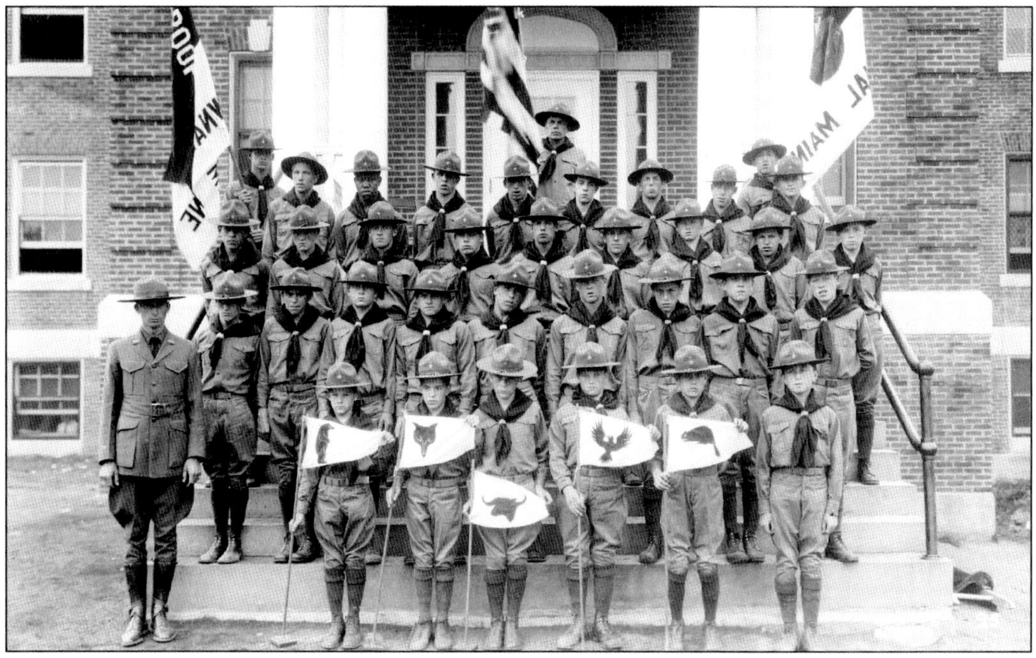

This 1927 photograph shows a Boy Scout troop on the steps of Hedin Hall. Charles O. Wyman (back row, second from left) escaped from the institution in 1928, hiding out in a local barn before hitching a ride to Bangor and reuniting with his family. He had been taken from a poor farm and placed here in 1920. His story became well known when he returned to visit in 1989.

Nine

THE PEOPLE

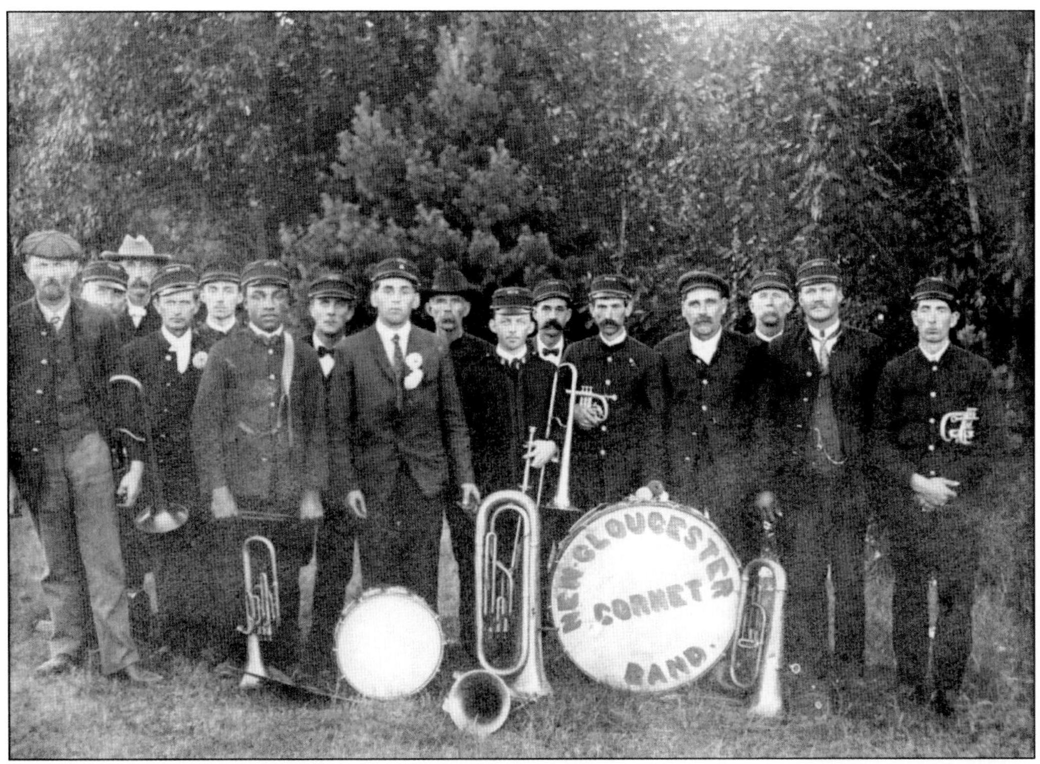

Members of the New Gloucester Cornet Band are Stan Woodbury, Ebben Nevins, Walter Small, Harry Woodbury, Albert Eveleth, Sammy Hicks, Herman McIntire, Bert Segars, Rufus Waterhouse, principal Walter Sullivan, Bert Weymouth, Jim Segars, John Rideout, Herbert Blake, and Steve Libby. The New Gloucester Cornet Band played marches, overtures, and waltzes for many special occasions.

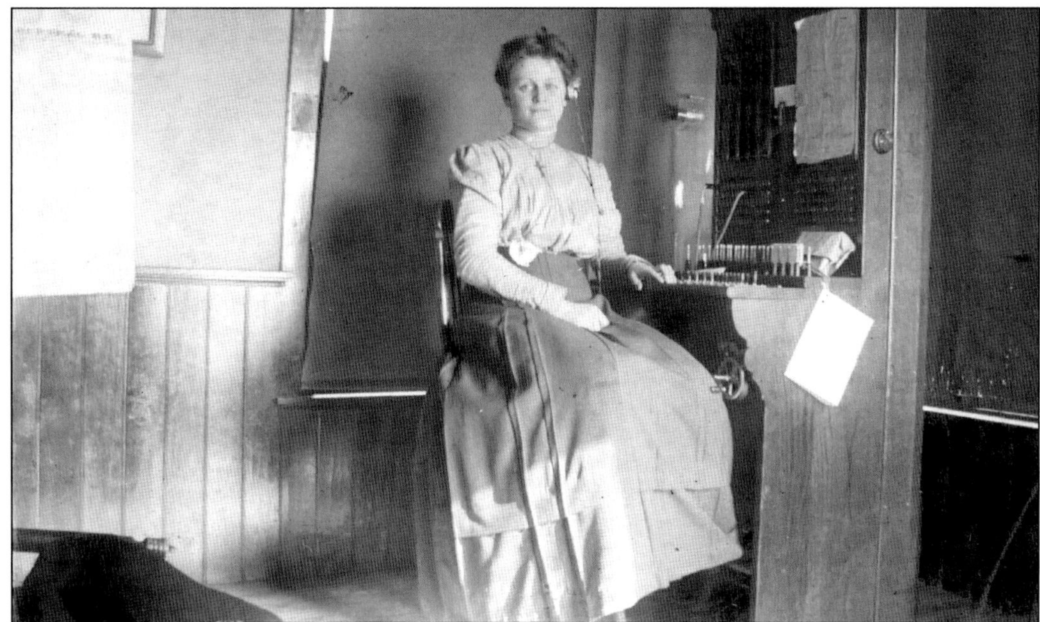

Florence E. Blake Houston is at the switchboard in the exchange for the Pine Tree Telephone and Telegraph Company in Lower Village. The company was organized on December 5, 1899, by president Charles Peleg Chandler, treasurer John W. True, and clerk Frank W. Winter. Offices were established in both Gray and New Gloucester, serving 164 telephones by the end of 1902. Recently it became part of Pine Tree Networks, with headquarters at Pineland Farms.

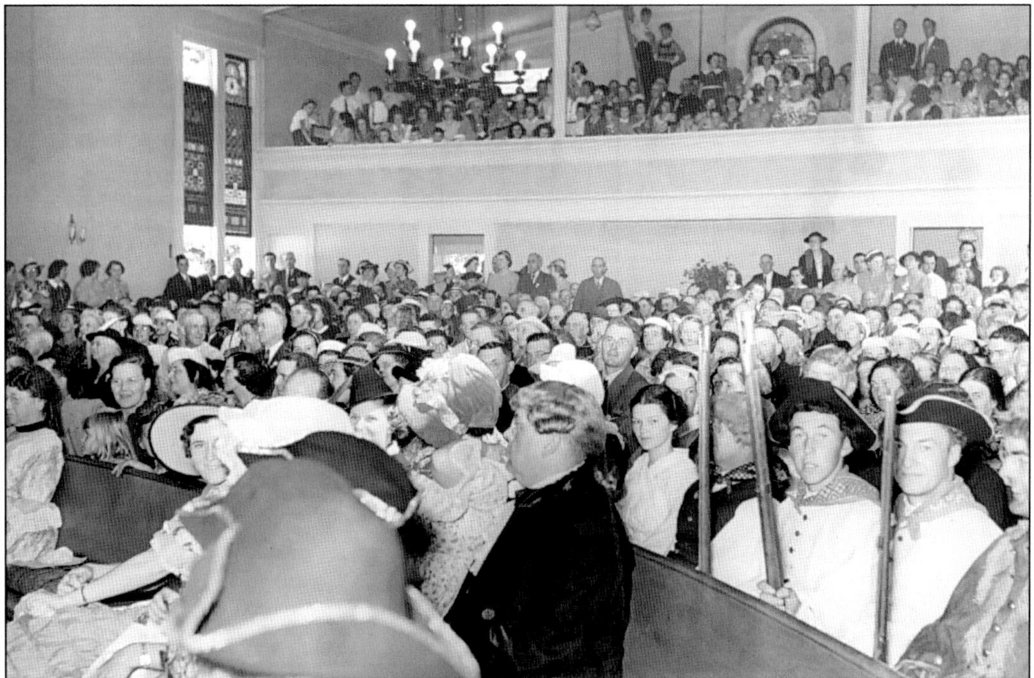

A pageant was performed at 2:00 p.m. on Sunday, September 4, 1939, at the Congregational church in front of a standing-room-only crowd. The town was celebrating the 200th anniversary of the settlement of New Gloucester. There is nothing like the sight of muskets in church.

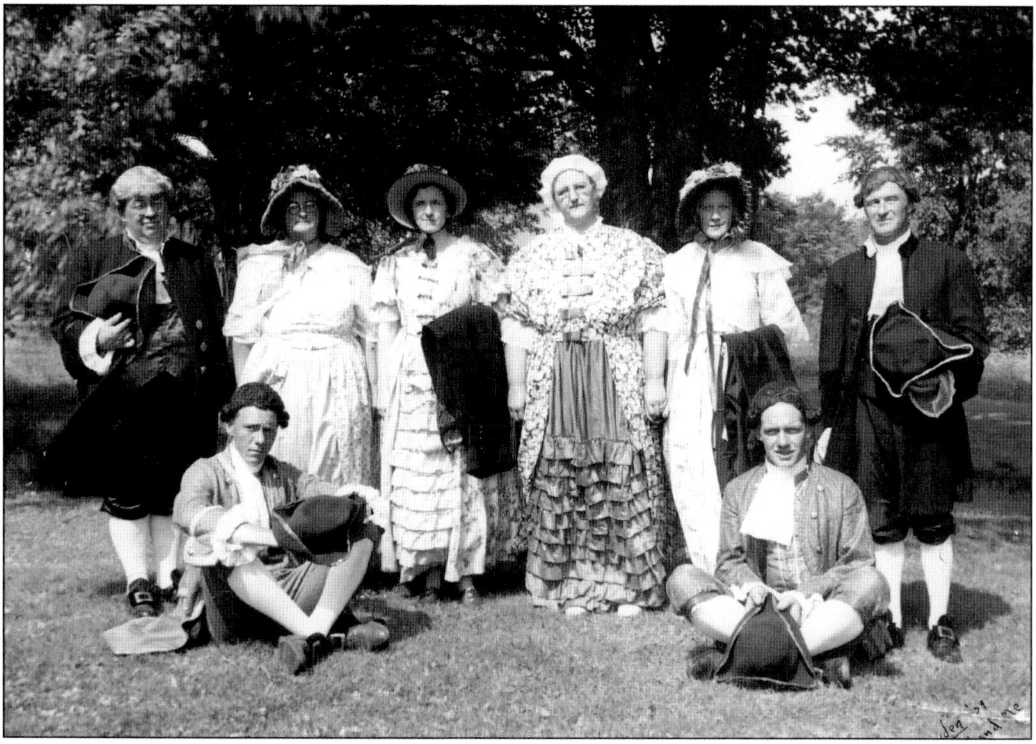

Some of the participants of the 1939 pageant are on display here. Seated are Harlow Humphrey Jr. (left) and Arthur G. Thompson. Standing are, from left to right, Lewis P. True, Alma True Tripp, Ruth Burton Ayer, Louisa C. Tufts, Helen Small Hinckley, and Walter R. Berry.

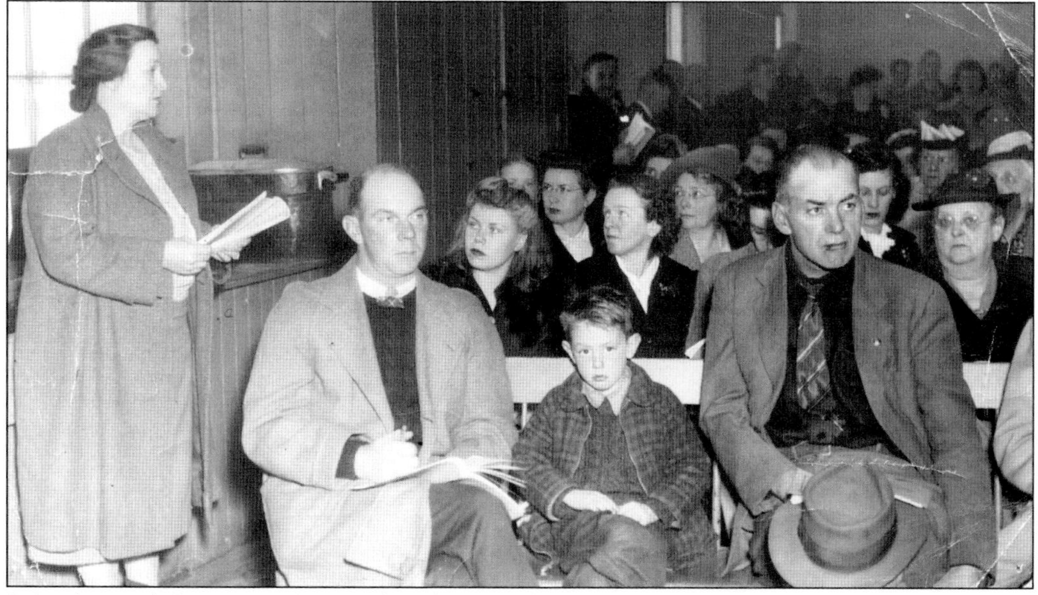

School consolidation was discussed at this Monday, March 10, 1947, annual town meeting held upstairs at town hall. Teacher and Consolidation Committee chair Thirza Waterman reports to the crowd, and, from left to right, Appleton Ford, Edward Ford, and Fred Blake listen in the front row. The town hall was also used for basketball games, dances, and plays.

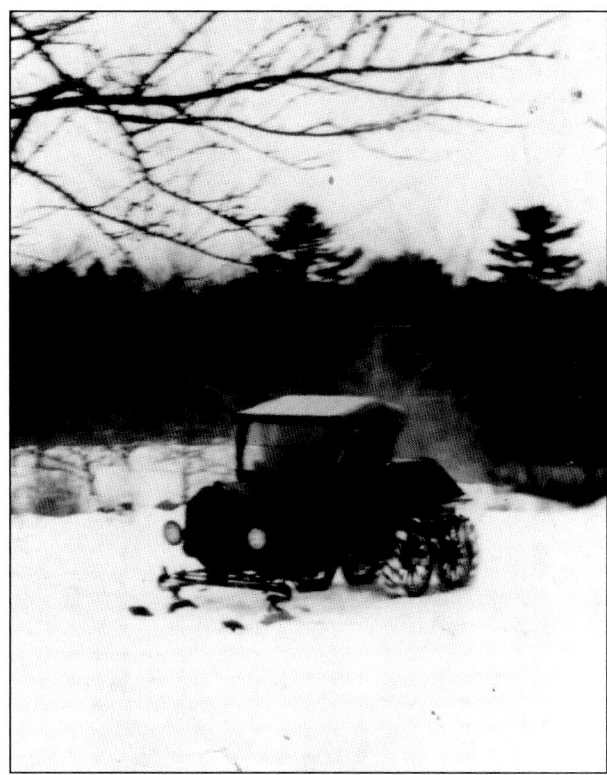

Dr. Linwood Sweatt's modified Model T is shown as a very early version of a snowmobile. The Sweatts moved here in 1925 and established a practice at 31 Cobb's Bridge Road. Sweatt (1894–1987) was very popular with the townspeople and was missed when he moved to Auburn in 1935. He returned in later years and retired to the shores of Sabbathday Lake.

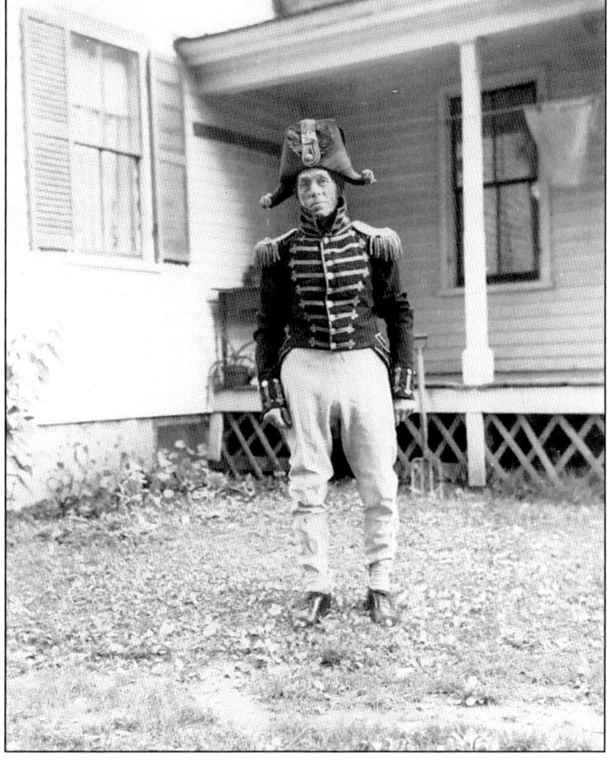

Christopher Lowe is posing in his wife's grandfather's uniform outside the family homestead. Gen. Charles Megquier (1797–1883) wore the 1828 Maine Militia uniform, complete with velvet-soft buckskin trousers. It is now at the Maine State Museum. The Megquier farm (built around 1810) is at 19 Megquier Road off Morse Road and was in the family for over 150 years. (Courtesy of the Lowe family.)

Col. Isaac Parsons (1740–1825) arrived in 1761 and built the gambrel on Cobb's Bridge Road. The "father of Maine agriculture" was so named due to his new and unusual method of growing corn—clearing, burning, and planting the land. He was married five times and requested in his will that his tombstone be of marble and taller than his wives' slate stones.

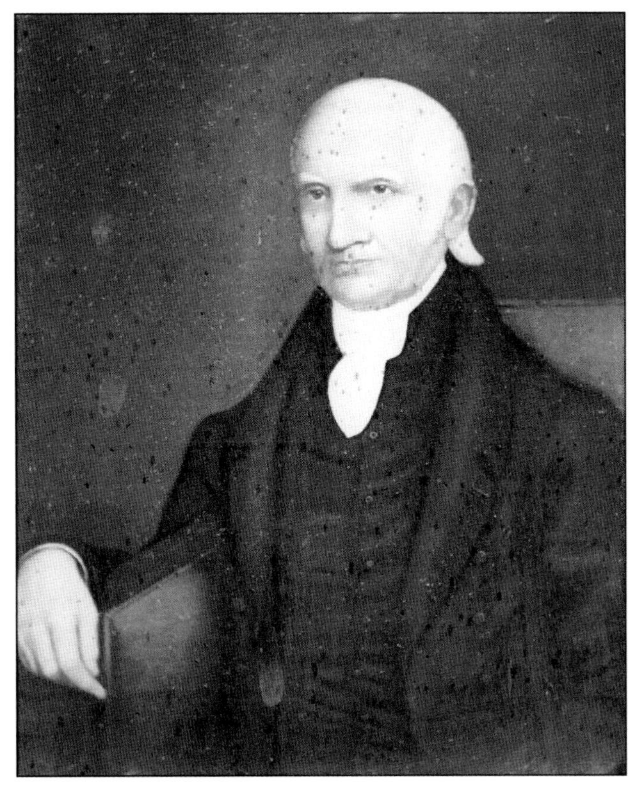

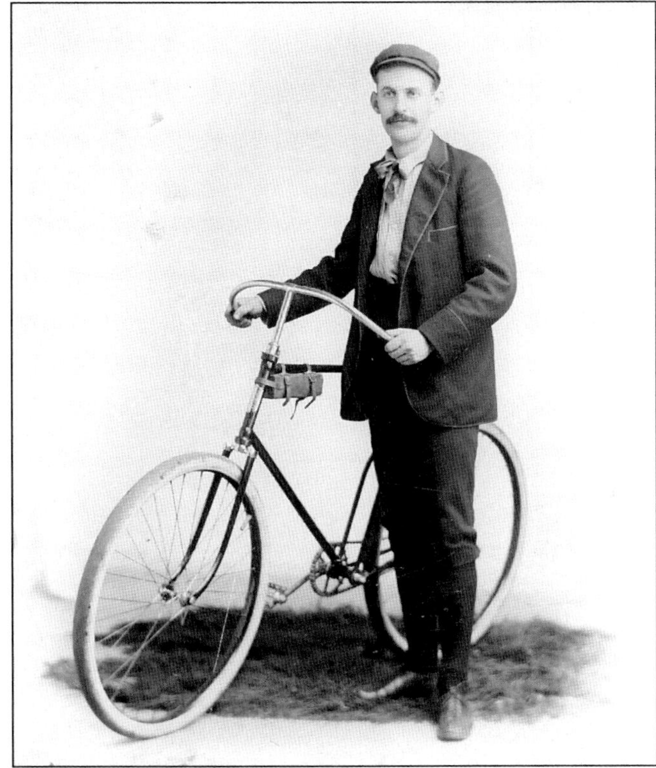

This depicts Charles Peleg Chandler (1857–1926) posing with his bicycle. Born in his grandfather's house by the mill at Upper Corner, he attended the local grade schools and Bailey School before he was sent away to Eaton School in Norridgewock. He was manager of Chandler Brothers and president of Pine Tree Telephone and Telegraph Company. (Courtesy of Stephen Chandler.)

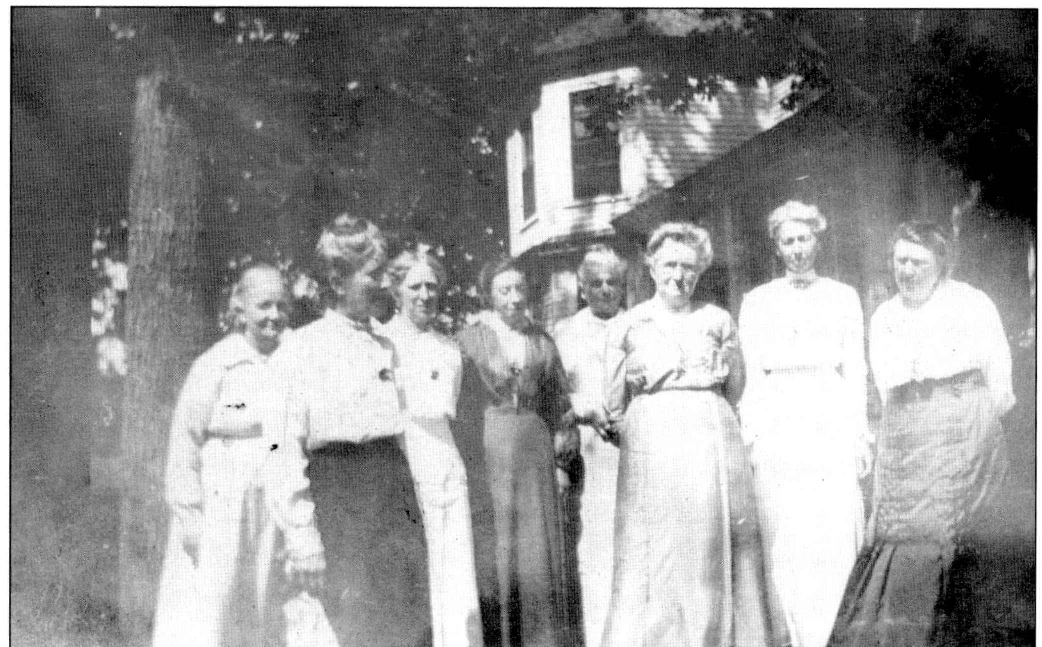

Members of the "Jolly Ten" are pictured on a day when only eight from the New Gloucester Women's Club are present. The literary club was organized in 1911. From left to right are Carrie True, S. Melissa Richards, Marcia Sweetser, Cora Chandler, Jennie Sturgis, Flora Berry, Lucy Fogg, and Alice Berry.

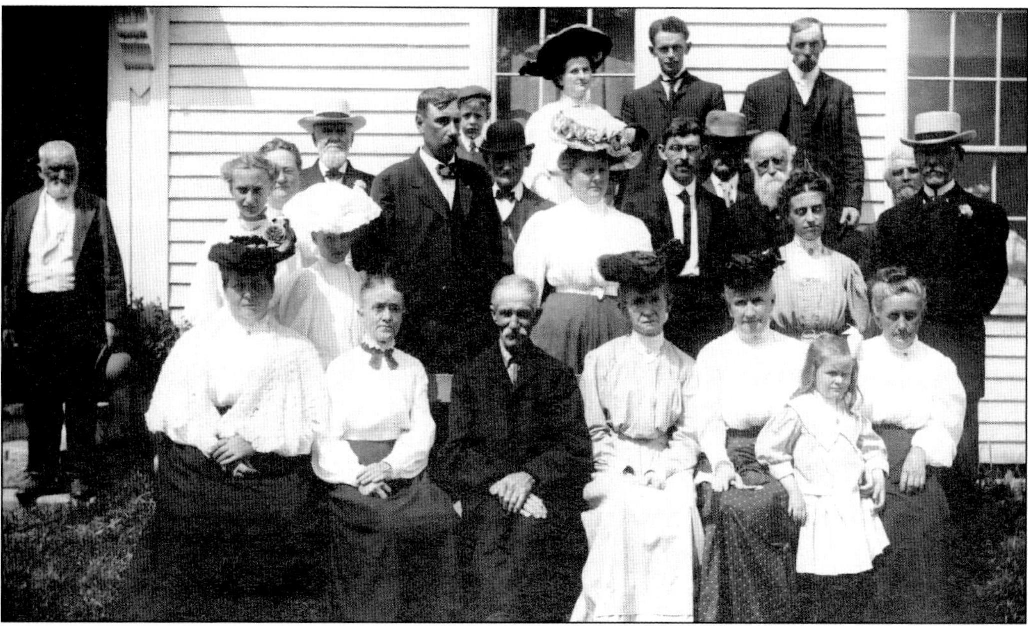

Descendants of Rev. Ephraim Stinchfield (1761–1837) gathered at his old homestead at 320 Penney Road on July 1, 1907, to celebrate the 125th anniversary of the founding of the Freewill Baptist Church. The owner of the house at the time was Stinchfield's grandson Cyrus Stinchfield (seated). The elder was the town's first native minister, and the "traveling parson" baptized 1,174 people. (Courtesy of the Blake family.)

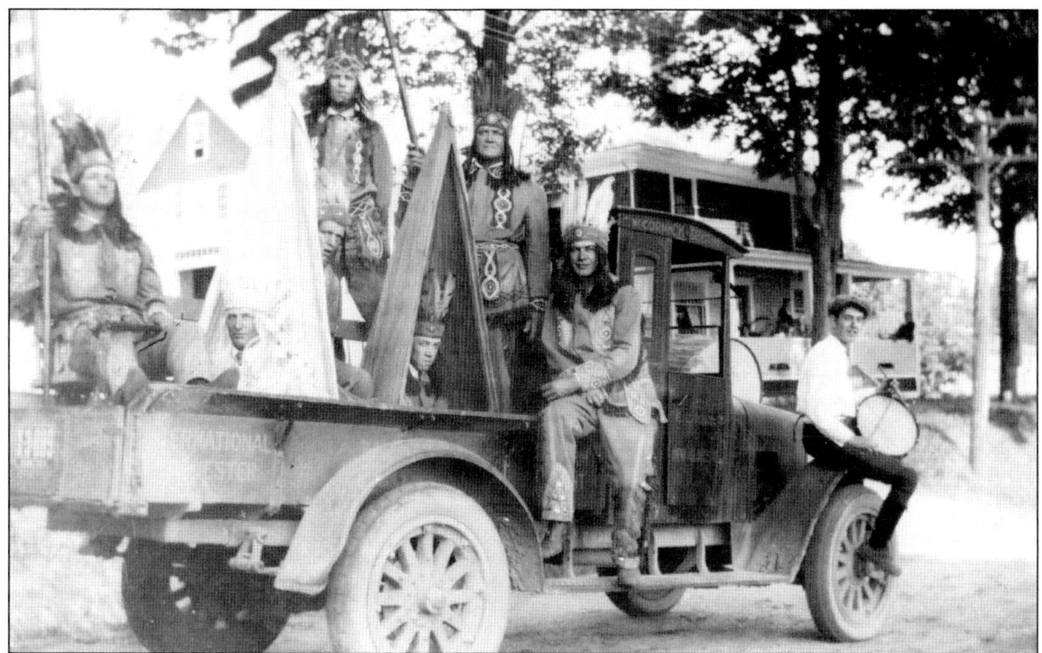

The Red Men Mishawaka Tribe No. 115 of the Improved Order of Red Men was formed in 1910 by 40 New Gloucester men. Durumquen Council No. 33 Degree of Pocahontas was founded in 1912, consisting of 69 men and women. Here the men pose on July 4, 1925, on the truck of Everett C. Roach at his home at 16 Cobb's Bridge Road. The local chapter dissolved in 1999.

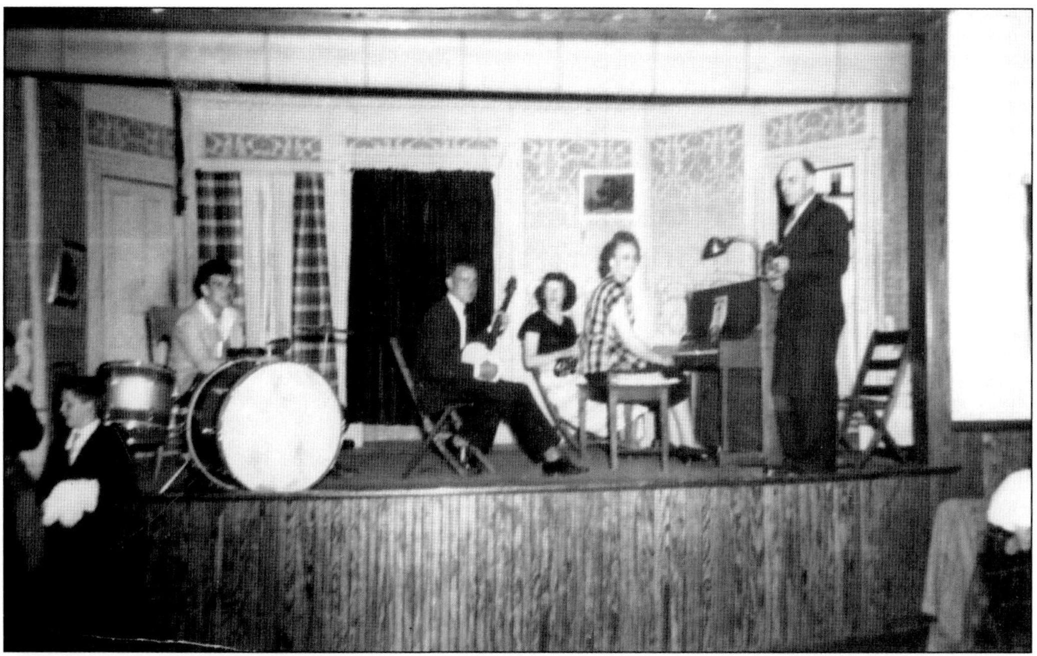

Playing in the band at the 1926 Grange hall are, from left to right, Roy Lowe on drums, Chester Berry on banjo, Norma Bishop Higgins on saxophone, Ruth Wills on piano, and Ed Lowe Sr. on fiddle. New Gloucester Grange No. 28 was organized in 1874. The building was sold to Arthur E. Thompson in 1955 to store apples and then to Thomas Moser for a furniture workshop.

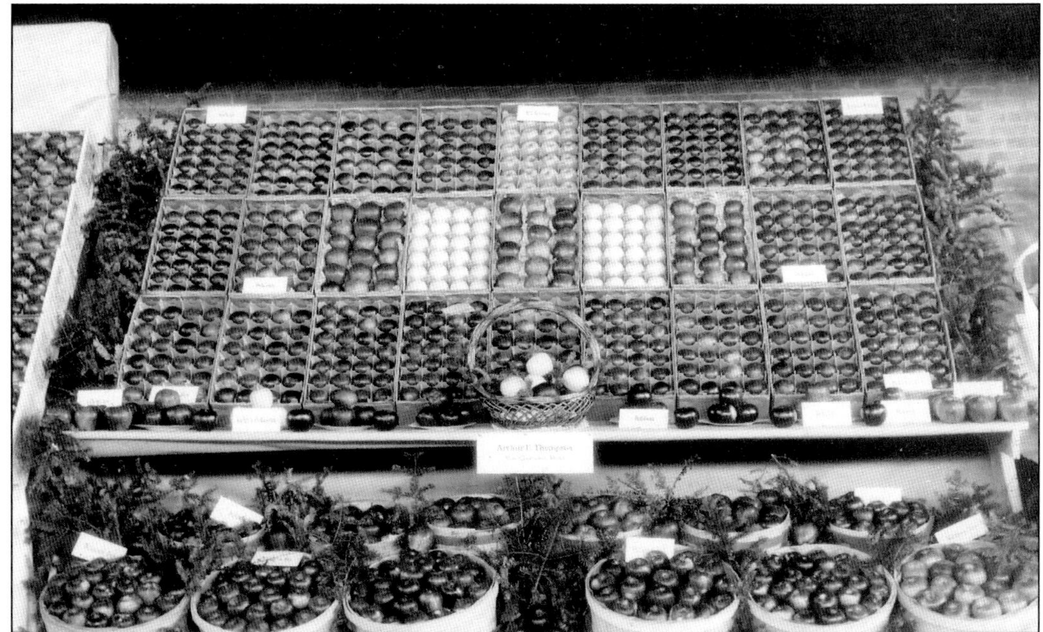

Thompson's Orchards at 276 Gloucester Hill Road was founded in 1906 by Arthur E. and Myrtle Thompson and is still run by the family over 100 years later. Arthur built up the orchard he purchased, taking it from 800 old trees to 2,500 flourishing trees. This image depicts one of Myrtle's prizewinning apple displays. (Courtesy of the Thompson family.)

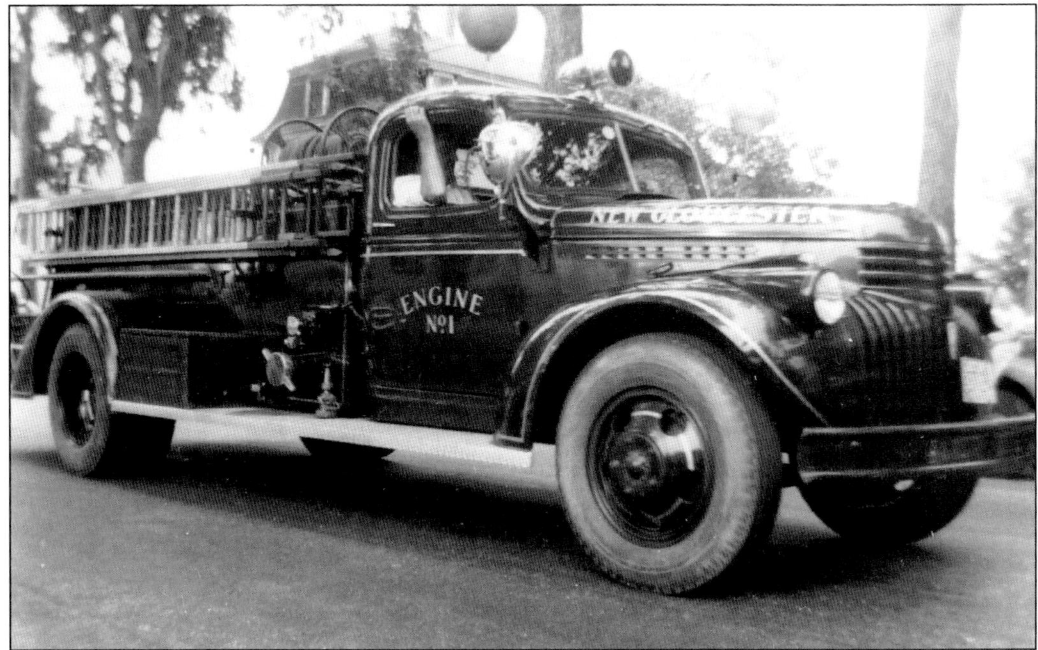

The 1946 Chevrolet Buffalo is on parade here in 1949. It was voted at a November 1928 special town meeting to form the New Gloucester Fire Department and to build a fire station between the town hall and library to house its new 1928 Ford Model A chemical unit. There have been seven fire chiefs, with Harry P. True serving longest, from 1929 to 1955.

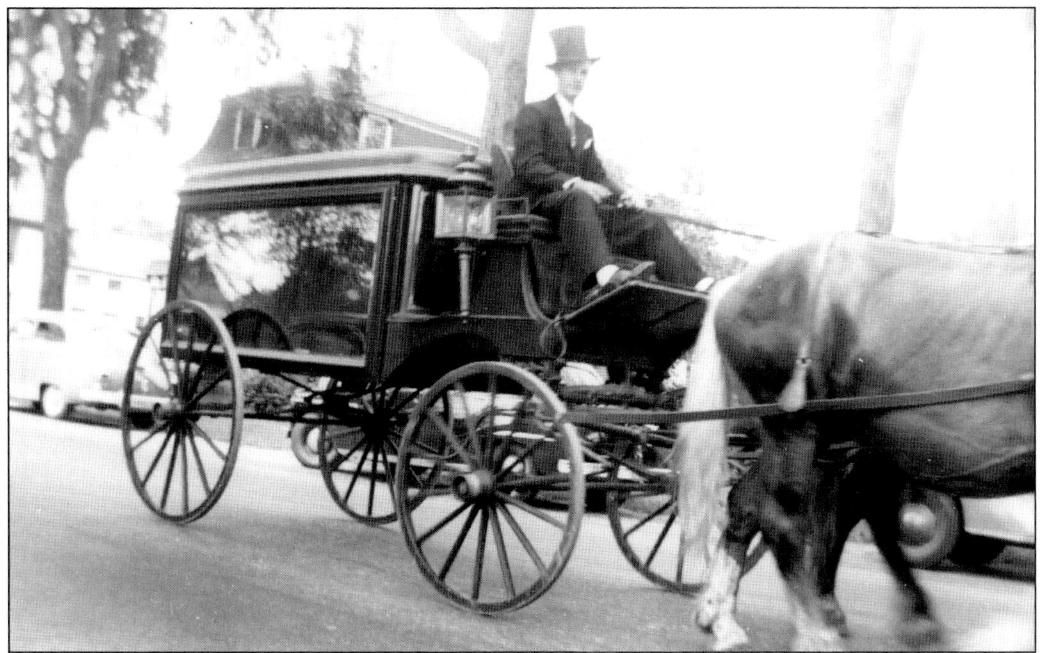

The 1909 town hearse is also on parade here in 1949. It was purchased from George L. Brownell of New Bedford, Massachusetts, for $525. It also had runners that allowed for winter use. The New Gloucester Cemetery Association was incorporated in 1927, with Fred P. Haskell serving as the first president and Lewis P. True as secretary/treasurer.

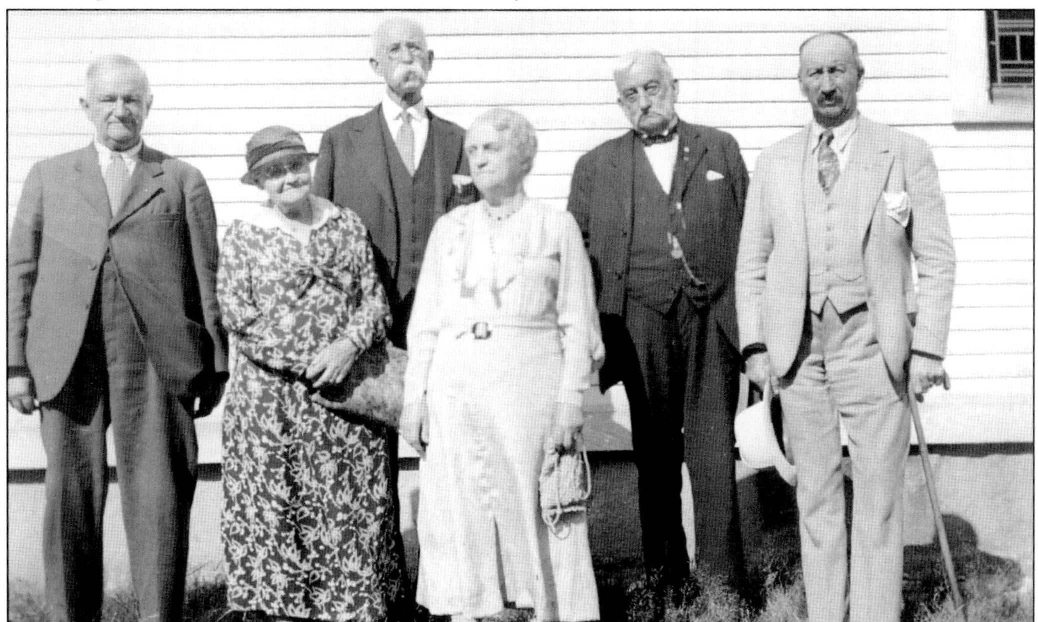

The first officers of the New Gloucester Historical Society are, from left to right, Charles H. Nelson, Alice Townsend Woodbury, John Woodman Rideout (president), Hattie Woodbury Bennett, A. Loring Richards, and Fred M. Nevins. It was incorporated on September 7, 1934, but the idea began in 1924 when it was decided to hold the sesquicentennial celebration at the site of the blockhouse.

Discover Thousands of Local History Books Featuring Millions of Vintage Images

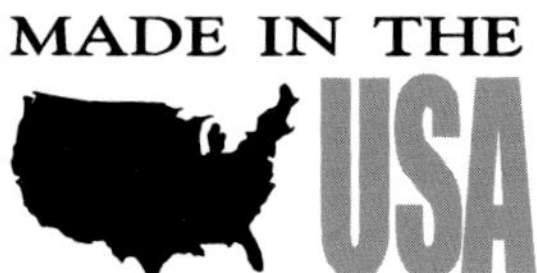